WHAT MADE THE STEEL CITY

ald
Print

Printed and published by:
ALD Design & Print
279 Sharrow Vale Road
Sheffield S11 8ZF

Telephone 0114 267 9402

E-mail a.lofthouse@btinternet.com

ISBN 1-901587-68-1

First published November 2007

WHAT MADE THE STEEL CITY

AN ENCYCLOPAEDIC DICTIONARY; WORDS, WORKS, PHRASES, PEOPLE, PRODUCTS & PLACES........ ALL YOU SHOULD KNOW ABOUT SHEFFIELD.

Compiled by Don Alexander

Why a Sheffield dictionary when there are so many books on the Yorkshire dialect?
Three reasons:

First, Sheffield is a boundary city, physically and linguistically, sitting between the North and the Midlands. It was a meeting point of Brigantes and Corieltauri, Romans and Brigantes, Mercia and Northumberland, paganism & Christianity, Dane and Anglo-Saxon, Bishoprics of Canterbury and York. Just in Yorkshire, it borders Derbyshire, Nottinghamshire and Lincolnshire.It is the regional big city for the Hope Valley, Bakewell and Baslow in the Peak; Dronfield and Chesterfield in Derbyshire; Newark, Worksop and Retford in Nottinghamshire; and Gainsborough in Lincolnshire as well as for the South Yorkshire towns of Rotherham, Barnsley and Doncaster.

When Sheffield's population grew in the 19th century from over forty thousand in 1801 to over four hundred thousand in 1901 far more people were sucked into our metal industries from Derbys., Lincs., Notts. and other Midland counties than from Northern regions. (My father's grandfather abandoned farming in Rutland to work at Vickers, and my mother's father left rural Derbyshire to become a grinder on Hollis Croft.) It follows that Sheffield dialect has as much of the Midlands as of the North. You are just as likely to be addressed as 'duck' (especially in the south of the city) as 'love'. The general Sheffield pronunciation of coat, **'cooat'** becomes **'coit'** in north Sheffield, Stocksbridge, Chapeltown, Barnsley.

Second, the metal trades here such as special steels and heavy engineering, cutlery, saws and other cutting tools, medical implants and scalpel blades, magnets, pewter and silverware are not, excepting silverware, found elsewhere in Britain to any significant extent, and bring their special vocabulary which becomes part of the Sheffield scene. For example, **'crozzle'**, the word and the product, recycled from the old cementation steel-making process and found on top of riverside, garden, pub and park walls, is to be heard and seen nowhere else in Britain.

Third, this book contains a selection of names of people, factories, products and places contributing to the Steel City's growth, history and fame. A sort of who's who, what's what, and where's where. There's an emphasis on the metal trades, of course, from the earliest recording of **cutlers** here in **1297**; to the Lords of the Manor, the **Shrewsburys**, ironmasters and controllers/ protectors of the cutlery industry up to **1624**,when cutlers themselves formed the **Cutlers' Company;** to the invention of **crucible steel**, the world's first proper steel in 1740**;** to the **Victorian giants** of steel who were the force behind the railways, the industrial revolution and the Navy, propelling British power and influence around the world. Without these latter men especially, Sheffield would have remained a small town pushed up against the Peak. National heroes, who are largely unsung in their home town are included**; Florence Nightingale**, who saved lives on the battlefield, and **Samuel Plimsoll**, who saved lives at sea. Also, powerful historical figures, **Bess of Hardwick** and **Mary**, **Queen of Scots** who spent the prime of their lives here, Mary albeit unwillingly. **Huckleberry Finn**, the most famous character in American fiction merits a mention because, on his adventures down the Mississippi he claims at one point to be a Sheffielder!

A line has to be drawn somewhere, so living people who bring renown to the city are not included, unless they are associated with a product, invention, building etc. (For instance how could the **gripple** be mentioned without reference to its inventor and producer, **Hugh Facey;** the world famous collection of Sheffield tools without referring to **Ken Hawley;** the nationally famous boxing gym in Wincobank without mention of **Brendan Ingle**.)

ACKNOWLEDGEMENTS.

I have to thank these groups of people for their use of the dialect words and phrases listed In this dictionary:

1. Childhood friends at infant school and on the streets in the 1940s at Neepsend. Some 10 and 11 year old more vulgar **dee-dahs** must be credited with the uncouth words and sayings. (They were ahead of their time because one hears the same vulgarities by today's 'comedians' in estuary English which sound merely smutty and not as funny as when heard from **deeing** and **dahing** young roughnecks of yore.)
2. Barnsley lads in KOYLI 1959/60.
3. Rotherham steelmen 1961 to 1983.
4. Sheffield factory men and women 1983 to 2001.
5. The general Sheffield and Rotherham public, passers-by or observers of the scene in market halls, pubs, trams and buses, football grounds, places of work etc. whose snippets of conversation in our vigorous dialect has interested and amused me since the late 1940s.

Listed below are some people who've been of much help, mostly without their realising. The ones highlighted have helped most:

Trevor Ablett, Fred Alexander, Mary Alexander, nee Hopkinson & **Mary Alexander nee Pybus,** Don Allison, David Arthur.
Andrew Boswell, **Cyril Boswell**, Mary Boswell, **Ray Bullen**.
Tony Capstick, **Ed Chapman**, John Clapham, Ron Clayton, Alan and Eric Cottingham.
Martin Dawes, Dave and Kate Dawson, Malcolm Davies.
Francis Evans.
Dennis Gibson.
Brian and June Hall, **Ken Hawley**, Roy Hodgson, **Bill Hukin**, Peter Harvey.
Paul Iseard.
Alan Jackson, Dave Jeffery.
Walt Kleman.
Trevor Lodge, Alistair Lofthouse.
Malcolm Marsden, Stephen McClarence, Daisy McDonald, Jim McQuaid, Jimmy Moors.
Laurie Nash, Nicky of Mexborough.
Jack Overall, Margaret Oversby.
Les Payne.
Reg and Jackie Reid, Mel Roberts, Rony Robinson, Andrew Robinson (article on Charlie Peace).
Stan Shaw, Fred Smith, Frances Soar, **Jack Sullivan**.
Lynda Taylor, Terry Tilbrook.
Paul Ward, George Welton, **Byron Willgoose**, Charlie Williams, Doris Wostenholme.

Caveat: Language is always in a state of flux- even dialect, and dialect, which in general is not written down, hasn't normally a standard spelling. My upbringing in the 1940's & 50's in industrial Neepsend fixed Sheffield words, sayings & pronunciation of that era & that place in my mind. It might not quite tally if you are a Sheffielder of another district & era. Spelling is as in my previous book **Orreight mi ol'** so, for example right is spelt **reight,** not **reyt** and **jennel** is preferred to **gennel.** Apart from words which are unique to the Sheffield Trades many dialect words in this dictionary are found elsewhere in Britain - for instance **mardy** is heard across a swathe of middle England, (though in Stoke & Manchester it is mainly shortened to **mard**).

Some previous Sheffield dialect books consulted:

The Hallamshire Glossary.	Rev. Joseph Hunter.	1829.
A Glossary of Old Sheffield Trade Words and Dialect.	B. Ronald Dyson.	1936.
Sheffieldish.	Derek Whomersley.	1981.

To compare dialects north and south of the Sheffield Region see:

The Yorkshire Dictionary.	Arnold Kellett.	1994.
Ey Up Mi Duck! Dialect of Derbyshire and the East Midlands.	Richard Scollins & John Titford.	2000

Photographs by Trisha Power, Ian Barnes, Rachel, Lucy & Don Alexander.

A

ah, **aah** (broad a), **aye** yes

aah do how do you do?

abaht about
al sithee at ten o'clock, or theer abahts

Abbeydale Hamlet a complete 18th century scythe works set around a courtyard, now a superb working museum for anyone with imagination and sense of history; the world's only complete **crucible steel (qv)** melting shop with teeming and ladling floor, cellar, stack, and clay-treading, pot-preparation area all accessible; water-powered forge and grinding hull, paint shop, various small workshops, offices, manager's house and cottages, two converted to a gift shop and café.
During the **Sheffield Outrages (qv)** non-union grinders, as well as facing the dangers of silicosis and stone breakage were threatened by gunpowder and rattening of their leather lineshafts. In November 1842 the tenant at Abbeydale, a Mr. Dyson had his grinding hull blown up, and 20 years later Joshua Tyzack was shot at three times driving his gig home. He was unharmed though a bullet made a neat hole in the brim of his hat.
Tyzack sons and Turner ran the works up to its closure in 1933, though it was re-opened for crucible steel production for a time in WW2. Sheffield Corporation wanted to demolish the works but they were saved largely through the efforts of what became known as the **Sheffield Trades Historical Society** (qv). Now looked after by the Sheffield Industrial Museums Trust.
As well as seeing the old stone buildings, waterwheels, extensive dam, nearby gardens and **Ecclesall woods,** it is especially pleasurable to see **Little Mesters (qv)** there such as Barry Gribban grinding chisels, or Ron Staley grinding scythes and hay knives for **Tyzack's (qv)**

aberra I'd better
aberra lerra gooan gerrit ersen I'd better let her go and get it herself
aberritinterz I bet it isn't hers

Admiralty (stress on the second **a**) Royal Navy building on Janson St. which closed in the 1970's.Their inspectors tested millions of tons of shell, armour plate & heavy gun steel & finished items especially during the two world wars.

affs, usually preceded by **this** afternoon
what tha dooin this affs?

afooer before
ah've eard ducks fart afooer I don't believe you

afternooin afternoon. North Sheffield to Barnsley. A feature by the late, great **Cappo (qv)** on Radio Sheffield was **Lurv in the afternooin.**

afters, used in the phrase **on afters** (working) on afternoons; on the afternoon shifts, usually 2 **while (qv)** 10. c.f. **on mornins** and **on neets.**

ageean again
al not tell thi ageean a father's warning to his son.
ee's at it ageean sithee
send' dog back on ageean! Loud advice from the Bramall Lane crowd during a boring cricket match, after a stray dog had entertained them by running on the pitch and stopping play.
ageean can also mean against; **purrit o'er ageean** (or **ageeanst) 'wall, will tha.** Put it against the wall please.

ahr our
ahr (owd) lass my wife
ahr kid my brother, or my friend
orreight ahr kid; nah then ahr kid.

aif half
aif a crown half a crown; two and a tanner; two and six (twelve & a half pence).
1940s schoolboy's doggerel;
Jack and Jill went up the hill
For a bit of hanky-panky.
Jill came down wi' aif a crown,
Jack must have been a Yankee.

aif-baked a simpleton
aif-deead very tired

Aizlewood Mill this imposing building used to house a steam-powered corn mill built 1861 to a **Flockton**(qv) design, once having a bridge over Spitalfields (where the new inner ring road runs),to Bridgehouses railway depot to bring corn from Aizlewood's Lincolnshire farms. Now a business centre.

Aldwarke (pronounced **Aldruck)** huge steelworks by the river Don, downstream from Rotherham; inheritor of the former **Park Gate Iron & Steel Co. & Steel Peech & Tozer (qv);** to-day's 2 x180 ton **arc furnaces** and modern casting & rolling plant can produce over a million tons of special & engineering steels a year, as much as could be produced by 20 **open hearth**, then 6 **arcs** previously. Ownership has now passed from Anglo- Dutch **Corus** to **Tata** of India.

Allick Alex
a mad Allick a harum-scarum

allus always

alsithee terneet I'll see you to-night

Andrews Toledo were a steel firm on **Neepsend Lane,** originally with **Crucible** melting furnaces, then **Open Hearth**, latterly **Electric Arc**, along with billet, bar and rod rolling mills. Their most famous order was for steel rod suspension cables for the Brooklyn Bridge, New York. To have seen in the 1940's men manipulating hot steel rod in their **rolling mill,** catching it with tongs, passing it from one pair of **rolls** to the next, as it increased speed elongating, whipping and snaking its way on the mill floor, was a huge privilege, though, as children, we didn't altogether appreciate it at the time. Theirs was a daily ballet, but one slip could mean serious burns, or even death.
After WW2 they were bought by Darwins, who then merged with Balfours. **Darwins Steel Castings who make stainless castings at Tinsley today are descendants.**
The Neepsend firm's founder, **Mr. J. H. Andrews (Mestrandrews,** as his workers would have called him) lived in a grand, stone-built home on Snaithing Park Rd. which became a regional N.C.B. headquarters, then a conference/training centre for DfEE (still known as **Manpower** in Sheffield), and now is a privately owned hotel.

annealing A steel heat-treatment, softening process in which the metal is heated to a set temperature, then allowed to cool slowly in the furnace.

Anston quarry magnesium limestone stone used for Beverley Minster, King's College, Cambs. & the Houses of Parliament.

'appen happen; perhaps; 'appen more common in the West Riding & Lancashire, or in radio/television comedy sketches set in the North.

arc - see **electric arc furnace.**

'ark listen
'ark at 'im listen to him; implies putting on airs.

arms race World wars 1 & 2, away from the battlefields were, to a large extent struggles between the Don Valley & the Ruhr steel firms, esp. WW1 at sea. This must have put paid to an international agreement in 1894 when a syndicate, of the three major Sheffield firms; Vickers, John Brown & Charles Cammell, along with Carnegie & Bethlehem Steel (U.S.A.), Schneider (France) & Krupp (Germany) controlled prices & divided orders outside their home markets.
The British Society for the Advancement of Science book for 1910 described Sheffield as **the greatest Armoury the world has ever seen**, and with the biggest three firms having their own shipyards on the Clyde, at Barrow, the North East and Birkenhead it was the power behind the British Empire.
Before WW1 especially the Sheffield firms were in an **arms race** among themselves.
Projectiles v armour;
'On one side of the road someone is inventing an armour plate that will resist the most formidable piercing shell made.....(whilst) an establishment on the other side is producing a shell against which nothing can possibly stand' (quoted by Dalton).

arrers darts

arse-booard, or **'orse-booard** board on which the grinder sits astride, extending to the grindstone; his weight converting it to a powerful lever for pressing large blades to the stone.

arse-end uppards upside down

assl I shall
assl clout thee if tha dunt geeoar threat by mother or father to awkward boy.

astha have you
astha gorra minit?
astha gorrit withi?
Astha bin Laikin' Barnsley terrorist?

Atkinsons the last major independent department store in Sheffield; others were Walsh's, Cockaynes, Roberts Brothers & Cole Brothers (now John Lewis). All but Cole's were completely destroyed in the 1940 **blitz (qv)** then rebuilt in Portland stone, as decreed by the city planners of the day. In WW1 **Atkinsons** had a drop stamping business at the back of the shop on the Moor making poppet valves for the infant aircraft industry, later taken over by **Daniel Doncasters (qv).**

Attercliffe industrial suburb in the East End of Sheffield, formerly with serried ranks of terraced houses cheek by jowl with big, black steelworks' sheds; home to a hardy & humorous people. (When the M1 opened and local garages offered 'last petrol before M1' a workmens' safety-shoes & working clothes shop countered with 'last overalls before M1'). In the low-lying Don Valley most Sheffielders say **dahn 'Cliffe ; he lives dahn'Cliffe.** Locals would say **on 'Cliffe,** or even **up'Cliffe. Sheffield Forgemasters** and **Firth Rixson** are still prominent in the landscape along with **Hallam FM Arena** and **Don Valley Stadium** (built for 1991 Student Games) and **Ice Sheffield** plus **English Institute of Sport** (built 2005)

Attercliffe Palace theatre rivalling Glasgow Empire as the' Comedian's Graveyard'

awak awake
he's worth mooer to me asleep than tha art awak unkind remark by **Samuel Fox**, steelmaker (qv) to a worker who reported a colleague asleep.
it's like shittin' in bed awak an' shovin' it aht wi thi feet extreme frustration in a Rotherham steelworks caused by conflicting demands of customers, colleagues and management.

awny only, because
What time tha cumin awny ah'm off aht at nine

'ayporth o' scraps please (at chip oyal) = half-pennyworth.

ax ask
'the antient form preserved by the common people' (**Hunter's** Hallamshire Glossary 1826) ; **'lets ax some friend....'** (A line in 'Smithy rhymes & **stithy (qv)** chimes) by Joseph Senior 1882); **ax** is also used in Gaskell's Darkshire in her novel 'North & South'; brought back into wider use by West Indian immigrants who came to work in steel & on the buses here in the 1950s & 60s.

azeegeniter has he given it her?

B

babby baby
'babby's rooerin' the baby's crying

badly poorly, feeling off 'hooks
backards (opposite to **forards)** backwards
backards rooad round
back dooer trot (when **'lav** was across the back yard) diarrhoea
back end autumn
back loader bus with open entrance near the back, enabling the more energetic to run after a moving bus, grab the polished steel pole and leap on, sometimes swivelling round it in the process.
back tonger man, usually in a steel sheet hand-rolling mill, who stands behind revolving, three-high, polished steel rolls; catches, using a pair of big steel tongs, the hot sheet as it comes through the rolls towards him and passes it back.
The process is repeated until the required gauge is achieved; a job needing strength, stamina, a keen eye & lightness on the feet. Now hand mills have largely been superseded by **continuous mills.**
back-wacks minor roads, lanes, alleyways, **gennels(qv)** off the main roads.

bags (me) foggy; bags (me) seggy (children's games) claiming first or second

Sir Donald Bailey (1901-1985) brilliant Rotherham-born, Sheffield University - trained civil engineer, inventor of the **Bailey bridge**, the first one of which was assembled by Sappers at the Somme barracks, Glossop Rd., near the university. Nearly half a million tons of steel = over 4000 bridges were built in WW2, shortening the war by a year, in General Montgomery's opinion. Eisenhower classed it as one of the three most important inventions of the war, along with radar and the heavy bomber.
The bridges were made from standard steel modules each of which could be handled by six men; all pieces could be transported on 3 ton lorries; quickly assembled bridges could be launched from one river bank for an assault; it was an easy, strong & flexible system supporting loads up to 70 tons and was used to cross canals and mighty rivers such as the Meuse & the Arno. Though intended as 'temporary' structures many hundreds have survived over 60 years, including one at Eastwood, Rotherham, restored a few years ago by the Royal Engineers. They were used extensively in war shattered Europe & are still made today for war - and earthquake-ravaged countries, testimony to Bailey's design.
Recently, one, dating from 1945 has been rebuilt in a **Forgemasters** shed by **Mandell Engineering,** and lifted by crane across the Don from Effingham Rd. to Attercliffe Rd. as part of the **Five Weirs Walk** (qv), replacing one a few hundred yards upstream formerly used by Hy. Matthews Timber whose building is about to be re-developed.

balanced handle **xylo (qv),** ivory, bone, plastic or pearl handle of a knife, so well made or weighted (e.g by a small piece of lead within the handle) as to keep the tip of the blade off the table cloth when laid down. On wooden tables knives would be sent spinning on their **bolsters (egg Waterloo (qv)** preferably**)** in competition with each other for the longest spin, or to see who the blades would point at when they stopped.

Arthur Balfour high-quality steel & tool firm founded as **Seebohm & Dieckstahl** in **1865.** Their name was changed to Arthur Balfour in **1915** when there was strong anti-German feeling (though Hy. Seebohm was of Bradford Quaker stock).By then **Balfour** had been with the firm 25 years and was MD and principal shareholder. After WW2 they merged with **Darwins** whose name lives on at **Darwins Alloy Castings,** Tinsley.

baltic very cold weather; a word heard around Mexborough, which is on the **Sheffield & South Yorkshire Navigation (qv),** the route for many thousands of tons of Swedish iron bars for converting into the celebrated **Sheffield shear** (qv) steel. Is it fanciful to believe that this extensive trade with the Baltic led to the word being associated with cold weather?
Baltic works **Beardshaw's** steelworks on **Effingham Road** now housing various small businesses. A memorial plaque on the wall commemorates 29 people who were killed by 36 bombs dropped nearby during a Zeppelin raid 26 September 1916.

band flat strap, power belt in **lineshaft** (qv); steel strip.
hot band hot rolled steel strip (rolled e.g. at **Brinsworth Hot Strip Mill).**

band saw made from narrow steel strip replacing circular saws in woodyards

band corrosion fault that sometimes occurred across a steel knife blade just above the bolster, caused by heat when hard-soldering the handle to the tang.

Banner Cross Hall site of an Elizabethan Hall, the current neo - Gothic, turreted hall was built ca.1820 for a Scots family (hence local roads named after Scottish towns) before it became home at various times for steelmen **Vickers (qv), Flather,** and type-founder Stephenson of **Stephenson & Blake(qv).** Now HQ of builders **Henry Boot.**

Barlow knives pocket knives, usually with wooden covering (handle) though bone, buffalo & stag horn, xylo, ivory and even mother-of-pearl also used. They have a long bolster, usually brass & one or two blades (at one end). Barlow was a Victorian cutler from Wadsley or Neepsend known for cheap pocket knives exported to the USA in large amounts. They were the 'cheap and cheerful' knives of the day, rather like Richards **lamppost** brand in the 1950's and 60's. In Mark Twain's 'The Adventures of **Huckleberry Finn'(qv)** Huck describes 'a little one-horse town in a big bend' (of the Mississippi) where loafers sat on boxes all day long whittling them with their Barlow knives. He had earlier spoken of a 'bran new Barlow knife worth two bits in any store'. To-day they are made in high quality by Sheffield firms **Wostenholm (IXL** mark stamped on bolster), **Rodgers, Wright, Ablett, Stan Shaw,** and **Taylor's Eye Witness (** eye trademark stamped on bolster)

barm yeast
barm pot silly person

Barnsley chop very large lamb chop

Barraclough, Ken 1917-1990 with degrees in chemistry & metallurgy, he became expert on the Sheffield Trades, light & heavy(qv). Steel-making was his speciality & at **Brown-Firth Research Laboratories(qv)** he was known as **Mr. Vacuum Melt** for his work on highly sophisticated processes for ultra-pure steels & alloys for industries such as power, defence & aerospace. He had great admiration for the old Sheffield steel men & their methods and wrote papers, newspaper articles and books on **blister/ cementation/ shear, crucible & Bessemer steel**(qv).

Bassetts sweet firm next to **Owlerton Stadium** best known for 'Bertie Bassetts' liquorice allsorts named in 1899 when a salesman from the Sheffield factory dropped various samples on a client's floor & the shopkeeper ordered **allsorts** mixed together.
Now called **Cadbury,Trebor Bassett** they currently make Maynard's wine gums, & Trebor mints as well as their traditional allsorts on the site.

Batchelors Peyse factory off 'Wicker at **Blonk St.**, then **Clay Wheels Lane**, Wadsley Bridge, now Worksop. They invented mushy peas at the Blonk St. site; (lately occupied by Hancock & Lant, furnishers, currently being converted to flats & shops: a nice old crucible steel stack is being preserved, the remnant of a small steelworks there). The Worksop factory, producing Oxo as well as some Batchelor's products, is now (2007) part of Premier Foods who intend to expand and make other products there, including Bisto & Sharwoods' sauces.

bath ticket ticket given to schoolchildren in the 1940's & 50's for a swimming session at corporation baths such as Corporation St., Hillsborough & Upperthorpe.
tuppence ' apenny an' a bath ticket a small monetary cost or award.

bay; front bay; back bay varnished wooden–slatted or upholstered bench seats in U-shape in the upstairs front or back of a tram. Boys would run upstairs shouting 'back bay, back bay'-their favourite seats.

Bayles, Peter author who gave Sheffield knives a nice tribute in his 'The Writing Schoolmaster'(1590); 'First therefore, be the choice of your penknife; a **right Sheffield (qv)** knife is best.'

bearstake base of old tree trunk-see **'line-shafting'**

Beauchief Abbey pronounced **Beechiff,** a tower church. built upon and surrounded by Norman ruins, in idyllic countryside on a 14-mile **Round Walk (qv).** As well as performing their religious duties the monks worked iron forges on the river Sheaf in the twelfth and thirteenth centuries. In **1496** they granted Roger Eyre lease of a bloomery and two woods for ten years on the Sheaf at Millhouses.
Two graves caught my eye in the Abbey grounds; one "Jacet **Christopher Pegge** de **Beauchief** 1799", a relative of **Strelley Pegge - see Thomas Boulsover.** The other of a young man, Courtney Gorell "who died of yellow fever at Pernambuco in the Brazils aged 20 years, February 25 1857."

Beatson Clark & Co. Ltd. Rotherham glass manufacturer of best quality bottles esp. for the pharmaceutical industry. Est. **1751**

beck small stream. **Beck Rd., Shiregreen**.

John Bedford set up the **Lion Works** on Mowbray St. in **1864** after making files in **Oughtibridge**, then at **Portobello**. Lion Works became famous for its beautifully-made, strong & reliable tools inc. files, spanners & hammers. They were absorbed into **Spear &Jackson/Js. Neill** in the 1960's. **John Bedford** was chairman of **Sheffield Infirmary** & returning from a board meeting at the hospital one evening, his carriage & pair fell off **Middlewood Rd**. fifteen feet into a field. He never recovered and died at his home, **More Hall** in **1898**.

beer note given to furnacemen to allow them past security and into a nearby pub for their beer allowance.
beer-off off-licence shop. (To-day Scouse/ Manchester 'offie' prevails).

beggar used in the phrase, **it's a beggar** = it's a devil e.g. **It's a beggar when you've got to buy your own beer!**

belluses bellows, in home or forge.

belly; How's thi belly for spots? How are you?
Mi belly thinks mi throoat's cut I'm very hungry.

belongs. He belongs on' Manor he lives on the Manor estate

berry; We berried him last week bury

Sir William Bennett (1816-1875) composer, friend of Mendelssohn & became prof. of music at Cambridge.

Emil Berek born in Poland ca. **1923,** fled for France when his country was invaded by Germany & Russia in **1939.** After WW2, following service with the French Resistance & the British Army, he settled in Sheffield where he worked for **J.Y. Cowlishaw,** pocket knife cutlers. Eventually he bought them out and set up on **Athol Road,** specialising in army knives and a range of slim all-stainless pen knives he helped design for Wilkinson Sword, mainly for the American market, where they were known as 'Slim Jims'. He was killed with his wife in a car crash in **1974,** but, like countless others in the trade, left a legacy of fine Sheffield craftsmanship.

Bess of Hardwick born at the old Hardwick Hall in **1518** she has been described as Sheffield's 'most formidable and shrewd woman.' She first married aged 14 Robert Barlow of Barlow Woodseats Hall, Johnnygate, just south of to-day's city boundary. Robert died in his teens leaving her a rich widow. Her second husband was Sir Wm. Cavendish, much older than her, and she had her children by him. Cavendish bought Chatsworth, began to rebuild it; died after work started & Bess had it completed.
After a third marriage to another nobleman, Wm. St. Loe (another old man, another death & another fortune), she set her sights on the richest of them all, Sheffielder
George Talbot, 6th Earl of Shrewsbury (qv).
She made it a condition of their marriage that two of his children by a former marriage should marry two of hers by Wm. Cavendish. Thus her eldest son, Henry Cavendish married Shrewsury's eldest daughter, Grace Talbot, and her youngest daughter, Mary married his second son Gilbert Talbot at **Sheffield Parish church** in February **1568**. By arranging this she set up a dynasty through the dukedoms of Devonshire, Portland & Newcastle with links right up to today with the Royal family.
In **1569** Queen Elizabeth commissioned **Shrewsbury** & **Bess** to look after **Mary Queen of Scots (qv)**- to be her gaoler in effect - and on **28th November 1570** she and her retinue were escorted to Shrewsbury's huge **Sheffield Castle (qv)** (now estimated to have been the size of Warwick castle). She spent 14 long years here and at **Sheffield Manor** putting a great strain on their marriage. Bess is said to have suspected her husband with the Scottish queen and shortly after Mary was finally escorted from Sheffield in **August 1584** they split up, Shrewsbury leaving to live with his mistress in Handsworth.
Having been involved in the building or re-building of some of the region's finest houses. Bess then went back to Hardwick and had the current Hardwick Hall, 'more glass than wall' built with her initials **ES, Elizabeth Shrewsbury** standing defiantly, in stone on top of the towers.

Sir Henry Bessemer (1813-1898) inventor of the world's first bulk steel-making process. When he announced in a scientific paper; 'The manufacture of malleable iron and steel without fuel' in **1856**, that steel could be made in tons rather than pounds by blowing air through molten cast iron in a converter for twenty or thirty minutes, he was ridiculed by Sheffield steelmen. Their melters & teemers had perfected the art in **crucible steel-making (qv)** of producing steel in the largest pots they could handle, of a consistent quality never achieved in the world before. They judged Bessemer's process to be dangerous, and only capable of producing poor-quality steel.
Bessemer had problems, especially with phosphorous content, but he persevered and decided to 'beard the lion in its den', building his own steelworks right between **Cammell's (qv)** and **John Brown's (qv)** in Sheffield's East End. A few years later **John Brown** was himself producing Bessemer steel, rolling it into railway lines and paying Bessemer £1 per ton royalty. This didn't signal the demise of crucible steel; in fact production soared because the harder, better quality steel was needed to work (saw, cut, file, machine, etc.) Bessemer's bulk mild steel. **Hy. Bessemer & Co.** made forgings, including railway tyres and axles on the Carlisle St. site until 1929, ironically no longer using the Bessemer process, but a 25 ton acid Siemens Open Hearth furnace. The firm continued as Baker & Bessemer in Rotherham but the 1905 Bessemer building office block still stands on Carlisle street.

best bib and tucker dressed up to the nines

bilbo knife, dagger (Bilbao)

billet mill steel primary mill rolling blooms down to round, or more usually square billets from 2.5 inch to 7 inch square, cut to lengths up to 40 feet.

billio, like billio very fast; he ran **like billio**

Bill's mother's
It's black o'er Bill's mother's Looks like rain yonder. It looks as though it's **gooiner sile it dahn.**

bi-metal tool composed of two metals e.g. hacksaw with high speed steel cutting edge welded to a flexible mild steel base; or edge tools, scythes, axes etc. with shear or crucible steel cutting edges forge-welded to an iron base.

Birmingham screwdriver a hammer

Bishops' House Elizabethan half-timbered house, now a small museum, at the top of Meersbrook park. Once owned by the **Blythe** family, an early **Wm. Blythe** had 2 sons, one of whom became the bishop of Salisbury in **1494**, and the other became bishop of Coventry/Lichfield in **1503**, hence the name of the house.
The Blythes were farmers/ **scythe manufacturers** and a later Wm. Blythe had estate valued one third farm and two thirds **scythes**, of which he had **1000** in stock when he died in **1631**. He had rented space at **Heeley mill** and at local smithies for his outworkers.

black bright very dirty face; used by mothers of their offspring, it recalls too an image of **miners'** faces in the days before pit-head baths, when they made their way home, black with coal dust, glistening with sweat.

Blackburn Brook a small stream between Rotherham and Sheffield, it deserves a mention becausemonks of Ecclesfield priory built a water-powered corn mill there. (Along with the eleventh-century **Worsborough Mill (qv)** it is one of the earliest recorded water-powered mills in the region.)

blackclocks black beetles lurking behind the skirting- boards

blade shapes of tea/dessert/table knives include: **straight/parallel/finger point/ (French) slipper.** The former were more popular from early times to about **1930**; the latter are more popular now.

The Blades nickname of team and supporters of the red & white half of the Steel City which reflects pride in the ancient knife-making tradition. See also **Bramall Lane.**
The Blades, Sheffield United Football Club won the league in 1898, and the F.A. Cup in1899**,** 1902 and 1925. Optimists among us eagerly await further success. Pessimists & **Wednesdayites** might argue that **United's** halcyon days were in the 90's- trouble is they mean the 1890's**!** Diehards among each team's supporters worry that the other **teeam** might do well- currently **Wednesdayites,** who call the **Blades** the **Blunts** are fearful that **United** are becoming top dog; see **Owls.**

Blanco oval-shaped block of chalky white polish for military belts & webbing as well as for sports shoes and plimsolls. Despite the name it was also made as a dark green paste for the subsequently merged Light Infantry- KOYLI, DLI etc. in the 1950's/ 60's.
The manufacturer was **Joseph Pickering & Sons Ltd**. who succeeded John Needham, (founded 1824 on Harvest Lane), then moved to Mowbray St. before building the impressive **Albyn** courtyarded complex on Burton Rd., Neepsend. Less 'bull' in the Forces led to the demise of **Blanco** but another branch of the firm made cardboard boxes, mainly for the cutlery & tool trades, in a nice, brown-tiled building on Moore St., the facade of which has been preserved. **Pickering's** still make boxes in a factory on Little London Road.

blank basic cut-out, stamped or forged shape of spoon, knife, spanner, chisel, spade etc., etc.

blartin' rortin', roartin', rooartin'(qv); loud, vulgar shouting. cf. **blortin'** in 'Eyupmiduck', a book on Erewash Valley dialect. Less common than **rooartin',** the Sheffielder heard using it most (he talked, e.g., of Shirley Bassey **blartin' out**) spent his boyhood in the Midlands.

bleedin'ell, bleeder though not, of course, unique to Sheffield these curses were very common in working class areas of the city in the 1940's/50's and 60's, far more so than the now ubiquitous 'F' words. The worst curse a mother would give to her male offspring would be to call him **you little bleeder.** When opposing fans stood together on the terraces & the **kop** & Rotherham United beat Wednesday at Hillsborough 5-3 a Rotherham man was pleased to hear a Wednesdayite comment, **'they're fast these bleeders, aren't they?'** Ever afterwards he called Sheffielders working with him at **Park Gate Iron & Steel Co.; "them bleeders from Sheffield!"**

blister steel steel made in **cementation (qv), converting** furnaces, so called because the surface of the wrought iron bars was blistered when converted to steel. **Blister steel** bars were mostly then hot forge-welded into the celebrated **Sheffield shear** or **double-shear steels**, or broken into pieces & melted down into the even more celebrated **Sheffield crucible steel (qv).**

the Blitz, blitzed, bombed out Blitz is the German for lightning (Blitzkrieg, sudden attack; lightning war). A German Zeppelin had bombed Sheffield in **1916** during WW1, killing 28 people, but that was a comparatively leisurely attack, compared with the heavy bombardments by the Luftwaffe in WW2 on the nights of **12th/13th December & 15th/16th December 1940**.
As early as 28th November **1934** in a speech to the House of Commons Winston Churchill had warned that Birmingham and Sheffield would be prime targets, as well as London, in a future war. Professor J.B.S. Haldane wrote in **1938; There is half a square mile of Sheffield which is more vital for the production of**

munitions than any other part of Britain.
Perhaps he should have said ten square miles to include the East End & firms such as **Steelo's (qv)** in Rotherham since, though desperate attempts were made to shift some of Sheffield's special steel industry to Gateshead, Manchester & **Darley Dale** near Matlock (**Firth Rixson** still have forging operations there), the city remained the nation's main armourer in WW11, as in WW1.
On the two big night raids by a total of about 400 German bombers 760 people were killed or missing, 3000 houses, shops and businesses were destroyed and 82000 properties were damaged. People recalled the flames, the noise, the smell of cordite , burnt out trams, bombed buildings, much of the town centre destroyed, including major stores such as Walsh's, Robert's Bros., Atkinson's, Burton's, Marks & Spencer, Redgate's, Cockayne's, C. & A., and the Brightside & Carbrook Co-op. The worst single incident was the death of 70 people in the Marples hotel. A woman described the blitz as the biggest fireworks display ever.
The attack was seen from surrounding towns:
Roy Castle (then living in Holmfirth); "We often watched the bombardment of Sheffield as it took a pounding, the sickening rumbling as bombs exploded relentlessly, lighting the distant sky."
Ruth Robinson (then living in Barnsley aged two and a half, wakened by her mother to look at the sky over Sheffield); "...the sky looked as though it was on fire. It was such a bright, vivid red & the wheels of the tower at the pit were etched black against it."
Brian Blessed (then at Mexborough); "As a kid I used to see Sheffield burning, shrapnel would fly as far as Mexborough."
Margaret Claxton; "We stood at a bedroom window, four miles north of Doncaster, watching Sheffield burn. The blaze was so huge that, though we were 20 or 30 miles away, the whole sky was red."
However, the Germans were unsuccessful in their aim of disrupting Britain's war effort at source. Their raids were code-named **Operation Crucible** and their bombers even had specific targets, e.g. Woodhouse & Rixson forge, but very few steelworks were hit.
In his book **The Sheffield Blitz. Operation Crucible** Alistair Lofthouse shows that British deception in the Peak District may have misled German bomber crews on their way to Sheffield into believing that the city's western outskirts were between Strines & Fox House. If they had been more accurate and had unleashed all their bombs on the East End (and west Rotherham) destroying the lower Don Valley works, they would not only have caused havoc with Britain's war effort, but would perhaps have killed thousands more people, since, as well as men working nights in the works, the whole area was very heavily populated, with serried ranks of houses cheek by jowl with the huge works.

bloody-minded not a local expression, but a local trait. Sheffielders like to think of themselves as friendly and easy-going, and, of course this is true but there is a streak of lawlessness & unconformity in the region. From **Robin Hood (Robin of Loxley)** to those who supported the French & American revolutions-see **Boston Castle**, Rotherham and the plaque to **Samuel Holberry (1814-1842)** in the **Peace Gardens.**
From the Victorian grinders' union **Sheffield Outrages (qv)**, to support for the Russian revolutions in 1905 & 1917. (Support for the Reds didn't involve giving much cash;
on 21st February 1905 the Pen & Pocket blade forgers Assn. **Resolved that we grant £1 to the Russian workmen in their struggle for reforms).**
From **Dr. John O'Dwyer Creaghe** who threatened the **bum-bailiff** with a poker at his practice at Hill Top on **'Cliffe** & founded the **Sheffield Anarchist,** described as 'one of the most scurrilous journals ever to appear'; to **Elliott (qv)**, the **Corn Law Rhymer,** and **Joseph Mather,** who wrote scurrilous poems about 'Old Niddlety Nod', the **Rev.**
Wilkinson (qv), Vicar of Sheffield & J.P. We must mention too **Samuel Plimsoll (qv)** shaking his fist at the Speaker and being ejected from the House of Commons.He stood by his principles even though he had to sell his home, **Whiteley Wood Hall (**dubbed White Lie Hall by his enemies) to pay legal fees, and **the Plimsoll Line** on ships reminds us of lives at sea saved by **the Sailor's Friend.**
Sheffield ramblers were heavily involved in the **mass trespass** for right of access on **Kinder Scout** in **1932.** In more recent times we had councillors **Blunkett, Billings & Betts** who were bent upon turning Sheffield into a 'Socialist Republic' until the scales fell from their eyes with the collapse of communism in the U.S.S.R. & Eastern Europe. On the periphery of the region we still have **Wedgy Benn,** who Harold Wilson said 'immatures with age', **Arthur Scargill,** brooding on what might have been, and **Dennis Skinner,** the venerable'beast of Bolsover'.
To finish this section, three vignettes on Sheffield workmen, who are much more important than poets or politicians in the advance of the city;
The 20 stone head melter at **Cammell's** didn't stand when Queen Victoria's carriage rolled into **Cyclop's works** for her to watch the casting of a huge propeller for one of Her Navy's battleships. He sat on his three-legged stool, finished his mug of tea, put out his pipe, then stood to give the go-ahead to hundreds of men with **crucibles** full of molten steel, to be wheeled to and poured into the casting pit.
John Ruskin (qv), quite a rebel himself, tempered his tribute to the Sheffield cutler as the best in the world by including the proviso **'when the workman chooses to do all he knows'.**
In his recent autobiography, 'The Cutler's Tale', **John Price,** a Birmingham man with a holloware factory in Brum & a cutlery factory in Sheffield, says his father could get away with slanging matches in Birmingham, but not in Sheffield. **'He never did understand the Sheffield mentality'.** He claims one problem was that they couldn't employ a **Wednesday** supporter in the polishing section, or, at the other end of the factory, a **United** supporter in a **Wednesday** team of workmen.

bloomery furnaces Roman/medieval shallow pits where iron ore & charcoal were heated together, using the natural draught of hilltops or bellows. The iron did not melt but formed a 'cake' or bloom which still contained a lot of slag which had to be hammered out.

blooming mill, blooms a **primary** steel mill rolling 7 to 12 in square **blooms,** which have been cogged down in a **cogging mill (qv)** from ingots. Often today the ingot process route is avoided & blooms & billets are continuously cast in a **continuous casting machine (qv)** directly from molten steel.

Bluecoat school a charity school founded in 1706 for orphan boys, it was for over 200 years at the corner of East Parade & Campo Lane in town, moving in 1911 to a fine building on Psalter Lane, site of a former quarry; see **Brincliffe quarries.** In 1939 it was requisitioned by the Army for a transport depot and is now, with 1960's additions **Sheffield Hallam University's Psalter Lane** campus with an excellent reputation for setting new designer/silversmiths on the road to fame and, hopefully, fortune.

the **Blunts Blades** **Wednesdayites'** nickname for the

bob a shilling (5 new pence); a word not peculiar to Sheffield, but this nice play on the word filtered down to schoolchildren in the 1940's:

If tha Bob dunt gi ahr Bob
that theer bob that tha Bob owes ahr Bob
ahr Bob 'll gi tha Bob a bob in 'eye!

If **tha looks as though tha's lost a bob an' fon a tanner** you are looking miserable, because you've lost 12 pence and only found six. Finding **a ten bob nooat** would make you very happy indeed.

bobar (of a child) poo, or to do a poo; jobbie.

Bole Hills area of Crookes on a high edge overlooking a steep slope down to **Rivelin valley**. **Bole Hill** also occurs at the top of Cobnar Rd. being the name of a lane, a farm & a high area of **Graves Park**. There are other local sites, all high land where wind could provide the draught for smelting iron ore or lead.

bolster, bowster the projecting shoulder of steel on a knife between the blade & tang. A nicely balanced knife with **xylo (qv),** bone or **ivory(qv)** handle can be spun like a top on the bolster. Various bolster shapes include **bullet** bolster, **egg** or **egg waterloo(qv)** bolster, **flush** bolster, **yankee** bolster. **Coddy bowsters** are bolsters pinned onto a flat tang of a cheap knife. **No-bowster** is a wooden-handled trade knife, (butcher's etc) having no bolster. An **integral bolster** has tang, bolster and blade forged from one piece of steel or it may be part of a one-piece all-steel complete knife. A pocket knife might have a very short **bearded** bolster, or a **long** bolster (see **Barlow** knife.) Pen and pocket knife bolsters are usually made of brass or nickel silver.

The cheapest bolster is a **spelter** bolster which is made of zinc poured into small dies usually **egg waterloo** shape into which is inserted a **whittle-tang (qv)** knife stamped out of steel sheet. This type of knife has largely been ousted by cheap Asian imports.

Before the widespread manufacture of hot forged stainless steel knife blades in the 1920's/1930's the best Sheffield cutlers hot forged iron bolsters onto **shear (qv)** or **double shear** steel. Look for a faint **thumb-mark (qv)** impression on the back of the blade where the two metals joined.

bolsterstone a narrow hard-grit grindstone 1.25 to 1.5 inch width x 22 inch diameter for grinding bolsters and removing fash.

Bolsterstone An attractive Pennine-stone village near **Stocksbridge** overlooking the beautiful Ewden Valley in north-west Sheffield. When the rooks are busily building their nests, and the wind is soughing in the high trees by the fine old stone church, 'Wuthering Heights' is brought to mind. What a pity some of todays' felons can't take their turn in the stocks outside the church, to give us a healthy glimpse into the past. The oldest **glassworks** in South Yorkshire was established here ca. 1650. The village today has a well known choir.

bonny, bonny babby, bonny lass in Scotland & Northern England means pretty, though in Sheffield it implies being also pleasantly plump.

bonser, a bonser excellent, e.g. a great shot (football).

booan bone
rag an'booan man rag and bone man
got a booan on; hard on; got onk on to have an erection.

booit boot; more common in north Sheffield**;** Chapeltown to Barnsley.
Booitstraps former name of a folk club in Chapeltown.

bosh vessel holding water or oil for quenching heated blades.

boss a man may address another man thus, or as **squire, youth,** or **sir** if he doesn't know him, or has forgotten his name. The purest local words in such cases, however are; **laddo(qv)** (more common in Sheffield & to the north of the city) and **surrey(qv)** (more common in Derbyshire & Notts.)

boss also means to forge, in Sheffield: Fred James, bowie knife maker, interviewed by Valerie Answer ca. 1980, talking about forging bolsters in mild steel; ' We had to heat them up in the hearth fire to **boss** them in the bolster.'

Bottom mill walk up Sharrow Vale road past the stainless steel jaguars of the car show room, look over the wall to your left and you will see beautiful Georgian mill buildings fronting a mill pond set in nice grounds. The pond and the bubbling river Porter that feeds it are home to ducks, moorhen & coot as well as the occasional heron, kingfisher & dipper; an idyllic spot in the midst of a busy city. It was built as a **snuff mill** in 1763, and is now Britain's only remaining such mill, now powered by electricity though still capable of using its 19ft. waterwheel if necessary. Still run by descendants of the **Wilson** family, clay pipes are now made as well as snuff. The mill's proper name is **Sharrow Mill,** the familiar name being adopted after a family feud led to the rival **Top Mill** or **Westbrook Mill (qv)** being built at the top of Sharrow Vale road. This was bought by British American Tobacco, then closed down.

Prior to the building of the Sharrow Mill in **1763** there was a cutler's grinding wheel on the site with records going back to **1604**. **Joseph Wilson** had introduced **snuff grinding** in the **1740's** using tobacco from Virginia, before concentrating totally on the then fashionable product.

Joseph gave some land to set up **Clifford House Church of England School** on **Psalter Lane.**

Thomas Boulsover (1705-1788) a cutler, granted the freedom of the Cutlers' Company in 1726; invented **Sheffield Plate (qv)** in 1743 after accidentally fusing copper and silver while repairing a knife handle at his workshop on the corner of Tudor street & Surrey street- see tribute to him including bronze profile near **Graves Art Gallery.** He found the metals, when fused, could be rolled & worked together, and began making buttons, and later, buckles and snuff boxes in the new metal, 'the poor man's silver' at new premises on Baker Hill, between the bottom of Norfolk street and Shude Hill. This was in partnership with **Joseph Wilson,** (who later started making snuff - see **Bottom Mill**), and with financial backing from the delightfully-named **Strelley Pegge** of Beauchief Hall.

In 1757 he moved to larger premises near today's Crucible theatre, and even though he concentrated on small items such as buttons, it was a very profitable trade (John Read of **Sheffield Smelting Company** once paid him £100 for silver sweepings from his workshop floor), and in the same year he bought **Whiteley Wood Hall** in the Mayfield valley from **Strelley Pegge**. (This superb hall - a later owner was **Samuel Plimsoll q.v. -** was demolished in 1957 in what today would be regarded as sheer municipal vandalism. The remaining outbuildings and grounds, now used by the Girl Guide Association, are impressive enough & give some idea of how imposing the hall must have been).

At almost the same time as Boulsover was realising the possibilities of fused plate after his accident with a knife handle in 1743, **Benjamin Huntsman (qv)** was working on his revolutionary **crucible steel (qv).** Boulsover's invention was the trigger for Sheffield's vast silver industry; other Sheffield platers such as Hancock; Tudor & Leader; Gainsford, Bradbury etc. attracted to the town by the trade and manufacturing the full range of holloware- tea pots, candlesticks etc. in a wide variety of patterns**;** formation of the **Assay Office (qv)** in 1773; the massive Victorian firms **Mappin & Webb; Walker & Hall; James Dixon(qv)** etc; today's renaissance with craftsmen and women drawn to the city by the facilities & opportunities here... Huntsman's invention was the trigger for the even vaster Sheffield steel industry.

Why are the world's first fused plate and the world's first 'proper' steel mentioned in the same breath? .... Simply because the plate wouldn't have been successful without the fine steel used to make rolls and dies to work it. The skills of the diesinker in cutting out intricate silverware patterns in blocks of steel are incredible.

Boulsover himself was drawn to the steel business, and though he kept on making buttons in Sheffield plate, he built workshops in the Porter valley to roll crucible cast steel into sheet with which to make superior saws. He built stone cottages for his workers by a dam and wheel, which he enlarged to power the rolling and grinding.

Take a walk upstream from **Shepherd Wheel (qv)** and before you reach **Forge Dam** see the memorial plaque to Boulsover set in stones from his demolished mill, and donated by steelman David Flather when he was **Master Cutler** in 1926. Nearby is Boulsover's dam, a nice stretch of water in beautiful surroundings, now popularly known as **Wire Mill Dam** after the trade of a subsequent owner.

Bowser is how Sheffielders would have pronounced Boulsover.

bow(s) scissor finger hole(s)

bow dresser man who grinds/polishes scissor bows.

Bowie knives big fighting, hunting, frontiersman knives made in Sheffield ever since **George Wostenholm (qv)** supplied at least a dozen to Colonel James Bowie himself. They still make them today, beautiful decorative knives, blades etched with 'Americana'; the bald eagle, stars and stripes etc and slogans such as 'Land of the free' and 'Remember the Alamo'.

Other firms making bowies today include **Jack Adams, A.Wright, Stan Shaw, Stuart Mitchell** and **Reg Cooper.**

Boxing Day massacre when Wednesday, near the bottom of the league, beat United, near the top, 4-0 at Hillsborough in 1979.

Joseph Bramah (1749-1814) b. Stainborough, Barnsley engineer, invented the hydraulic press; (one is in **Kelham Island Museum** that was used at the Royal Mint for the Bank of England). The massive 10,000 ton **forging press** at **Sheffield Forgemasters,** which can shape 200 ton blocks of hot steel as if it were butter, is testimony to the efficacy of hydraulic power, originally harnassed by **Bramah.**

He also invented an improved lock; the **Bramah lock,** and the **Bramah pan water closet,** patented in 1778. This latter, an example of which is at the renovated **Butcher Wheel** building on **Arundel Street,** was superseded by a superior water closet invented by another local man, **Thomas** - no schoolboy titters please - **Crapper,** born at **Thorne**.

The **Bramah lock** was much respected and gets mentioned in The Pickwick Papers **(1836-1837).** There are references to **Bramah** keys at a lawyers, and old Mr.Veller (Weller), speaking to his son Samivel (Sam) about his fear of being chased by a certain buxom female complains; "If I wos locked up in a fire-proof chest vith a **patent Brahmin,** sh'd find means to get at me, Sammy."

A branch of the **Bramah** family were involved in the Sheffield metal trades on Devonshire street and are now at Holbrook. They made beautiful satin-finished stainless steel holloware (teapots, gravy boats, mixing bowls, toast racks etc.) in the 1950's/60's, then moved over to aerospace parts when teapots with wobbly lids & other holloware, poor quality but dirt cheap, came flooding in from the Far East. Now in the world-wide **Doncasters** group of companies they make, for instance, jet engine cowls for Boeing. Doncasters are better known in Sheffield as **Daniel Doncaster,** or **Donny's (qv)**

Bramall Lane, Brammer Lane, 'Lane home to Empire Day celebrations and WW1 recruitment campaigns, as well of course to **Sheffield United Football Club,** the **Blades,** founded **1889**. The ground was opened 34 years earlier however, on April 30th **1855**, as home to **Sheffield United Cricket Club**. Two of its members, anxious to keep their men together during the winter months formed **Sheffield Football Club (qv)** in October **1857**, the world's first football club. Yorkshire County cricket team was also founded in Sheffield & **Bramall Lane** became its senior ground. Having a football pitch next to a cricket pitch though, was unsatisfactory –you needed binoculars to watch **Jimmy Hagan** weaving his magic way if you were stuck at the cricket pavilion end- so the cricket pitch was dug up, a stand was built and Bramall Lane became a proper 4-sided football ground.

Memories of cricket persist; the knowledgeable, witty and irreverent crowds; the Cricketers Arms pub on Bramall Lane; even in an infant school 1940's cheeky, robustly - sung rhyme:

'One day dahn at **Brammer Lane**
we were playin' at cricket;
'ball went up mi trouser leg
and hit mi middle wicket!'

brat white apron worn by cutlers, silversmiths and **buffer girls (qv); buff brats.** Sometimes leather aprons used if working on heavy or sharp objects; **saw smithers (qv)** working on and handling circular saws up to six feet diameter at firms such as **Spear & Jackson, Atkinson Walker, Sanderson Kayser (qv)** would wear **armoured brats,** leather brats reinforced by rows of metal studs for protection.

braungin' boasting, boastful, clever dick; he's a **reight braungin' chuff.** Can also imply moaning, **whittling (qv).**

bray to hit, beat, hammer;
ah'll bray thee;
'window wor brayed in.

bread cake made of plain bread, as used in making jam butties, or chip butties; may be offered as **cakey bread** to tiny children to make it sound more appetising.

bread saw bread knife with fine serrations.

Harry Brearley (1871-1948) inventor of stainless steel in 1913. A remarkable man, eighth of nine children, born in a back yard off Spital St. in what was known as a 'House, Chamber and Garret' dwelling. Three rooms and the **house (qv)** was only 12 ft. square, so Brearley much preferred life on the teeming streets with **Little Mesters (qv)** workshops, and railway warehouses, grain stores & stables to explore. He couldn't remember anything about school and soon left to work, underage, at a workshop making clogs 8 a.m. to 11 p.m., then at Moorwood's iron foundry varnishing kitchen stoves. Finally his father, steel melter at Firth's, took him on as his cellar lad in the crucible furnace in 1882, the fourth of his sons to work for him. Harry's brother, Arthur, in the next furnace, looked after his 11 year old brother who relished learning something of the art of the steelmaker, working 5.30 a.m. to 6.30 p.m.

When Firth's found he was below the minimum age required by the Factory Act he was discharged, though was taken on later as a bottle-washer, at twelve years old, by the chemist at the firm's laboratories in 1883.

This man took him under his wing, teaching him glass blowing; sent him to learn soldering in the plumbers' shop, and woodworking in the joiners' shop; bought him a 600 page algebra text book, which Brearley treasured, and got him to go to nightschool.

Ruskin's 'Unto this Last' was a revelation, and the youngster wrote a library copy out in full by hand.

When his mentor emigrated to Australia, Brealey moved, as chemist to Kayser Ellison's in 1901 (subsequently known as **Sanderson Kayser (qv)**), another high class steelmaker.

C.W.Kayser, German born who came to Sheffield as a scissor forger, was mean - he took one of Brearley's two pencils with the observation that 'only one could be used at a time' - but allowed him to do private analytical work on steels and publish a book on the subject. Brearley thus became a very skilled man with his diligent chemical analysis of steel, and also pioneered instruments to measure steel's temperature in a furnace, forming his own firm, Amalgams Co. to manufacture pyrometers.

The steelworks' chemists came into their own with the various grades of alloy steels, but Brearley much admired the skills of the Sheffield steelmen, personified by his father & brother, Arthur. So long as the wide range of carbon steels were made 'the good melter was not handicapped by the want of a chemical laboratory. He knocked the end off the cold ingot & saw in the fractured surface more than a college full of analysts could tell him. If the ingot contained blowholes or showed signs of being cast from too high a temperature it was scrapped: the 'topping' operation secured what chemical analysis cannot ensure, viz: sound ingot material.' If sound the experienced melter had the extraordinary ability of judging 'from the appearance of the fractured surface the degree of hardness..... & the particular category into which it should be classified for making this or that kind of tool.' He could 'distinguish..... a variation in hardness corresponding to a fiftieth part of one percent of carbon....a fine art.' This remarkable faculty 'was exercised by workmen who had nothing to say for themselves. A description of how they distinguished the fine shades of difference between fractured surfaces has never appeared in print & probably never will'

He took a job in Riga, then in Russia, for Firth's in 1904 to manage a partly built steelworks they had bought to make files, then later to make shells after the revolt in 1905 (precursor of the October 1917 revolution). He took skilled Sheffield men with him, including his brother, Arthur, though one Sheffielder, supposedly an expert hardener, was not up to the job. This man was a 'romancer of the first water' who confided 'the secret of hardening shells is to heat the buggers'. His shells failed firing tests & Brearley took over the hardening shop.

Back in Sheffield Brealey was made head of the new **Brown-Firth Research** laboratories on Princess street, (buildings which are now home to **English Pewter Company,** while steel research is carried out today at nearby premises by **Allvac (qv)**) It was at these laboratories that he discovered **stainless steel (qv)** in 1913, while experimenting with chromium additions for improved rifle barrels. It is thought that rejected polished samples were later found to have remarkable resistance to rust, & Brearley had the perception to forsee many uses for the steel as well as its revolutionary use for knife blades. See cutlers **R.F. Moseley.**

A dispute with Firth's over the discovery led to him joining rival steel firm **Brown Bayley** in 1915.

Breweries Sheffield, Rotherham & Barnsley rivalled Burton-on -Trent for beer production a hundred years ago, but the big firms have now all gone. Some favourites were:

Barnsley Brewery, Oakwell Ales, opened 1861 and closed a hundred years later.

Bentley's of Rotherham.

Duncan Gilmour

Hope & Anchor, latterly of Claywheels Lane, Wadsley Bridge, well known for a black Sheffield stout, **Jubilee Stout,** which rivalled Mackeson's and Guiness. Drunks and students are recalled singing a patriotic refrain; 'Land of Hope and Anchor,
Mother of the free.........'

Hope & Anchor exported their stout to Canada in a deal with a Canadian brewery which introduced Carling Black Label to England. Jubilee Stout has faded away whilst Carling has gone from strength to strength to become the best selling beer in Britain.

Mappin's, Masbro Old Brewery, Rotherham. It was founded in 1835 and the man who was the power behind it, John Newton Mappin, died in 1884. He founded the **Mappin Art Gallery,** Weston Park, and was related to the Mappin of **Mappin & Webb (qv),** world-famous silversmiths.

Less high minded Rotherham lads used to sing, after a jar or two;

'We are the boys from Mappin's brewery
Sup like hell and fart like fury'

Richdales, 'for rich ales' towered over Bramall Lane ground.

Hy. Stones, Stooanses Cannon Ales of Neepsend, the favourite beer for most steelworkers, some calling it 'Jungle Juice.' The brewery, along with Bramall Lane & Sean Bean, featured in the film; 'When Saturday comes.'

Tennant Brothers impressive Exchange Brewery near Lady's Bridge was built in 1852, and there are substantial remains, converted in the last ten years into offices and apartments. They brewed a very strong bottled beer, Tennant's Gold Label, which was in the Guiness Book of Records for its strength at one time. Whitbread's took them over in 1962 and closed them down in 1993.

Ward's, or **Waard's** on Ecclesall Rd. was the last big local brewery to go, its clock tower, maltings and other buildings converted to apartments, with pleasing stainless steel sculptures of hops to remind people of its heritage. Established in 1840 it was, along with **Stooanses,** Sheffield's most popular beer, and there was much anger when Sunderland owner, Vaux were more interested in the value of the site for development, than in the brewing tradition.

Fortunately, Sheffield is in the vanguard for Real Ale pubs and there's a Neepsend trail covering pubs on Shalesmoor to Kelham Island, to Neepsend to Penistone Rd., Owlerton.

There are micro breweries including **Abbeydale; Crown** (Hillsborough Hotel)**; Farmer's** (Bradfield)**; Kelham Island; Port Mahon** (Cask & Cutler)**; Thornbridge; Wentworth. The Gardeners Rest** pub at Neepsend is set to brew its own ale nearby. The biggest, and holding most awards, particularly for its Pale Rider beer is **Kelham Island Brewery.**

Brick works There were scores of quarries and brick works in the region e.g. Sheffield Brick Co. off Chesterfield Rd., and off Rutland Rd. making house bricks; Hepworth near Penistone, well known to-day for clay piping; but refractory bricks and products for the steel and glass industries were, and are the local speciality. Current manufacturers include, Steetley, Vesuvius, and Sheffield refractories; previous stalwarts were Pickford and Holland on Archer Rd., Dyson at Attercliffe and Totley, and Wragg at Loxley.

Dyson now make other products, and the main Pickford & Holland site has grocers Sainsbury on one side of Archer Rd. and Aldi on the other, the sound of shopping trolleys superseding the sound of industry.
This was an interesting area; beehive furnaces, towering chimney, rock crushing machinery, quarry eating into Hutcliffe wood, remains of a **ganister (qv)** mine loading bay (still visible) on Hutcliffe wood road. Men would get from the quarry site to the main works using a tunnel under Archer road. They shared this with local foxes doing their rounds. The sounds of rock being crushed competed with nearby Laycock's drop stamping clutch discs. The foxes were attracted by the sound of chickens and pigs in the allotments above the quarry.

Brincliffe Quarries Psalter Lane, Quarry Lane, Brincliffe Edge, now **Hallam University Psalter** Lane site; former source of sandstone for local buildings, and of **Brincliffe Blue**, a fine gritstone which, along with **Wickersley**, was the best stone for making grindstones for the finest work on knives and razors.

Brindley & Foster were church organ builders at Columbia Place, 30-46 **Suffolk Road** from **1854** to **1939. Thomas Wm. Handforth,** born at Hunslet, Leeds in **1867,** when organist at **Sheffield Parish Church** (now the **cathedral)** composed a 'Celebration March; the **Brindley March**' when the organ was refurbished by the firm, and therafter, whenever a new organ was built at Columbia Place, the march was played on it. This information thanks to **Martin Dawes,** the **Star,** August **2007. Martin** goes on to say that Mancunian **Bryan Hughes,** is writing a history of the firm.

British Army knife not your namby-pamby Swiss officer's version laddie, the tough British Army knife has been made in Sheffield for a hundred years or so, stamped with year & government arrow head.
Older ones, WW1 & 2 are very collectable, especially by Americans who like to find one for every year. Heavy duty blade, spike, tin opener and screwdriver, shackled; originally with black bexite covering, criss-crossed for grip, now all stainless. The Navy knife is bigger, as befits the Senior Service.

William Broadhead saw grinders' union man heavily involved in the **Sheffield Outrages (qv)**

brock badger; **Brocco Bank**, Hunter's Bar.

brokken broken; 'Here am I, brokken hearted, paid a penny, & only farted.'
(Childish ditty from the 1940's when you had to put a big old penny in the door of a public **lav,** when you wanted a **bobar (qv).)**

Brookes & Crookes not one of the largest cutlery firms but a good example of many hundreds of small to medium size firms making products that are to Sheffield's eternal credit. Founded in 1858 in the **Atlantic** works, **St. Philip's Road**, their bell trade mark graced fine razors, table knives and pen knives right until 1957, by which time demand for high quality products was in decline.
A speciality of the firm was a patented cartridge extracting knife, and other multi-blade, multi-implement folding knives, incorporating such things as pruner, saw, magnifying glass, cigar cutter etc.

Broomhill Sheffield 10 in the lush, hilly, wooded West End. John Betjeman's poem; **'An Edwardian Sunday, Broomhill, Sheffield'** is marvellously evocative and he had much affection for the, then black, sandstone houses, probably including those in even grander **Fulwood** and **Crosspool**. In an article on 3rd July 1961 in the Daily Telegraph & Morning Post he wrote; 'Greek, Italian, Gothic, they stand in winding, tree-shaded roads, these handsome mansions of the Victorian industrialists who had made their pile from steel and cutlery.... They lived in what is still the prettiest suburb in England...'
Broomhill itself is busy and chic, made livelier by thousands of students. The whole area, including **Fulwood**, **Crosspool**, **Dore** & **Totley** is constantly portrayed in national surveys as one of the richest in Britain, but with the green belt / **Peak Park** in the adjoining western heights forbidding expansion there is, unfortunately, pressure to fill extensive, Victorian gardens with cramped, expensive new homes.

Spence Broughton hanged for highway robbery in 1792, his body was left on Attercliffe Common in a gibbet to decompose as a warning to other evil doers. A modern replica hangs outside a pub on **Broughton Lane** opposite **Hallam FM Arena**.
There is a nice anecdote in the South Yorkshire, Derbyshire, Notts. & Lincs. Quarterly, June 1900 (seen in the Local Studies Dept., Central Library):
A Sheffield workman called Smithers made a bet with a friend called Mathers that he daren't take a basin of broth at midnight to Spence Broughton's skeleton hanging high in its gibbet. The bet was accepted & Mathers carried the broth up a ladder placed against the gibbet. Smithers was hiding behind the gibbet planning to scare off Mathers.
Mathers held out the steaming broth to the skeleton & said;
'I've brought thee some broth, Spence lad.'
Smithers replied in a ghostly voice;
't's too hot'
Mathers insisted;
'then blow on it lad'
..... He won the wager.

Sir John Brown 1816-1896 his father, a slater, wanted him to be a draper, but young John said he would be a (steel) merchant, because a draper only deals with local people whereas a merchant trades with the whole wide world. From humble beginnings he became one of the Victorian giants of Sheffield steel.

By the time he'd expanded his works on the greenfield site that was the East End, by the river Don, he lived in an imposing house; **Shirle Hill** at Nether Edge. He was so important that the P.M., Lord Palmerston visited him to discuss arms and the Navy's requirements. He was too busy to go to Westminster. He later moved to **Endcliffe Hall,** built at enormous expense.

His main markets were **1**. The railways. He invented the conical, spring-loaded steel buffer 'to prevent damage from the violent concussion of railway carriages'; forged wheels, tyres and axles; made carriage & engine springs; rolled railway lines from **Bessemer steel (qv). 2.** The Navy. Like neighbouring steelmen, Cammell & the Vickers Brothers he eventually had his own shipyards. His were on the Clyde and built ships of the line for the Navy using heavy gun forgings, cast gun turrets, rolled armour plate (by 1861 a typical size had reached 20ft x 4ft x 5inch thick) from his Sheffield works. After his death the yards built cruise liners too in the early 20th century, culminating in the Queen Mary & the Queen Elizabeth in the 1930's.

Brown's began to have a close relationship in late Victorian times with Thos. Firth & Sons, another of the giants of Sheffield steel. The two firms collaborated on research and by 1908 **Brown-Firth Research Laboratories** were established in a solid red-brick 3 storey building on Princess St., subsequently home to the invention & perfection of stainless steels-see **Brearley & Hatfield.** (The building is now occupied by English Pewter Company with steel research carried out nearby on Attercliffe Common by **Allvac,** one of the successors to the Victorian firms.) The two firms amalgamated when the steel trade faltered after WW1 and became known as **Firth Brown Ltd.** Post WW2 and with the Labour government's second nationalisation of 'the commanding heights of the economy,' local control of this and other major British steel firms passed to the government and civil servants in London.

brush; livin' o'er 'brush unmarried couple living together.

Brush House, the Brushes built 1790 on the site of an old farm called **Brushes farm,** by 1900 it was the home of steelman **Charles Kayser (qv),** who was said to have added the distinguished castle-like tower to remind him of his German homeland. In 1920 the house was transferred to Sheffield Education Authority and the first pupils of the new Firth Park Secondary School were admitted in the same year. The first headmaster, a remarkable character, Dr. Lloyd Storr-Best knew ten languages, including ancient & modern Greek, was a fine gymnast, and was friends with leading Sheffield industrialists. An all boys school the lads were known as **Redcaps,** sang the school song in Latin (six verses), and generally lusted after knowledge and girls. In 1937 the school became **Firth Park Grammar School** and the reputation of its 650 boys for football, music and languages especially, was notable until 1969 when it 'went comprehensive.' Every pupil learned French with a choice of G.I.R.L.S. in the second year onwards (= German, Italian, Russian, Latin, Spanish).

Every one of you will have memories of school-teachers. Mine are;

Dr. Eker (Joe Plug). A Jewish refugee from Austria, he made boys learn French phrases by heart, and countered any question about inconsistency in grammatical rules by saying: 'I don't know, I didn't invent the language'. He would creep towards a wrong-doer singing 'I taut I taw a puddy cat a-creeping up on me' and, bursting upon him, 'I am dat great big puddy cat, Sylvester is my name!'

Spike Johnson, history teacher and author of the history of the Brushes, graphically showed how barges progressed through Brindley's tunnel by laying on his back and pedalling his feet in the air.

Joe Over (hymn; 'Guide me oh, though great Joe Over') taught Italian & French. Irascible, he had an iron hand, replacement for his own shot off in the Great War, with which he used to swipe errant boys.

Ken Bown taught Spanish and was a week-end flyer for the R.A.F. Cynics claimed his was the Meteor jet flying slightly askew in a formation at Norton airshow.

Gagan, one of the best three maths teachers in England, he told us. Called everybody Bill. Sarcastic, he clipped a tired-looking lad rhythmically on the head to the verse; 'Oh sleep it is a lovely thing, beloved from pole to pole.' Told a lad from Intake he'd not much output, again with a clip to the head. Gave a lesson on the English language after an Attercliffe lad, accused of spoiling a text book had countered vigorously 'It weren't spoilt, 'book'

'Duke' Weatherall, assistant head, drew a graph of Le Grand Meaulnes' emotional feelings, when guiding pupils through this classic French tale of adolescence. A bald man, he advised against going at things bald-headedly, 'even if you are like me'.

Dr. F.T. (Hefty or Fred) Wood was old fashioned, wore spats, innocent of schoolboy guile, he was author of a standard English language grammar, which, he claimed, was used in twelve different countries, 'even in Malaya.' At this a lad in the front row turned to the rest of the class and said; 'Aye aye, local boy makes good!'

brussen , a brussen bloke small, stocky, bold, perhaps prickly, bad tempered man; **brussen** also used, if rarely to mean full up; **f.f.t.b.** fat, full to bustin.'

buff to polish cutlery to a mirror finish on a wheel,(buff). A standard wheel is 10/12 inch diameter, wooden with leather periphery, originally buffalo, hence the name. (Bullneck, sea elephant, and walrus hide were also used, the latter known in Sheffield as sea horse.) The leather would be treated with resin, melted in a small ladle over a gas ring. **Blade buffs** are wheels with their resin coating rolled in an abrasive grit, for glazing knives.

buffer girls often singing, often unsung heroes of the cutlery trade. They would mix together special buffing sand and engine oil, pick up about half a dozen spoons with one hand, and scoop up a handful of oily, damp sand with the other & present both to the revolving buff in a graceful, rhythmical, rocking movement. As with many skilled trades, they made it appear deceptively simple.

They wore **brats (qv),** aprons, were sometimes known as **buff brats,** and with legs covered by brown paper & headscarves topping dirty faces they were a powerful influence in the trade. Feared by young male apprentices who were sometimes black balled, and worse, they were given a respectful distance by the public as they emerged, in working gear, down the Moor, arms linked, laughing and singing.

buffit, buffet low stool; pouffe, puff.

bug blinding describes a workshop newly white washed. This isn't always popular with cutlers, buffers and grinders. The Factory Inspectorate required an annual limewash/white wash but **Ed. Chapman**, a pocket knife grinder for 57 years confirmed to me before he died, aged 102 in 2002 that he couldn't see his work so well against the glaring white background.

Cutlers at **A. Wright's** said the same when they moved from fine old premises on **Sidney St**. to equally fine old premises, newly white washed, on **Charles St**.

buggerlugs rascal.

playing silly buggers pretending to be ignorant to avoid a job, or duty.

bull week the week before Christmas in the cutlery trade with much overtime worked to pay for the holiday.

(cow week = 2 weeks before Christmas; **calf week** = 3 weeks before).

bulleead small fish=bull head or miller's thumb caught, along with stickleback and **taddies** by **Heeley** friends in pools in Cat Lane woods (now housing), and by **Neepsend** friends **up Rivelin.**

bumbailiff rent or debt collector, sheriff's officer, landlord's assistant, celebrated in the doggerel:

' We're reight dahn in 'coyal oyal
weer 'muck slarts (or slaps) on 'winders.
We've used all ahr coyal up
an' we're reight dahn ter'cinders.
If 'bumbailiff comes he waint know weer ter find us
'cus we're reight dahn in 'coyal oyal
weer 'muck slarts on 'winders.'

A translation begins; 'We are deep down in the basement where the dirt accumulates on the casement.......' A similar rhyme is known in Cheshire, and no doubt elsewhere.

Burgon & Ball **La Plata** works at Malin Bridge, on the site of a 1690's grinding wheel, have been famous for their one hand sheep shears for over 250 years. On a recent visit to the works packets of shears were labelled for export to Montana and Melbourne. Now they are made & marketed too for garden use; grass trimming and light pruning.

burnisher a woman in the silver trade, or man in the pocket knife trade who works silverware and steel respectively to a mirror finish, using steel-headed tools; a job requiring much patience & skill. Helen Aldridge, burnisher at **Dixon's** & **Walker & Hall's(qv),** when interviewed by Valerie Answer in 1980 listed the tools she used as 'leather away; half Dutchman; two-faced; a dot; a pin dot; round; little two-faced; an ounce steel; a little stone; a round stone.'

Men burnished steel parts of pocket knives using considerable pressure, with burnishing tools made sometimes from old files smoothed to brighten the backs of springs, for example, to look good and, in the case of carbon steels, to resist rusting.

burnt blades blades overheated on the wheel, spoiling their temper.

burrited heads **revit** (rivet) heads made from steel or brass wire hammered & polished on a knife handle, slightly protuding, in the shape of a little round cap.(cf. Spanish **el birrete,** cap).

W. & S. Butcher founded about 1725 by two brothers they became steel & tool manufacturers as, well as knife makers with a substantial American trade. Their imposing four storey red brick building built in 1835 & set round a courtyard was called **Butcher's Wheel,** following the fashion of the day in retaining the word **wheel,** though firms had moved from water wheels along the rivers to steam power in town. The building, on Arundel St. is now being converted to flats, with the ground floor used by the admirable **Freeman College(qv)** for traditional **Little Mester(qv)** metal workshops.

George Butler fine old Sheffield cutlery firm whose key trademark was granted in 1681, and 'ART' mark was registered in 1861.Their hand-forged, hand-ground knives, scissors and razors were top class. After merging with another fine firm, Leppington's and moving into their big factory, (now demolished) on Matilda St. for some years, they are now in Deeley's factory in Handsworth, owned by **Arthur Price of England.**

button making was a Sheffield speciality from **Boulsover's(qv)** Old Sheffield Plate to those made from stag & buffalo horn offcuts. Two branches of the **Singleton** family made mother of pearl buttons at **Hackenthorpe** & **Rosedale Rd**.(off **Ecclesall Rd**.). The cockney 'Pearly Kings & Queens' used to visit Sheffield to have their attire covered in **Singleton's** buttons.

butty workmate (mining); bread cake sandwich (chip butty).

buttyman sub contractor in the cutlery trade; a **Little Mester.**

C

C & A Dutch owned clothes stores known as **Cooats ats** in Sheffield & **Coits an' Ats** in Chapeltown and Barnsley. Sometimes too, known by words too vulgar to print.

cabbage to pinch, steal; **to cabbage a few yards** = to take a free kick or throw in further up the field than you should.

Thos. R. Cadman famous for open razors for which they were granted the **Bengal** mark in 1748.

cagmag cheap trifle comprising cake soaked in jelly topped with custard; gristly meat.

Cake & chips please when ordered at the chip shop **(chip oyal; chip og)** note that the Sheffield area fish cake comprises of two big slices of potato with pieces of cod between, the whole immersed in batter.

cake oyal mouth; **shut thi cake oyal.** (rude).

callin' (usually of women) chattering, gossiping. More usual in north Sheffield to the West Riding; see **cantin'**

Charles Cammell (1810-1879) one of the Victorian giants of Sheffield steel whose firm moved to the greenfield site that was the flat land beyond the **Wicker (qv),** alongside the River Don and the railway line to Rotherham. This was as early as 1845 and their **Cyclops Works** was followed by **Firth's, John Brown's, Vickers, Jessop's** etc. leading to the powerhouse that became known as Sheffield's **East End.**

Some indication of the power & influence of Sheffield steel firms at the time of the British Association for the Advancement of Science meeting in the city, 1910, is shown by the list of **Cammell's** undertakings at the time:

Cyclops Works; Armour plate, forgings, railway axles, tool steels, files.

Grimesthorpe Works; a mile further down the Midland Railway line, made heavy forgings & castings, gun forgings, steel tyres, springs, buffers, projectiles.

Yorkshire Steel & Iron Works, Penistone; railway tyres, axles, forgings, billets & bars.

Derwent Iron & Steel Works, Workington; 3 blast furnaces and a railway line factory that was moved from Penistone in 1882 to take advantage of world trade via Workington harbour. After well over a hundred years rail production has almost returned home: the **Corus** plant at Workington has closed in 2006 and a new one has opened at **Corus,** Scunthorpe.

Solway Iron Works, Maryport; 3 blast furnaces.

Three **Hematite** iron ore mines in Cumberland.

New Oaks Collieries, Barnsley

Cammell Laird, Shipbuilding and Engineering Works, Birkenhead. Like their Sheffield neighbours, John Brown & Vickers, they wanted to control building of battleships from rolling armour plate, and forging the guns to launching the ships.

The Coventry Ordnance Works Ltd, joint owned with John Brown.

Cammell eventually merged with **Vickers** becoming **English Steel Corporation** until nationalisation after WW2. In 1863 they had installed the world's first hydraulic press (invented by **Bramah (qv)**) which is a forerunner of **Sheffield Forgemasters** 10,000 ton press. Their **Cyclops Works** lives on, now home to aerospace steels specialists **Allvac (qv).**

You can see Norton Hall, now apartments, Charles Cammell's home for some years, set at the top of the beautiful **Grave's Park,** near fields grazed by highland cattle, and next to the picturesque Norton church and the **Chantrey (qv)** memorial. He moved from Norton to an even bigger home, **Brookfield Manor**, nestling at the foot of hills leading to North Lees and Stanage Edge, with a long drive leading in the opposite direction down a flat valley to Hathersage main road, near the George inn. Look at the stone gatehouse with his trade mark camel and **PERSEVERANDO**.

candle end knife with plain handle rounded at the end.

Cannon Hall a Barnsley museum of South Yorkshire Life, once home to the **Spencer** ironmasters. **John Spencer** leased **Wortley Forges (qv)** in **1658.**

canker illness little boys were threatened with if they sucked copper coins. **Tha' ll get canker.**

cantin' gossiping

capertling flirting

Cappo the much loved Tony Capstick from Swinton Bridge Rotherham, brilliant, funny comedian on **Radio Sheffield** with a keen interest in dialect. One feature was a selection of romantic recordings which he introduced as **Lurv in the afternooin'.** He had a hit song based on a nostalgic Hovis record, and **laiked (qv)** as a policeman in 'The last of the summer wine'.(He explained **'laiked** meaning played, not shirked).
He liked to play with words; If **oyal** is hole, what is **oil**?....Answer; **greease.**

Carbrook Hall an Elizabethan building succeeding other halls on the site since 1176, now a pub in the shadow of the huge **Sheffield Forgemasters (qv)** electric melting shop. The hall was home to John Bright, a keen Sheffield parliamentarian in the Civil War, and Cromwell, who visited Carbrook, made him governor of **Sheffield Castle (qv)** during the siege of 1644. It is interesting to think that Cromwell saw the same fine oak panelling and fireplace that we can admire today.

Carl Wark a plateau on the moors above Longshaw and Fox House & below Higger Tor, with iron age fortifications, including an impressive wall along the top of the north side, which otherwise would have been easy to scale by a determined enemy. The wall, still defiant since when it was built between 2000/2500 B.C. is made of stones big enough to deter thieves & vandals over the centuries.

Lawrence Field on the Longshaw estate has evidence of iron age dwellings and it is easy to visualise these people, when threatened, trudging up to Carl Wark to repulse any attack.

captain a general word used by a man when addressing another man informally. There are many others; boss, bud, cocker, squire, jarv (heard in Mexborough), **surrey (qv),** youth (south Sheffield to Notts.), **mi ol',** ahr kid, kiddo, lad (but not **laddo (qv)** which is used specifically when you've forgotten someone's name).

Edward Carpenter (1844-1925) homosexual poet & pioneering socialist, he admired Sheffielders, if a touch condescendingly:

"From the first I was taken with the Sheffield people, rough in the extreme, twenty or thirty years in date behind other towns, and very uneducated, there was yet a heartiness about them, not without shrewdness, which attracted me."

Carr's Silverware, Holbrook founded and owned by **Ron Carr** who started on his own making & selling hallmarked silver ingot necklets and has gone on to develop the largest silverware manufacturing firm in Britain, if not in Europe. He has bucked the trend for traditional large firms to 'downsize' and his skilled workforce produce an ever expanding range of silverware & cutlery in modern, as well as resurrected Victorian designs. Along with boffins at **Sheffield Hallam University** Carr's have invented **Lustre silver;** sterling silver that does not tarnish, though, of course, sweaty finger marks need to be wiped off as soon as possible.

Large areas of the superb West End of Sheffield are being spoiled by landowners, including the church, selling out to developers who cram as many expensive houses as they can into the gardens of large Victorian houses, felling some of Sheffield's two million trees in the process. Ron Carr has bucked this trend too and, as well as saving & enhancing a big garden at Whirlow has built an impressive new home (which Roger Redfern includes in his book; 'Sheffield's Remarkable Houses')

casey caseball, old fashioned leather football which became very heavy on muddy fields.

cast steel stamped on a knife = forged from **crucible (qv) cast steel** as opposed to **shear steel** or **stainless steel.** Stamped on a saw could mean **crucible, open hearth** or **electrically melted steel,** depending upon the saw's age.

Castleton small **Peak District** village with big attractions: caverns, Norman castle, blue john stone, Winnats Pass, Mam Tor, stone hoses, stone pubs, stone church, stone Y.H.A., Britain's deepest cave, Titan recently revealed under Cave Dale.

Catcliffe Cone the oldest surviving glassworks cone in Europe, it was one of two built about 1740 by William Fenny, previously works manager at **Bolsterstone (qv) glasshouse.** Fenny's Bolsterstone glass products were high quality and 'were carried to London and other places and sold at higher than market price by the name of London glass or some other name.' Fenny married Mary Fox, daughter of the owners who passed the business to their son. Fenny wanted to set up his own business in Bolsterstone but his mother-in-law's will stipulated that he shouldn't make glass within ten miles of the village. Hence his choice of Catcliffe, near Rotherham, ten and a half miles to the south east.

Benjamin Huntsman, inventor of **crucible steel (qv)** in nearby Handsworth, knew of the glassmaking process in crucibles and was possibly influenced by the Catcliffe works- though glass melts at 1100 degrees centigrade and he would have to attain 1600 degrees in his furnace and hold it there for 4 hours or so to make reliable **cast steel**.

Caudwell's Mill an interesting stone-built working flour mill at Rowsley, near Bakewell, powered by 2 water turbines. Its restoration was thanks to Mike Tilley, a member of **Sheffield Trades Historical Society (qv).**

cellereead cellar head; space at the top of the cellar steps, home to the fridge perhaps, or brushes, shovels & shoes with dank smell of whitewash.

cementation steel was made in brick built conical cementation furnaces not unlike those used to make pottery and glass.

Flat bars of wrought iron, typically 3 inch x ½ inch x 10/12 feet long, interspersed with charcoal, were piled inside open-topped **sandstone chests** known as **'coffins'** (usually 2 per furnace) measuring 4ft x 4ft x 12ft. The chests were sealed on top by an airtight thick layer of **wheelswarf**, the 'sludge' mixture of water, steel & stone particles from grinders' troughs, and heated over 5 to 12 days to between 800 and 1150 degrees centigrade, depending upon the grade of steel required. The wrought iron, which is virtually carbon-free, was

converted to steel by carbon from the charcoal seeping into the bars, the gas released giving them a blistered appearance, when they were extracted after several days cooling. The **blister steel** bars were often reheated in bundles of 9 or 12 and forge welded together under a tilt hammer to produce the famous Sheffield **shear steel,** which was sometimes cut and again forge welded to produce the even more celebrated **double shear steel;** the ideal steel for knife blades, being capable of being sharpened to a vicious edge.
Upon **Huntsman's** invention of **crucible steel (qv)** blister steel bars were used**,** broken into small pieces as the raw material for this, the world's first cast steel made to consistent, & reliable formulas.
The cementation process originated in Germany and arrived in Sheffield between 1650 & 1700. Both the furnace and the furnace man were known as a **converter (qv)** since they converted iron into steel. One of the earliest Sheffield steel makers, **Samuel Shore,** with at least 2 furnaces by 1709 'bound a steel **converter** to work his furnaces & his only, for ten years at 6 shillings per week plus 6 pence as charitable grant to his mother'.
Originally furnaces were of 5 tons capacity but eventually the norm was 25/ 30 tons. By 1835 there were 56 cementation furnaces in Sheffield & 554 crucible melting holes. Just 21 years later there were 206 cementation furnaces producing 51,000 tons of blister steel, most of which, apart from that for shear steel knives, was used in 2113 crucible melting holes. At about this time **Bessemer (qv)** had invented another & much bigger type of **converter** which converted molten **cast iron** into bulk steel by blowing air through the iron & **reducing** carbon content to make **mild steel**- see the monster hanging near the entrance to **Kelham Island Museum.**
See what is possibly the world's only surviving cementation furnace on Doncaster St., near Hoyle St. This was built in 1848, one of 5 that **Daniel Doncaster (qv)** began in 1831, in his father's orchard. The survivor celebrated its last converting charge in 1951, when it was said to have been fired 10th October and drawn on 31 December to produce '4 temper shear steel'.

chairs; **She's got all her chairs at 'ooam** She's a bright lass.

chaiteead daft person

Sir Francis Chantrey (1781-1841) Victorian England's greatest sculptor with fine examples of his work at Lichfield Cathedral, Westminster Abbey, St. Paul's and the Cutlers Hall. He was born at Norton and is buried there in the grounds of the fine old Anglican church. A simple but impressive memorial stands by the road.

chapel 'at pegs used in the phrase; eyes, or nipples, **'standing aht like chapel 'at pegs'.**

charcoal made from oak in Sheffield for the **cementation** steel making process. See the memorial in Ecclesall woods to a charcoal burner who was burned to death.

Chatsworth England's most famous stately home and gardens date from between **1687** and **1707** and have been owned by the Devonshires ever since. The earlier, Elizabethan Chatsworth had belonged to **Bess (qv) of Hardwick's** second husband Sir William Cavendish, who had commenced rebuilding work in 1552. When he died in 1557, the house was left to his young, ambitious wife who completed the work. **Bess's** 4th husband was the powerful **George Talbot, 6th Earl of Shrewsbury (qv)** and when they were instructed to guard **Mary, Queen of Scots (qv)** they held her at Chatsworth for a few months in **1570** before all moving to Shrewsbury's main properties in **Sheffield;** the massive, secure **Sheffield Castle** & **Sheffield Manor (qv).**

Geoffrey Chaucer (ca 1343-1400) said to have lived at one stage of his life at Hatfield, but in any case we'll call him an honorary Sheffielder, since, apart from all the **theeing** & **thouing** and talk about having a **wesh,** he made the first known mention in literature of a Sheffield knife**.** In the 'Reeve's Tale' the rough, tough, quick tempered & uncouth miller is described as having a Sheffield **whittle,** a general purpose knife, in his stocking**:**

"A Sheffeld thwitel bare he in his hose"

There is some uncertainty whether this means the knife was against his midriff rather than against his leg, but since he had a cutlass (panade) in his belt as well as a dagger ('a jolly poppere') in a pouch, a position against the leg, as the Scottish soldier's dirk, seems more likely for the Sheffield product.

chavel chew, or fray a rope or band (powerbelt in works).

chavvy young child, or **babby.**

checks, milk checks from the Co-op, (often pronounced **Corporative** with the accent on the 'a' –see also **'Stooers**), these are small, plastic tokens about the size of a penny left on the doorstep for pint glass bottles of milk. Colours, changed when the price of milk goes up, are usually blue, green or yellow.

cheeap cheap

Chesterfield ancient market town with famous crooked church spire (football team are called the **Spireites).** Industry was mainly **coyal,** chemicals and engineering**;** much metalworking remains, iron & steel castings, for example and estates such as **Sheepbridge** are hives of activity. Some industry spilled over from Sheffield when land was hard to find, and also when business rates soared in Labour's looney left stronghold. **Sissons,** former Sheffield silversmiths moved first to **Calver Mill** to make stainless steel sinks & baths etc.,then to their current site at **Sheepbridge,** and at the other end of the scale, **Cottam's** moved their

forge making horse shoes from Darnall to Chesterfield Industrial Estate. More recently, with space and grants available, some Chesterfield firms have moved the other way; **Trebor** sweets to the **Bassett** site; **Markham,** world famous heavy engineers and makers of tunnelling machines, merging with the even more famous **Davy** at **Darnall** as **DavyMarkham; Chesterfield Special Cylinders,** the U.K.'s only maker of high pressure gas cylinders, some up to 12 metres long, to the **East End,** near **Forgemasters,** one of their main suppliers.

James Chesterman (1792-1867) invented the spring rewind for window sashes & measuring tapes in 1821; then the retractable steel tape in 1853, after working with **Samuel Fox (qv),** to master the method of continuously hardening & tempering steel strip. The **Sheffield Flood (qv)** of 1864 destroyed his factory on **Nursery St**. and it is said he pushed a handcart with remnants of his machinery to another fruit & vegetable growing area, which is now **Pomona St**. off Ecclesall Rd. There the impressive **Bow Works** were built and remained in production until Chesterman, along with Rabone of Brum were swallowed up by **Stanley Tools (qv).** Bow Works is now part of Norwich Union.

cheyse cheese. It's **cheyse ageean in'snap tin!**

childer children

chimley, chimbly chimney. Those were the days, when terraced houses in serried ranks **puthered (qv)** out smoke from their **chimbly pots**. Mixing with the smoke from hundreds of steelworks, that's when pollution really was pollution.

choil indentation at end of a blade enabling this to be ground without the bolster getting in the way; **choil it** is an archaic expression for 'clear off.'

Christian: act/eat like a Christian behave properly/ don't **gollop** your food.

Cholera Monument slim 70ft. recently repaired tribute to 402 victims of the **1832** epidemic, including the **Master Cutler,** John Blake. The site is in parkland above **Granville Rd**. with panoramic view of the city centre over the **Midland Railway Station,** and of the distant moors beyond **Bramall Lane.**

chuff a classic Sheffield swear word, similar to, but not quite, sod; idiot; bastard; twat etc. Can be insulting, or can even be affectionate, depending on tone & context:

He's a reight chuff

Shurrup chuff an' tha'll learn summat.

In Shakespeare's Henry 1V there's a nice case of the pot calling the kettle black when Falstaff seems to use the word in the Sheffield sense:

Hang ye, gorbellied knaves.....ye fat chuffs.

chuffin'ell the kind of expletive you might use if you hit your thumb with a hammer, being more acceptable than the now ubiquitous 'f' word.

Chuffinelles a very Sheffield name for a female group founded by the much lamented Lynda Smith, comedienne, script writer and TV star of 'Have I got news for you'

clag, claggy mud, muddy. **Claggy** also used of traffic to mean blocked, snarled or clogged up.

clart'eead; cloth'eead dozy, idiot

clarty sticky mud, muddy.

clawk to claw; **cat's clawkin' 'Plumbs' covers.**

clem; clam; clemmed; clammed the first meaning is to be hungry with the 'a' version more popular in Sheffield; 28th March **1674** disturbances by cutlers' apprentices who **'did in a tumultuary way assemble themselves together.....saying they were clammed by reason of the new (grain) measures'**
Prof. Mel Jones quotes an anonymous 1870 letter from a striking miner to Mr. Chambers (of **Newton Chambers, qv);**

"Sir. Prepare to meet thy God. as i insist on thee being a dead man. before long.........if thou means to let us **clam & starve.** we mean to have it out of you you bugger as thy Days are numbered. so prepare to meet thy God. your truly one who wishes you in hell fire."
Manchester favours the 'e' version; **'we may clem to skin & bone.'**(Gaskell's 'North & South').
The second meaning of **clammed,** like **starved** in Sheffield is to be very cold or **frozen.**
You can be **clammed; starved; frozen** without necessarily being **nesh.**

'Cliffe; dahn'Cliffe; on'Cliffe Attercliffe

Clifton House & Park now a museum of **Rotherham** life & its prominent iron & steel, glass, coal & Rockingham pottery industries, it was built & set out in **1783-84** for **Joshua Walker** who had inherited a valuable share of the **Walker Ironworks (qv).** He had married into wealth too, despite the name; Susannah Need, and they bought **Blyth Hall,** Worksop, as a second home.

clinks small surface cracks on a blade.

clipt point butcher's or pocket knife blade with point trimmed off at an angle, like a putty knife.

clock cowd; clap cowd gone cold (usually of meal or tea)

clog, clogs worn, for example, by **rolling mill hands** & children in the **1940's**

clog iron cheap, or poor quality steel. Sheffield men making aerospace steels have been known to describe Rotherham steel as **clog iron,** & Rotherham men making engineering steels have similarly insulted Scunthorpe steel.

clever clogs clever dick

fussy clogs sometimes said about a teenage girl fussing about what clothes to wear.

gie it some clog boot the ball upfield
clog's 'll spark terneet we're hitting town tonight
from clogs to clogs in three generations rise & fall of a family business.

clomp sound of heavy tread of shoes or boots

clonk on 'eead blow on the head

clooers clothes
Ah could sleeap on a clooers line said to be from when tramps slept for a nominal charge at West Bar hostel while standing with their arms over a rope to keep them upright. Interestingly, Sam Weller talks to Mr. Pickwick in Dickens' classic novel, "The Pickwick Papers," of the dregs of humanity who weren't even "**up to the twopenny rope.**" He explains that coarse sacking was stretched as beds across ropes, and these ropes were suddenly released at 6 a.m. dropping the inmates to the floor and ensuring they didn't **lig** any longer in kip.

clooers 'orse clothes horse, also known as a **winter(h)edge**

close-plated knife steel blade with a very thin sheet of silver soldered on to avoid tainting by acidic food. Stainless steel made the process obsolete.

closet outside toilet; W.C.; lav; throne. Closet was a word quickly picked up by Poles who came here after WW2 and one told of a fellow ex-R.A.F lad who, desperate for a 'slash', shook the locked door of **Cole's Bros**. Department store vigorously. He'd mistaken the word **closed** for **closet.** No doubt he would have been called a **closet 'eead** = idiot; wazzock.

clout both meanings; a blow or cloth are known nationally: **dish clout; ne'r cast a clout till may (or May) is out.** Shakespeare mentions **swaddling clouts.** When it means a blow, however, there is a Sheffield feel about it:
Assl (I shall) **clout thee if tha dunt gie o'er**
Assl clout thee in a minute mother threatening an obnoxious son with a **scutch** to the back of the head, or a swipe with a wet **dish clout**.
1940's childrens' doggerel:

Good King Wenceslas
knocked a copper senseless
outside Marks & Spencer's
'copper came out an' gave him a clout
an' that made Wencelas senseless

cob as well as the national meaning of a round loaf of bread, it has been heard to mean 'to throw':
Cob it o'er 'wire throw it (the ball) over the(telephone) wire.

Wm. Cobbett not a Sheffielder but made a nice, if exaggerated comment in his 'Rural Rides', 31st January 1830:

'They call it black Sheffield, and black enough it is; but from this one town & its environs go nine-tenths of the knives that are used in the whole world'.

cobble sometimes a yellow/red hot bar or rod of steel going through a pair of rolls, often at speed, depending upon its diameter and the number of passes it has undergone, is not caught correctly by the roller, or his assistant with his tongs, and the steel snakes & twists out of control around the rolling mill floor. This is called a **cobble.** Hand mills in particular are dangerous places to work in, and when all rolling was by hand in Sheffield burns were common. It was not unknown for hot steel to go right through a man's leg, one victim being a certain **Charlie Peace (qv).** Children would stop on their way to school in the 1940's to look through rolling mill gates, mesmerised by the men in steel-studded clogs moving quickly and assuredly on the steel plates of the mill floor, catching the hot steel and returning it through another pass in the rolls. The men, some little more than boys, were as nifty as footballers or ballet dancers on their feet, but one slip or a **cobble** could maim them for life. Hopefully the few remaining hand mills are safer these days, though when a member of the BBC's Time Team had a go putting a billet through a pass at **Pro-Roll Ltd.** he had to be prevented from being dragged through the rolls.
Most rolling mills today are continuous, with a train of stands reducing, say, a steel billet 3" and up square x up to forty foot long, (heated to the correct rolling temperature) down to, say, 3/8 inch diameter as it passes through a series of rolls. The steel moves faster & faster as it shrinks & elongates through each mill pass emerging finally at high speed & in the correct diameter, to be then coiled or cut to length. If the increasing speeds at each mill stand are not synchronised an almighty **cobble** can ensue, with steel twisting in fantastic patterns to the roof. These mills are safer because men operating the controls are sitting in a **pulpit (qv)** but production delays are expensive as the twisted steel has to be cut into pieces, put in **scrap pans** & sent to the melting shop.

cod; codder first hand forgeman

cog down; cogging forging or rolling steel **ingots** into **blooms (qv)**
cogging mill primary reversing rolling mill that **cogs ingots** down to **blooms.**

coils steel sheet, strip, bar, or rod rolled into coils, or wire drawn & coiled.

coil set if a coil of steel strip is uncoiled & cut to length into flat strips, the strips from the beginning or end of the coil may arch resuming its bent shape after several hours, or even days. This is called **coil set.**

coining the end of a spoon blank is cross rolled to form the flat shape of a spoon bowl. After then clipping to shape the handle is **coined** with the design under a drop stamp.

coit coat. Still heard in north Sheffield: Ecclesfield, Chapeltown, Stocksbridge, Penistone & Barnsley, though in most of Sheffield & Rotherham you are more likely to hear **cooat (qv).** That it was heard further south in Sheffield is seen in Muriel Hall's 'More of Mayfield Valley' when she quotes a gamekeeper, who met a poacher with his **coit** slung over his shoulder on a freezing day:

"Nah then Walt, tha'll freeze ter deeath – get thi coit on. I'll help thi."

The poacher backed away because he had hares up each sleeve.

pigeon coit pigeon cote

collyforblin' messing about, doing nowt useful.

commando knife slim pointed killing knife, blackened for use by the Paras; SAS; SBS; designed by Fairburn-Sykes in WW2 and made in their hundreds of thousands by **Ibberson; Rodgers; Wostenholm** etc. They are still made, in their hundreds, by these & by Jack Adams, & Reg Cooper.
A German parachutist in the Luftwaffe in WW2 wrote to the **Famous Sheffield Shop** claiming that the Sheffield knives were copies of German knives made by such as Eickhorn in Solingen. He added, however; **'I know that the British ones are better made than the German ones'**, partly because Ibberson & Joseph Rodgers knives had
synthetic (bexoid) handles which could be gripped better than the German wooden handles. A German book on the subject; 'Kampfmesser' gave the production of commando knives in WW2 by the two Sheffield firms as a quarter of a million & he wondered where they had all got to!

conkers children's game played throughout England when chestnuts were shed (before teachers & HSE, mindful of hovering lawyers, cast their baleful eyes on the sport). Sheffield practice was to call a winning conker; **conker one, conker two, conker three** etc., depending upon the number of its victories.

continuous casting process devised by BISRA steel research laboratories on Hoyle street, whereby molten steel is poured from a ladle into a water-cooled tundish, and extrudes billets or slabs continuously. Obviates the need for the traditional ingot/primary rolling route, (though some special steels must still be processed by the ingot method).

converter furnace for converting iron into steel, or man in charge of the process. The word applies equally to the **cementation furnace (qv),** which adds carbon to wrought iron to make **blister steel(qv)** and the **Bessemer furnace (qv),** which reduces carbon in cast iron to make mild steel. See the world's best preserved cementation furnace on Doncaster street, and Bessemer converter at **Kelham Island Industrial Museum (qv).**

cooam comb; **com** is also used (pronounced as German **komm). Gi'us com** is perhaps a bit more abrupt than **Gi'us cooam.**

cooartin' courting; **Ah tha cooartin'?**

cooat coat; (more common than **coit qv)**
It's a top cooat cowder on 'tops It's an overcoat colder on the moors.

'copper the copper; a large open receptacle, rounded at the bottom, set in bricks at about waist height with **coyal** or **cowk** fire underneath to heat water for washing clothes, (or bathing toddlers). Normally made of copper, but could be cast iron. The local dialect word for this is a **set pot (qv).**

cornish mantelpiece; (perhaps from cornice).

Coro; Corro Coronation Street; older Sheffielders prefer **Cor(r)o** to **'Corrie'**, which is now universal around England, not just in the North West. Generally in South Yorkshire a word is shortened & given an **'o'** ending rather than an **'ie'**, or **'y'** ending when speaking informally; e.g.: **wello** (wellington boot); **Steelo's (qv)** (Steel Peech & Tozer, Rotherham); **kiddo** (cf Welsh boyo); **laddo (qv)** which is not quite 'laddie', because **laddo** tends to be used when you've forgotten somebody's name. Names too, get the **'o'** treatment; **Deano** (Dean); **Dobbo** (Dobson); **Jacko** (Jackson); **Robbo** (Robinson); **Hendo's** (Henderson's Relish).

Corporation hair oil **tap watter**; the poor man's Brylceem. Dates from when Sheffield Corporation ran the water supply.

corsey/causey; corsey edge pavement; pavement edge; causeway, in the sense of a paved footpath.

corten steel perfected in Sheffield & Rotherham by **British Steel Corporation** (now **Corus**) which weathers to a surface oxidised coating leaving the core protected from rusting. Used on buildings - see at the Riverside, Kelham & for sculptures - see Angel of the North.

Robertus le Coteler merits inclusion since he, along with **Jordanus Cissor, Simon Cissor** & **Stephanus Cissor** were listed in the Yorkshire Lay Subsidies, **1297** in the reign of Edward 1 (**1272-1307**), making them the earliest known cutlers in the "ville de Schefeld."

country knives stamped or etched with the customer's name; e.g. shops such as Harrod's or John Lewis, rather than having the maker's mark.

covering scales of a pen/pocket knife which may be of steel, nickel silver, silver, gold, ivory, pearl, tortoise shell, wood, buffalo or stag horn, cow bone, plastic, bexite etc.

cowd, clock-cowd, clap-cowd cold; e.g. dinner gone cold.

cowks **1.** Cokes, cinders **2.** Worn grindstones. A table knife grinder would sell his stone on to a grinder of smaller objects such as pen knives or razors. Steel wears stone down comparatively quickly and hundreds of thousands of **cowks** were used as stepping stones across the rivers; piled as pillars supporting outbuildings **(Abbeydale Hamlet); cut in half & used on top of walls (Norfolk Park,** Granville Road entrance**);** as steps up embankments **(Shepherd Wheel));** in the home; by the fire to hold the poker etc., or by the door as a walking stick or umbrella stand. Many were simply discarded in a nearby stream to be retrieved by householders over the centuries to feature in their walls & gardens. See **grindlecowks.**
3. Hunter's ' The Hallamshire Glossary' 1828 gives **cowks** also to mean apple **cores**. I had thought this meaning extinct, when, to my delight my 88 year old friend, **Reg Reid, 179 years later-** on the fourth of October **2007** to be exact- shouted to a bloke sitting on a bench, eating an apple, **"Save us 'cowk."**

John Yeomans Cowlishaw cutlery firm founded 1845, best known for silver fruit knives, now prized by collectors; **hallmark JYC** granted **1854**. Cowlishaw shot himself in 1895, shortly after the death of his wife, but his firm lived on at least until the 1970's when it was owned by **Emil Berek (qv).**

coyal mined locally since at least the 13th century; seams near the surface to the west (Ringinglow) & down to the town centre (site of **Hallam University** & the 'Hole in the Road' etc.) Cambridge Street in town was once Coal Pit Lane; Drift mines led into the hills at Greystones and, (on beds of **ganister (qv)**), at places such as **Ughill, Hutcliffe Wood Road, & Parkwood Springs.** The **Fitzwilliams** of **Wentworth Woodhouse (qv)** were involved in coal mining from the fourteenth century; the **Shrewsburys (qv)** from the fifteenth & sixteenth centuries, then the **Norfolks** up to the nineteenth century. The latter's 'superintendent of coal works', **John Carr (1756-1823)** developed flanged iron rails for use underground.
Coal powered the Industrial Revolution, just as Sheffield steel underpinned it. Sheffield men such as **Cammell & John Brown** mined coal as well as making steel. Deeper & thicker seams were, and are, exploited towards the east in an arc from Barnsley in the north, to Rotherham, Doncaster, Worksop & Chesterfield. Seams such as Barnsley, Park Gate, Silkstone & Markham spring to mind. Just a few of the collieries, now closed, that meant so much to our region: **Handsworth, Nunnery, Tinsley Park, Park Gate, Smithy Wood, Orgreave, Manton, Markham Main, Creswell, Kiveton Park,** 1867-1994, **Denaby Main** 1868-1968, **Dinnington** 1905-1991, **Manvers Main** 1868-1988, **Bentley** 1905-1994.
Mines still producing: **Maltby Main** 1910, now linked underground with **Silverwood**, 1903; **Rossington** 1916; **Hatfield Main** 1911. **Maltby** supplies the huge Drax power station and has reserves which should last beyond 2020.
Constant accidents are a price of coal mining. Most of us, born before 1940 will recall seeing or hearing of relatives having a bath in a galvanised steel tub in front of the fire, their backs blackened & bloodied by coal. Death was not uncommon, mostly in ones or twos, so it took large-scale tragedies to disturb the national consciousness. Taking the Barnsley area alone see:
1.The poignant memorial at **Silkstone** churchyard commemorating 26 children aged 7 to 17, drowned by storm water in 1838 at **Huskar Pit**.
2. The **Darfield** churchyard memorial to 189 miners killed in an explosion underground at **Lundhill Colliery** in 1857.
3.The **Ardsley** memorial to 354 miners killed in an explosion at **Oaks Colliery** in 1866.

Coal was mostly moved by rail; when by road the biggest hauliers were :

Burnett & Hallamshire, 'Billy Burnco'.
Stevenson's, huge black lorries, white lettering.
Tommy Waard's (qv) , Thos. W. Ward.
Wood's (our name is Wood, we sell coal).

creeam cream
creddled born (cradled ?) in Mexborough

Creswell Crags neanderthal ice age caverns where mammoth & hyena etc.bones have been found. Sheffield University archaeologists have recently revealed ice-age rock art unique in Britain.

cricket when the football season ended young lads would turn to cricket in the parks; on the **recs.(qv)**; or down the **entries(qv)** along thousands of terraced streets. Wickets would be chalked on the galvanised steel bin placed at the bottom of the **entry** & the captains would **'wet for it',** if no coin was available, to choose who would bat first. **Wetting for it** meant covering your mouth with your hands and spitting on one palm. The other lad had to guess which palm was wet. A cricketing dispute would be settled by the batsmen having to **hit or miss, run two.** If you hit the ball and smashed a window you, or more likely your **mam,** had to **pay for your own china.** A ball hit over the gasworks wall was **six and out.**

crocodile brand of machetes made by **S.&.J Kitchin** on Saxon Road.They also made reaper blades & other agricutural tools before moving to Chesterfield, where they are now mainly stockists.
Their brand and other Sheffield brands of machetes were used all over the world & especially in Africa & South America. The Mau Mau atrocities in Kenya before that country's independence from Britain, were found to have been committed by terrorists wielding these Sheffield slashing tools.
John Steinbeck talks of machetes from Sheffield & New York, but eventually factories in South & Central America were set up to make them, largely from hot rolled steel strip made in Rotherham at **Brinsworth Mill.**

crocus powder red iron ore ground up finely for polish in the cutlery trade.

crozzle a unique Sheffield word & product: **wheelswarf**, a 'sludge' of water, stone and steel particles collected from grinders' **trows (**troughs) & **slap boards** was caked on top of the charcoal-covered bars in their sandstone chests in **cementation** furnaces. This, compared to a 'pie crust', about six inches thick, kept heat in & air out. When broken off at the end of the process it was cut into chunky pieces and used on the top of walls around the city, and ,especially on walls along the rivers. It was black, 'volcanic', and left glassy–sharp on the top to deter small boys from climbing the walls. The walls are mostly over a 100 years old now, made when the **cementation** process was in its hay day, and many have been demolished, especially in the last 2 or 3 years; e.g. the huge stone, **crozzled-topped** wall fronting the Queen's Road site of Arnold Laver's timber yard, now a B & Q warehouse. Nice examples remain at the side of **Sanderson's** goit by the river Don; at the entrance to Norfolk Park on Granville Road; on Stafford Road; and Roe Wood boundary wall on Norwood Road. There is said to be an out-building in Lynwood Gardens, Broomhall with a domed roof made of **crozzle** blocks. The house and gardens were home to **Francis Newton** and **crozzle** was brought from his Infirmary Road steelworks. **Hunter, 1828,** gives **crozzils** as 'half burnt coals'.

crozzled toast or meat, especially bacon, blackened & burnt at the edges.

Crucible Steel invented by **Benjamin Huntsman (qv)** in Sheffield ca **1740**, it was a revolutionary metal; the world's first cast steel made to various consistent recipes, and of such reliability that it gave Britain a 50 year lead over the rest of the world. The embargo on trade during the Napoleonic wars led to Napoleon offering a large cash prize to anyone on the continent who could match this **'English Cast Steel'.** 'Spies' coming to Sheffield included a Frenchman, a Swede and **Friedrich Krupp** of Essen who anglicised his name to Cropp when he booked in at a Sheffield hotel. **Crucible steel** was extremely difficult to make & **Huntsman** spent years perfecting it with the main problems being**: a/** reaching the high temperature **(1600** degrees centigrade) needed to melt the pieces of **blister steel** that formed the basic raw material, and retaining this temperature for a refining period of four hours. **b/** finding a clay or mixture of clays that could be made into crucibles strong enough to hold metal at this intense heat, (steel melting point being 5 to 600 degrees centigrade higher than brass, glass, and even iron).
Other Sheffielders were first to emulate **Huntsman's** process. Our men achieved incredible skills in treading the clay & making the crucible pots; in choosing the raw materials and getting the furnace heat up to 1600 degrees centigrade; in judging by eye the stages of a melt and when to pour; in combining skill and strength pulling out the **crucible** from the fire; in holding the glowing hot **crucible** with iron tongs and carefully **teeming** up to 60 lbs. (27 kgs.) of molten steel cleanly into a refractory-lined iron mould. Imagine the strain, imagine the heat. The **teemer** would suck on his silk **sweat scarf** as he poured the steel- any splashes hitting the sides of the mould could solidify early & and lead to surface defects in the **ingot.** He would wear water-soaked sacking from the waist down to protect against heat, splashes and sparks of molten metal. The youngest member of the team, the **slagger-off** would ladle water from the nearby trough and throw it on the sacking if necessary. It was not unknown for a **melter** or **teemer** to plonk himself in the trough to combat heat and fire. Before the ingots were forged into bars with amazing accuracy, a piece would be broken off the end and the **melter** could tell by examining the fractured surface what the steel would be best used for: scythes or knives or saws or files etc. Metallurgical analysis of the smallest gradations of carbon content in the steels later confirmed the **melter's** skilled judgement in choosing the right steel for the job.
Thanks to **crucible steelmaking** the parish of Sheffield grew from 14,105 in 1736 to 112,492 in 1841, and the town gained world wide fame. A Swiss metallurgist described **Marshall's (**forerunner of **Vickers')** steel as **'without contradiction, the most beautiful steel in commerce'.** The **Bessemer (qv)** bulk steel process and the giants of Sheffield steel such as **John Brown, Charles Cammell,** and **Vickers** ensured an explosive growth of population from the 112,492 in 1841 to 400,000 in 1900. **Bessemer** steel superseded iron, but the more expensive, more special **crucible** steel didn't peak until 1870 when 100,000 tons were produced. Many hundreds of **crucibles** were wheeled to the casting pit in a marvel of organisation when big pieces were made for the Navy. Gradually the **Siemens** process, then the **electric arc,** followed by **high frequency** melting and **vacuum** remelting superseded the **crucible** method in the 20th century, though the last **crucible melt** wasn't until 1972 at **T.W.Pearson's works** on Matilda Lane in 1972.

cruddy grotty, e.g.heavily tea-stained mug in a factory.

cuckoos faulty work in the cutlery industry; work returned for rectification before leaving the factory, upon which fellow workers would greet the guilty man or woman with loud **cuckoo** calls.
Tha's got cuckoo for 'em
They gen him 'cuckoo
She'd cuckood 'em (done poor work on knives, etc.)

culinder used in the crude phrase for someone who dithers faced by too many choices:
Thar't like a fart in a culinder – can't gerraht fer oyals.
Also used in Glasgow & probably elsewhere, though without the Sheffield dialect.
In the German classic about the horrors of WW1, "All quiet on the Western Front", the University of Stirling editor translates a German phrase about a "Gruppenfuehrer" running around "wie ein Furz auf der Gardinenstange"(like a fart around a curtain pole) as, "He goes rushing around like a fart in a colander".

cut ; chuck it in 'cut throw it in the canal cut – showing that fly-tipping idiots have always been with us.

The Company of Cutlers in Hallamshire After the 7th and last **Earl of Shrewsbury** died in 1617, leaving no one to look after the 300 year old cutlery industry from **Sheffield Castle** or **Sheffield Manor (qv),** many cutlers refused to 'submit to the ordinances of the trade; took as many apprentices as they wished and at whatever terms they thought fit.' More seriously, according to their critics, they ' were emboldened & do make such deceitful unworkmanlike wares & sell the same in divers parts of the Kingdom, to the great deceit of his Majesty's subjects & scandal of the cutlers of **Hallamshire'.** Perhaps this was over egging it, but the upshot was that permission in Parliament was given in **1624** for the charter of incorporation for **The Company of Cutlers in Hallamshire.** The Company employed 'searchers'; officials who were empowered to enter houses & workshops and seize 'deceitful, unworkmanlike wares'. Thanks to banding together, too, the cutlers could better fight against the protectionism practised by the London cutlers, who were fearful of their Hallamshire rivals, sensing they would soon dominate the trade. Although governments then were more attentive to industry than they are to-day, the Company had to work for many years to ensure that the Hearth Tax didn't apply also to the hundreds of smithies, often in outhouses attached to Sheffield homes. The Company regulated training of apprentices & use of **marks** for all craftsmen making knives, scissors, shears, sickles & scythes, as well as checking quality. Numbers of cutlers & edge tool manufacturers were initially **498** in **1624**, rising to **2000** in **1679** and **4000** in **1800**. In Victorian times the steel, engineering & tool industries overtook cutlery as the town's leading wealth creators and employers, & in **1860** steelmen were admitted as **freemen** of the Company; **Thomas Jessop** being the first steel manufacturer to be made **Master Cutler** in **1863**. Today the **Master** and **Mistress Cutler** are leading citizens, ranking with the **Lord & Lady Mayor** and fulfilling a hectic round of civic duties.

Cutlers' Hall **The Company of Cutlers in Hallamshire** has had three Halls on the same site; in **1638**, **1725** & the current one in **1832**. This is on Church Street opposite the **Cathedral**, and is a pillared, classical building with a pair of the Cutlers' Coat of Arms standing proudly on top, with their elephant head, crossed swords and motto: **'Pour y parvenir a bonne foi'.**
The Company has built up a magnificent collection of cutlery and silverware over the years, and some of this is brought out for the annual **Cutler's Feast** in the sumptuous main hall, with Ruskin's tribute to Sheffield workmanship around the walls, high above the diners. A new **Master Cutler** has been chosen every year since **1624**, and over the years prominent people have addressed the gathering, including Winston Churchill, Margaret Thatcher and, probably more important for trade, the boss of Ford Motor Company. (Cameron, the current leader of the Conservative party has refused to address the 2007 feast, showing the current lack of any political interest in industry.)

'Cutlers was a popular abbreviation for the **Cutlers' Hall** as **the** dance venue in the post WW2 years.

cutlers assembler of knives; pocket knives & scissors. Now, loosely, anyone working in the trade.
cutlery in the trade is used only for items with a cutting edge such as knives & scissors. Spoons and forks are called **flatware.**
cutlin' assembling and hafting knives.

D

dab, dabs sweat; **Ah've gorra reight dab on.**
dag hand ; to be a dag hand to be skilled at; a 'dab hand' at something.

dahn deer; dahn Attercliffe; dahn Neepsend; dahn 'East End; dahn Rotherham (way)down there; down Attercliffe etc.

dairy maid obsolete = **watter wheel**. A Grinders' Misfortune Society was formed in **1804** and a song;'The Grinders' Hardships' sung at their annual festival:
" There seldom comes a day but our **dairy maid** goes wrong

and if that does not happen, perhaps we break a stone,
which may wound us for life, or give us our final blow,
for there's few that brave such hardships as we poor grinders do."
(Not to mention the insidious threat of silicosis; "grinders' asthma").

dam ; by-pass dam mill pond; where part of a river's flow was diverted along a leat into a dam to store for turning a water wheel, or wheels, to drive machinery for grinding, forging and rolling steel. The main stream continued on its way at a lower level and parallel to the dam, receiving the wheel's water back after usage, further downstream. With at least twenty such sources of power along each of the five rivers; **Don**, **Loxley**, **Rivelin**, **Porter** & **Sheaf**, and other mills along outlying streams such as the **Moss**, Sheffield's dominance in the knife, scythe and similar trades was assured. See **Abbeydale Hamlet** and walk along the river valleys to see evidence of the days of **water power**, which lasted right from the 12th to the 20th century, with its heyday from 16th to 19th. It is hard now to imagine the idyllic **Porter**, **Rivelin** & **Loxley** valleys resounding to the sound of industry. Industry moved downstream, largely into the Don Valley,though there is a powerful cluster of forges by the **Loxley** near where it joins the **Don,** and further up the **Loxley,** in idyllic surroundings is a gem of a works; **Pro-Roll Ltd.**, one of Sheffield's last remaining hand mills, no longer powered by its water wheel, but modernised and surviving by rolling small lots of expensive special steels and alloys.

the Dam Busters the R.A.F. breached German dams supplying the industrial heartland of the Ruhr, with no little help from Britain's industrial heartland. The R.A.F. practised on similar dams; Derwent & Howden, and the revolutionary 'bouncing bombs' were forged at **English Steel Company's River Don** works (formerly **Vickers & Co.**, now **Sheffield Forgemasters**).

danny (child's) hand.

Darbyshur Derbyshire:
Darbyshur born, Darbyshur bred,
strong in'aarm, weak in'ed.
(Some claim this should read **wick** in'ed = clever).
Darbyshur gritstooan Derbyshire gritstone, a hardy, bold, goat-like, inquisitive local moorland sheep. Watch your sandwiches on Stanage Edge!

Darnall still industrial, though the stream of thousands going on shift at **Davy's (qv),** bottom of Prince of Wales Rd., is reduced to a trickle of hundreds, & **Craven's** railway carriage builders are no longer. Comparative newcomers, such as **Mayflower Engineering** (on the site of a **Sanderson-Kayser** steelworks, & helping to preserve a rare **crucible steel (qv)** melting shop there); **Wentworth Pewter** & **Geo. Robson Conveyors** ensure continuing local manufacturing excellence. Darnall was a solid, proud working class area, even boasting its own Duke. **The Duke of Darnall** was an eccentric, Chaplinesque figure who used to walk around town, mainly on the Wicker, Waingate or Fargate, in the middle of the road, in black suit & bowler; white spats and rolled umbrella, with which he directed the traffic, leaping out of the path of trams if they refused to stop. He lived in sin with **Russian Edna,** a prostitute who was later murdered: a huge story in those years after WW2 when murder was extremely rare.

datal crazy; gormless
on datal working & paid by the day; not on shifts or piece work **on days** working the day shift, perhaps 6 **while** 2.

Davy Brothers founded 1830, world-famous heavy engineering firm at **Darnall** which has survived various changes of name & ownership: **Davy-United** to Kvernaland to AK Heavy Engineering, and now, back in local ownership as **Davy-Markham.** Markham, established 1889, were Chesterfield engineers famous for making winding gear for mines & huge tunnelling machines such as those that gouged out the Channel tunnel. (London, Paris, Moscow & Barcelona are among the world's underground railways that also used **Markham's** machines).
Davy were, & are best known for making rolling mills for the world's steelmakers. The tradition is very much alive today & some of the heaviest forgings & castings made in the world (at **Sheffield Forgemasters/ River Don Castings**) are machined, assembled & taken apart again for shipment to the U.S.A, Germany, Italy & China. The latest, heaviest ever work were 300 ton housings for a Chinese heavy plate mill, to roll plate for China's rapidly expanding navy & power industry. Davy's design/ draughtsmen's work was taken over by VAI of Austria who were in turn taken over by Siemens & are now based at Sheffield City Airport, under the name **Siemens VAI Metal Technologies.** This firm has further orders for wide plate mills of Sheffield design, manufacture and commissioning. Not to be outdone by China, India has ordered 2 heavy plate mills from them. **Davy** & successors have led in this technology since they first built 4 huge plate rolling mills In 1905! (Two were for Sheffield firms **John Brown** & **Charles Cammell**, one was for Japan, and the fourth-destination unknown, in those far off days, when British governments supported British industry).

Apart from steel mill plant the Darnall firm has worked on the Thames Barrier; Sluice gates in Singapore harbour; footbridges for Gateshead & London ; the Manchester 'Big Bang' sculpture, and the huge steel blocks to anchor the Wembley Arch.
See the massive River Don steam engine for a reversing plate rolling mill, one of the four built by **Davy** in 1905 & now at **Kelham Island** museum.

dead can mean **very. It were dead good= it were reight good.**

deead dead

dee (1) die. What did he **dee** of? He **deed** of a Tuesday. Tha'll **dee** if tha worries; tha'll **dee** if tha dunt.
dee (2) thee
dee, dah, dissen = thee, tha (thou), thissen.
Dee, dah't daft, dee = You are silly, you are.
Nah denn dee, what da dooin' wi'dissen?= Now then you, how are you? **Purrit dahn deer will da.**= Put it down there will you.
Wednesday an'United are both gooin'ter loise this affs- ah'll tell di dat much. A substantial number of Sheffielders have advanced linguistically and pronounce an initial 'th' as a soft 'd', as shown above. This is such a unique, localised phenomenon that people in surrounding towns: Barnsley, Rotherham, Mexborough, Wath, Dronfield, Chesterfield, Worksop etc.call Sheffielders **DEE-DAHS.** Barnsley **Tykes** & Rotherham United **Millers'** supporters chant out **dee-dah, dee-dah, dee-dah** at Oakwell & Millmoor, when their team is playing a Sheffield team and a Sheffield player gets injured, imitating both an ambulance & the Sheffield accent......... It was observed at the last World Cup that Brazil had a Sheffielder in goal: his name? **Dida.**

deer stalker high-class bowie knife; hunting knife with, perhaps, 8 inch spear point blade.

devil, divil a tool with a straight slit embodied in the steel face of a **stiddy** (cutler's anvil) to straighten up twisted blades.

diamond cut diamond-shaped scorings on wooden handled trade knives, or on bexite (a black plastic) army knife **coverings (qv).** Gives a firmer grip.

Dingles derogatory term given by Sheffield United fans to Barnsley supporters.

dinky knife tiny, fixed-blade knife, with blade often in a leather sheath for carrying in a lady's handbag.
die sinker man who cuts patterns into, or standing proud on, solid steel blocks for a wide variety of goods; cutlery, tools, holloware parts, engineering products, using simple tools such as hammer, chisels, specially shaped files, and emery powder to polish them. Cutting dies is an extremely skilful job and the 'male' & 'female' parts have to fit perfectly in the drop hammer to stamp out the relevant part in steel or silver. Once an original has been cut copies can be made by spark erosion.

dip hot dripping; bacon fat

dish clout dish cloth

Division Street stretching from near the **City Hall (qv)**, past the old Sheffield Water Board building (now a café) & the old Fire Station (now a nightclub), to Devonshire Street. **Tha could see reight dahn Division Street** said about a woman wearing a very low-cut dress.

James Dixon & Sons was established in **1806** on Silver Street as a maker of **Britannia metalware (qv),** which is, in fact, our modern day pewter. By **1822** the firm had moved into the imposing Cornish Place works, by the river Don at Neepsend, and it became one of the largest Victorian silver & E.P.N.S. works, with over 800 workers at the turn of the century. The avant-garde Glaswegian designer, Christopher Dresser, worked with **Dixon's** around **1879**, and when any of the half dozen or so E.P.N.S. teapots made by them to his designs turns up at auction they realise about £100,000 each. **Dixon's** today make reproductions, every bit as good, which you can buy for less than a £1000. (See sample in the **Millennium Galleries**). A more important designer for **Dixon's** was their own **Charles Holliday,** a graduate of **Sheffield College of Art,** who worked for the firm from the late1920's to the 1960's. His work included altar cross & candlesticks for Sheffield Cathedral; the 'Blue Riband', fastest Atlantic Liner trophy; sixteen Grand National trophies, & the 1961 U.S. Masters Golf trophy. Of course, designers need skilled men to make their designs, (unless they are designer-silversmiths such as **David Mellor** & **Brian Asquith),** and the 1961 Masters trophy, a beautiful replica of the Fort Augusta clubhouse, was made by a young silversmith called **Trevor Collins,** and **chased (qv)** by **Richard Axelby.**

The silver trade was hit by the advent of stainless steel and the demise of British passenger liners, but **Dixon's** lives on with **Cooper-Cobb** & other firms in **British Silverware Ltd.** previously in the **Solpro** group on Attercliffe Common, now trading separately. Some craftsmen from **Dixon's,** including **Hugh Crawshaw; Walter Hayes** & **Peter Perry** set up successful firms on their own. The Cornish Works were converted into apartments in the late 1990's.

Dizened up over-decorated; all dolled up with lots of jewellery, perhaps in a**shunkley (qv)** dress. Must be from **bedizened. Hunter's** 1828 **Hallamshire Glossary** gives **dizen;** 'to dress one's self out with showy finery.' Can also be inanimate: 'Peggy's curtains were **that dizened up** they looked like a French woman's knickers'.

dodo dummy; (baby talk, mother to child).

dog; he dunt keep a dog an' bark hissen (railway cleaner explaining why her husband wont get his own meals.

dog oyal kennel; also figuratively; **to be in'dog oyal**= to be in trouble, e.g. with the wife for returning late from the pub.

on' dog shelf on the floor; **on' flooer** (in a workshop).

dolly, dolly-bag 1/ small mesh cotton bag about 4 inch width holding a solid piece of blue detergent, all of which was thrown in the **wesh** tub (**dolly** tub) 2/ a

wesh-day tool like a small wooden three to five-legged stool with long handle and cross piece for turning clothes in the **dolly** tub. See **dolly posher** below.

dolly a wheel of calico discs having circular runs of stitching, all clamped together revolving on a glazer's spindle, & used for polishing cutlery. **dollying** final polish with calico wheel

dolly- posh; dolly-handed left- handed

dolly-posher; posher; dolly peg; posser wooden implement ; long- handled, with 3 to 5-legged stool-like base with which brawny-armed women stirred clothes in the **dolly-tub,** or **peggy tub.** Can also be a long, wooden-handled implement having a domed copper tool to agitate clothes.

River Don old name **Dun;** 'Dear to me were the banks of the Don', especially to lads as young as eight who swam in its murky waters, among multi-coloured swirls of machine oil from the steelworks. This river with its 4 Sheffield tributaries and the **Rother** further downstream, are the main reason for the region's industrial greatness. See **Sheffield Rivers.**

Don Valley Stadium built for the World Student Games in 1991 on the site of the former **Brown Bayley** steelworks. Home to **Sheffield Eagles** rugby league club; national athletics meetings & pop concerts by such as the Rolling Stones.

donkey stooan white or pale yellow stone for whitening the edge of steps & window sills in cramped working-class areas.('Donkey' was a brand name). A piece of donkey stooan was given you by the **rag & booan** man in the 1940's / 1950's in exchange for old rags.

Donny Doncaster; famous for **coyal** and the railway industry. Doncaster Locomotive Works, **'The Plant',** made steam-powered railway engines from 1867 to 1957, including famous **'namers'** such as The Flying Scotsman & Mallard. The town still makes tractors, though at the other end of the industrial scale, confectionary; well-known firms such as Parkinson's (Doncaster butter scotch, a brittle toffee), and Nuttall's (mintos) have disappeared.

Donny's **Daniel Doncaster's,** a Sheffield steel firm at the confluence of the rivers Loxley & Don off Penistone Rd. They were founded as forgemasters in 1778 and are now a world –wide firm with 30 factories, mainly in Britain but with 7 in the U.S.A. and one each in Mexico, Belgium and Bochum, Germany. Their Sheffield works include precision forges doing complex shapes in advanced materials, including cobalt chrome, titanium and stainless steel orthopaedic implants, as well as turbine aerofoils, (from the end of 2005, when they shut their Leeds plant and brought manufacturing to **Penistone Rd**.) They make investment castings off the Parkway; centrispun castings in the **East End;** fabricated and machined aerospace assemblies at **Halfway** (**Bramah**); and superalloys at **Killamarsh** (**Ross and Catherall**). See the listed **cementation furnace (qv)** on the street named after the firm.

dooer; dooer oyal door; doorway.**Put 'wood in 'oyal =shut that dooer.**

Dore Sheffield's most westerly and richest suburb, climbing above Totley to where the city becomes the Peak District. In his poem about his favourite English suburb, **'An Edwardian Sunday, Broomhill, Sheffield'** John Betjeman talks of mill workers going on tramway excursions to Dore & to Totley (with a little poetic licence because trams only ran to Millhouses.) Dore had a much earlier, more important mention in the Anglo Saxon Chronicle of AD 829; **'And that year King Ecgbert conquered the Kingdom of the Mercians, and everything south of the Humber……. And Ecgbert led an army to Dore, against the Northumbrians & they offered him peace & submission there, and on that they separated.'**

double shear steel high quality steel formed by hammering many **strings (**strands) of blister steel together; re-heating, folding and hammering again. This was the standard & best steel for the superb hand forged & hand ground pre-1914 trade/table & dessert knives; more flexible & easier to sharpen than both the purer **crucible steel (qv),** or the **stainless steel (qv)** which quickly replaced **double shear** after WW1. See **blister/ cementation/ shear** steel. Trade knives were finely **'ground to lift',** which the grinder tested by pressing the knife edge against his thumb nail. The steel knife edge should lift slightly then resume its shape when his thumb was taken away. It should do this all along the cutting edge- testimony to his grinding skills, and the flexibility of **double shear steel.**

douted, doused put out (of fire); **dout,** with this meaning, occurs in Shakespeare.

dozzle refractory product with central hole, heated & fitted on top of an ingot mould to act as a reservoir for molten steel, allowing the central solidifying contraction in the ingot to be filled. This gives a sound ingot, avoiding **'pipe'(qv),** a serious central defect which would be elongated in subsequent rolling. **Crucible steel** pioneer, **Benjamin Huntsman** also invented the **dozzle,** said to have been inspired when he saw clay drainage pipes at the side of a road and 'borrowed' one for his experiments. The defect called **'pipe'** is also avoided by **'uphill' casting** (**qv**) of ingots, and by **continuous casting (qv).**

D.R.G.M. mark stamped on cheap German goods that flooded England after W.W.1. It probably stood for Deutsches Reich something & something (the manufacturers probably wanted to hide the country of origin after the war & British propaganda had villified all Germans. Sheffielders, such as grinders **Eddie Chapman** & **Billy Hukin (qv)** said **D.R.G.M.**

stood for **Damn Rotten German Make.** German quality is now respected and we've reached the stage where Gordon Brown lectures them to say they should be more like us. That is, an economy that relies on manufacturing and is the world's leading exporter should, like us, rely on services, the housing market and shopping. What amusement & scorn this afforded manufacturers here, and, no doubt in the Ruhr.

dreeam a dream; dozy. He's a **dreeam;** tha'rt a **dreeam; a dreeam teeam.**

dress to cover the face of a **glazer (qv)** wheel with glued emery; **dressing hammer** special chisel-like faced hammer to cross-cut face of **glazer** wheel prior to caking with emery/beeswax.

hammer **driver** man who operates a **drop hammer**

drop hammer; tup hammer a forging hammer where the power of the blow on the item to be forged is caused by a 3 foot approx. free fall of the **tup.** The size of the hammer, a 1 ton; a 5 ton; a 25 ton, is based on the weight of the **tup.** To hear 1 & 5 ton hammers at the forges off Livesley St., Owlerton, is impressive, and even more so a 25 tonner in the still of the night near Meadowhall, as if cocking a snook at the retail emporium. When terraced houses were cheek by jowl with industry in the Don Valley, many a china cabinet would rattle to the vibrations of a nearby forge. Once steam driven, the remaining hammers today are electric powered. See also **helve hammer** or **trip hammer,** usually water-powered, where the hammer blows were delivered by the tilting action of the **helve** (huge oak beam).

dropped wrist rheumatic condition caused by repeated hammering over the years by a hand forger. Dried horse manure, collected by an apprentice, used to be placed in the recess of the **stock** (sandstone block, or oak base) housing the anvil (**stithy** or **stiddy).** This helped prevent the condition somewhat, acting as a shock absorber.

bread & **drippin'** a staple diet for children of the 1930's/40's/50's see **dip.**

duck term of endearment; friendly form of address among or between the sexes, or older to younger generation. More common in south Sheffield, Derbys., Notts. than in north Sheffield, Rotherham and Barnsley where **luv** predominates, though both may be used by the same person at different times! It shows again that Sheffield is a boundary city.

Ey up mi duck; Orreight mi ol' (luv) How are you? Both are book titles arrived at independently – the one about the dialect of Ilkeston & the Erewash Valley; the other about the dialect of the Steel City region.

It knocked mi duck off it knocked me for six (unpleasant news).

duff to avoid. " Charlie **duffed** Beatrice in the 1920's." "Solicitors **duffin'** Army in 1914-18 became steelworkers only to leeave as 'waar ended." (according to a 95 year old ex-crucible steel melter who died in 1994, & who was a cavalryman against the Turks in 1914-18).

duffers or **duffems** a derogatory term-see **Heeley.**

E

easiful heard in the phrase **'as easiful as an old sheep'.**

Ecclesall Woods 350 acres of ancient woodland. Such woods as these & **Greno, Beeley** & **Wharncliffe** were essential for the development of the **Sheffield Steel** industry. **Oak** trees provided charcoal for the **Cementation** steel-making process. A charcoal-burner who died when his hut caught fire, is buried in the woods; gravestone & railings paid for by friends......... Large bundles of **birch** twigs were collected, to be thrown on to hot plate & sheet during rolling- see the film at **Kelham Island Museum** of heavy armour plate being hot rolled at **River Don** works. The exploding sap blasted the scale off the hot plate as it formed, thus preventing it being rolled into the surface. If John Craven of BBC TV Countryfile, November 2005, was told correctly there are **176 woods** in Sheffield and **two million trees**.

Edward 111 (1327-1377) an inventory of his wardrobe ca. 1340 included **"cuttelum de Shefeld"**

'eead head; **big 'eead** braggart; **cloth 'eead** simpleton. **pob'eead** namby pamby- see **pob.**

'effin' an' blindin' using bad language

egg bolster, bowster **egg waterloo bowster,** with two ridges & two grooves, the most common type of bolster on **xylo-**handled knives-see **bolster/ bowster.**

eight; eyt eat: **Ah cud eight a meight pie.** Play on words in a Radio Sheffield phone in: "If someone was having their snap on 'Town Hall steps, what time was it by 'Town Hall clock?" Answer; **"Summat to eight."** Past tense & participle: **et; etten; gerrit etten-** get it eaten.

eight-foot a **jennel (qv);** passageway, traditionally 8 foot wide. Note, a female Scunthorpe P.C. talked on T.V. about a crime recently in a **ten-foot,**

so **jennels** in **Sunny Scunny,** like steelworks, are bigger than ours.

Ekky Road **Ecclesall Road,** a beautiful tree-lined thoroughfare runs from the old **'Waard's'** brewery, now appartments; past a small nature reserve opened about 25 years ago by David Bellamy, and a few substantial Georgian houses set back from the road; past pubs such as the Nursery, the Pomona, Champs bar, and the Portergate; past the college at the junction of Collegiate Avenue, its long high stone wall still bearing scars of the 1940 **Sheffield Blitz;** past cafes, restaurants and shops too numerous to list, though immodesty compels mention of **The Famous Sheffield Shop,** which sells the widest selection of Sheffield-made metalwares; past Methodist church and a small museum of traditional Sheffield life, open once a month; past the Polish club, Dom Kombatanta, and Catholic centre; to the mature trees fronting the Woofenden Homes at **Hunter's Bar.** The little river **Porter (qv)** bubbling out of the moors near Brownhills drops down the superb **Mayfield Valley** and eventually reaches **Hunter's Bar** through **Endcliffe Park** & under **Brocco Bank** It meanders through the bit of woodland in front of the Homes, slants under **Ekky Road** to emerge between Methodist church & pub. It then runs by the **Snuff Mill** on its way to join the **Sheaf,** near the Railway Station. The rooks left their rookery near **the Bar** long ago, the flat section of the road described being gridlocked for much of the day, but the road is lively, much loved by students, and some peace is offered in the nearby **Botanical Gardens (qv).**

Electric Arc steelmaking The standard process for making bulk special & stainless steels, in furnaces ranging from 10 tons to 200 tons capacity. A very powerful electric current passes through the furnace roof via 3 cylindrical carbon electrodes, which may be, say, 1ft.diameter x 9ft., leaping in an **arc** on to the **charge** in the furnace- usually graded steel scrap. The **arc** generates localised intense heat of 3000 degrees centigrade, which rapidly melts the **charge**. The time taken from one **melt** of steel to the next used to take 6 hours, but it now takes less than 90 minutes, even allowing for **fettling** the furnace refractory lining & loading the next **charge,** etc. The biggest **arc melting shop** in Britain, & one of the world's biggest is at **Aldwarke (qv),** Rotherham where 2 huge **arc furnaces** make ca. one million tons per year of special engineering steels; more than the 6 previous **arcs** at **Templeborough (qv)** (now **Magna** visitor centre), which it replaced.

Electro-slag refining . a method of making ultra- clean steels

Ebeneezer Elliott (1781-1849) owner of an iron foundry in Rotherham; bankrupt 1816; established a successful iron & steel business in Sheffield; leased Upperthorpe Villa from the **Blake type-founding** family after **John Blake,** in the year he was elected **Master Cutler,** died of cholera in 1832. **Elliott** achieved fame as a radical poet; the **'Corn Law Rhymer'** and earned a statue in **Weston Park,** as well as a plaque on Upperthorpe Villa, and an honourable mention in John Betjeman's poem on Broomhill.

Elsecar near Barnsley boasts a **Newcomen engine**, which is the only one in the world in its original engine house(1795), built to pump water from Earl Fitzwilliam's **Elsecar New Colliery.**

Friedrich Engels commenting on official 1844 reports on Sheffield he gave a sorry picture of our rapidly expanding town. Some children left school at 7 & none stayed beyond 12.The quality of schoolmasters left much to be desired- one a convicted thief who could find no other job. Youths spent Sundays gambling by tossing coins or organizing dog fights. In low beer shops crowds of young people all under 17 drank with their girlfriends or prostitutes. 'Crimes of savage violence are of common occurance' with explosives used to wreck non-union workshops. See **Grinders,** & the **Sheffield Outrages.**

English Steel Corporation formed 1 January 1927 merging the steel interests of two huge Sheffield firms, **Vickers & Cammell (qv).** The 1920's were bleak times for the steel industry. Forced to expand and concentrate on military work in WW1, when peace came firms had excess capacity and they had a struggle to regain pre-war non-military business. The Government of the day of course began to show interest again in steel in the late 1930's, & expansion was called for, though there were worries that all special steelmaking, and many essential products could only be made in the Sheffield region. That these worries were justified is shown in Stewart Dalton's book; 'Sheffield, Armourer to the British Empire', where he tells us that one 15 ton drop stamp at **E.S.C.** (ironically bought from a German manufacturer in 1936), was, for the first 18 months of WW2, responsible for every single crankshaft made for the Rolls-Royce Merlin engine which powered the most famous R.A.F. planes, including the Hurricane, Spitfire, Lancaster & Mosquito. 84 crankshafts per **shift** were made in 3 **shift working,** round the clock. Two larger drop stamps were then installed at **E.S.C.** and some at other works but every Merlin crankshaft for Spitfires was made at **E.S.C. River Don Works.** See **Sheffield Forgemasters.**

engravers & etchers engraving one-off intricate patterns, scenes, animals or lettering etc. on gold, silver, or pewter is a job for a skilled **hand engraver** such as **Malcolm Marsden** or **Peter DeVine.** Engraving names, dates etc. on pewter flasks, tankards, plates etc. and engraving on steel (which is too hard a metal to be worked by hand) is a job for a **machine engraver** using a pantograph. **Electric etching** machines, also worked by a pantograph system, can etch the **made in Sheffield** mark etc. on 15 or more knife blades simultaneously. **Acid etching** was an older, skilled method of transferring, often intricate, patterns on to steel, as still seen on **bowie knives (qv)** today. **Laser etching** has come to the fore in the last 15 years or so, and **laser machines** are even used at the **Assay Office (qv)** to hallmark precious metals, (though not exclusively since many people prefer the traditional, deep **hand-stamped** hallmark).

Enks Endcliffe Park

entry passageway through a row of terraced houses to the back yard. **'Goo an' play down your own entry'** – said to boys who played cricket down someone else's **entry,** the batsman holding a piece of wood, defending 'stumps' chalked on a galvanised dust bin. See **cricket** and **Bramall Lane.**

equal end pen knife with a blade at each end, usually a **pen blade** and a **pocket blade,** and handle that tapers equally to both ends. A pen knife that tapers wide to narrow is called a **lobster.**

Ey up hello; How are you? **Orreight?** Are you alright? Sheffield, the boundary city where North Midlands' **Ey ups** fight for supremacy with South Yorkshire **Orreights...**See **'Ey up mi duck'** (under **duck** above). You are unlikely to hear **'Ey up, Surrey' (qv)** in Sheffield, though **' Ey up, mi old flower'** is certainly heard as far north as **Barnsley.** In fact it became a catch phrase of the late lamented comedian, Charlie Williams there.

F

facing mark maker **filing the face** of a mark flat before cutting out the words or pattern.

factor factory/ business owner renting rooms and power to **little mesters,** whose work he bought, having it marked with his own mark and selling it.

fall autumn. Used in North America & Sussex, uncommon elsewhere, though it is listed in **Hunter's 'The Hallamshire Glossary'** of 1827.

Famished hungry, but in Sheffield (& Ireland) can also mean cold, as can **starving (qv).**

the Famous Sheffield Shop Ecclesall Rd., established 1983, retailer of **Sheffield-made** cutlery, tools, pewter & silverware, very little of which is available in big stores, seduced as they are by cheap goods from the Far East. Other outlets for Sheffield metalwares include **Sheffield Scene,** Surrey St.,est.1978 and **Morton's** of West Street, established about a hundred years ago as scissor makers.

Michael Faraday 1791-1867 had a small, but important connection with Sheffield in that he had steel melted at **Sanderson's** in 1820, with experimental portions of the more corrosion resistant metals; nickel, chromium, silver & even platinum & rhodium. The most corrosion resistant would have to contain 50% platinum – obviously not a commercial proposition! **Ken Barraclough (qv)** pointed out the above and went on that, with hindsight, Faraday didn't add enough chromium, & it wasn't until Sheffielder **Harry Brearley** (qv) experimented with chromium steels in 1912/13 that a successful stainless steel was achieved.

farrier's knife specially shaped knife to pare horses' hooves.

fart resounds down the years right from Chaucer's day - see **culinder.** A vulgar childish ditty, when a big old penny was put in the slot to use the toilet, was: **Here am I, broken hearted; paid a penny and only farted.**

fash rough turned up edge of a knife – usually when the softer, thinner **shear steel** is sharpened too fine. Sharp turned up edge produced when **blanking** cutlery or tools; shearing steel billets, bars, slabs, flats etc. ;slitting steel strip.

fast stuck. Not just a local word, even if it appears as though it ought to be. **He's gorris ' eead fast in'railin's.**

father pronounce with a broad 'a'. A toast to oneself; **Here's to me, mi father's son, not forgerrin missen.** Wilfred Pickles, highlighting the conservatism of some of the Sheffield trades, told of a journeyman file maker who carried a stout stick across his shoulders, with a bag full of files on one end, and a bag full of bricks on the other. When asked, "Why don't you put files in both bags? He replied, **What were good enough for mi father' s good enough for me.**

'Fatty' Foulke Willie Foulke played four matches for Derbyshire cricket club in 1900 but was best known as **the Blades** 20 to 25 stone goalkeeper for 11 years, & playing once for England v Wales in 1897. Tales surrounding him are legion, suffice to say he was one said to have lifted a referee up by the scruff of his neck, and it is claimed he inspired the chant "Who ate all the pies?"

fausse awkward. Now a very rare word, though appearing in **Hunter (qv),** 1827, as cunning; fox-like quality.

favour to look like; dustman to woman with multi-coloured hair pins, **"Tha favours 'illuminations"** (Blackpool illuminations).

feather edge cutlery pattern

feight fight. Childish play on words; **Wanna feight?** Answer: seven.

he **fell** o'er **hissen** to help us. did all he could

felt in the cutlery trade, a wheel made from solid felt for polishing items.

fetch; can tha fetch? vulgar 1940's infant schoolboys, 9 or 10 year olds: can you ejaculate?

fettle repair furnace walls after steel is cast, by shovelling **ganister** against them which adheres in the heat. Clean up a casting. In the home; clean up, sort something out, mend; **fettle'pots**= wash the pots; **get fettlin'** get working. cf **in fine fettle.**

fey, feigh to clean out mud from **dams (mill ponds);** to clean out **wheel swarf** =mud/ sludge composed of **sandstone** & steel dust that collects in water in the grinder's **trow** (trough). German **fegen,** to sweep, clean. **Ed Chapman** was a **pocket knife grinder** for 60 years, & in 2002, (when he was 102 years old!) talked a lot to the compiler of this dictionary. He said he had never used **sandstone** grinding wheels, which, as well as being more dangerous because of the possibility of fracture at speed, & the more insidious danger of silicosis, wore down quickly and **feying the trow** had to be done every three months. **Patent (qv) wheels** (made by Abrafact; Jowitt or Carborundum) lasted twice as long so **feying** was every six months. Sheffielders didn't waste much: the **wheel swarf** was sold to steelmakers who used it as a kind of 'pie crust' to seal the iron bars being **converted** to steel in **cementation furnaces (qv).** The steelmen later sold the 'pie crust' to be broken up in regular segments & used as **crozzle (qv)** on top of walls.

filers spoon & fork **filers** smooth the edges, now using special grinding wheels, though there may be some hand filing with sterling silver work, were the filings are then brushed up & sold as **sweepings (qv)** to **The Sheffield Smelting Co. (Thessco).**

finger, thumb, & rusty bum boys game in which one team bent down in a line & the other ran in turns to the line, leap-frogging as far as they could on their backs. There were some rules but the game usually ended with the collapse of the line under the weight.

See my finger, see my thumb see my fist, tha'll get some. (Childish verse, Hillfoot Infants School **1940's)**

Thomas Firth (1789-1850) became **head melter** at **Sanderson Bros.,** makers of the finest **crucible steel,** joined by his sons **Mark, (1819-1880)** on the commercial side, and **Thomas, (1821-1860),** in the works. The two brothers set up on their own in 1842 on Charlotte St., in a small way, employing their father as head melter, responsible for 6 melting holes, each probably holding 4 **crucibles. Mark Firth** developed the firm **Thomas Firth & Sons** into a huge concern in the East End, one of the giants of Sheffield steel. Mark was paternalistic & hugely popular, being at various times Lord Mayor, Master Cutler & benefactor to the city. He founded Firth College which became the University & gave a park & almshouses to the city. A workman describes how a Christmas dinner was held by the firm in 1851, with fires in a great shed that was to become a sheet rolling mill. 'Josey' Richardson, 21 stone head melter had his long pipe relit, from time to time, by a man holding a rod of steel heated at the end. Initially **Firth** disliked producing armaments, but as the other massive steel firms such as **John Brown, Chas. Cammell** & the **Vickers Bros.** vied with each other as armourers to the British Empire **Firth** eventually joined in. An **Arms Race (qv)** developed in the laboratories, melting shops, forges, foundries & rolling mills of the Don Valley; armour v guns firing shells to pierce it. **Firth's** didn't have their own shipyards but later merged with **John Brown (qv),** who did. **Firth 's** had Sheffield's first steam hammer in 1859, with a three ton hammer block. Later in the century they built the **West Gun Works** (now the **Gripple (qv)** factory), to house two 25 ton hammers that shook surrounding firms' buildings & machinery, and led to court cases. However we are told that the Princess of Wales, when she visited the forge with her husband to see an 81 ton gun being forged, 'did not shrink from the noise & the shock.' A few years earlier, in 1871, they had cast the 'Woolwich Infant' gun weighing 35 tons, & involving the teeming of a thousand crucibles.

When **Mark Firth** died in 1880 a two-mile funeral cortege followed his coffin to his impressive burial plot in the **General Cemetery.** Go & see the grand, but simple memorial, surrounded by short, red-painted railings which were cast at his works.

Eventually **Thomas Firth & John Brown** merged with **Vickers & Cammell's** and today their successors make aerospace steels **(Allvac)** and some of the world's biggest forgings & castings **(Sheffield Forgemasters). Firth Rixson** (below) have become a very powerful group. **Firth-Vickers** was established to develop the **stainless steel** interests of **Firth-Brown** and **Vickers,** with impressive new plant off Shepcote Lane. On nationalisation this became **British Steel Stainless,** then on privatisation it was sold first to the Swedes, then to a Finnish firm. This latter has built a new strip mill in Finland & bought the Shepcote Lane plant to close the Sheffield wide strip mill, and steal the order book. Stainless steel billets, rod, precision narrow strip, castings and forgings are still made in Sheffield steel mills, but with usage of stainless wide strip increasing around the world, Britain is in the sorry state of being the only country in the world to lose its production.

Firth Park opened by the Prince & Princess of Wales in 1875, a 36 acre estate which Firth presented to the town, followed by a glittering ball at his residence; stone-built **Oakbrook** on Fulwood Rd., now part of **Notre Dame** Catholic School. (At the ball the Wales danced to the specially composed ' **Oakbrook Galop'**)

Firth Rixson from their H.Q. on **Carbrook Hall Road** they control an impressive conglomerate, mainly **Sheffield** & **Rotherham** based, tracing their history to various independent firms as well as **Firth-Brown** and the smaller **Woodhouse & Rixson. (** The German pilots involved in the Sheffield **Blitz** in 1940 had plans of various steelworks to be bombed and **Woodhouse & Rixson** were important enough to be targeted. Fortunately, though the Luftwaffe caused havoc in the city centre, their raids, which aimed to cripple the steel industry, were an abject failure.)

Firth Rixson today produce **forgings** at **Meadowhall** & **River Don,** upstream from **Forgemasters; rings** at **Ickles; castings** at **Scunthorpe;** as well as having 4 **rolling mills** based at **Ecclesfield** and large **forging presses** at **Darley Dale.** (This plant, near Matlock was one of several built by Sheffield firms away from the **Don Valley** which it was feared presented too concentrated a target during WW2).

Firth Rixson have works also in Hungary & the U.S.A.

Firth Staybrite the celebrated 18% chromium, 8% nickel stainless steel, perfected by **Dr. Wm. H. Hatfield (qv),** successor to **Harry Brearley (qv)** at the **Brown- Firth Research Laboratories.(qv);** a steel eminently suitable for working into spoons, forks, bowls, tea sets, sinks, architectural fittings etc.

fish cakes a Sheffield & South Yorkshire battered speciality from the **chip oyal (chip og),** comprising pieces of cod deep fried between two big slices of potato; (not fish & potato mashed & mixed together, as in the rest of Britain).So, when it's 'frying tonight' & you want to try this speciality, ask for **' cake & chips please'.**

Five Weirs Walk a recently completed walk from **Blonk Street** to **Meadowhall** alongside the **river Don,** except where the river flows through a **Sheffield Forgemasters'** site, when a detour has to be made to **Attercliffe Common** round their **electric arc melting shop,** before regaining the riverside path on Carbrook Street. Beyond Meadowhall you can walk back along the **Sheffield & South Yorkshire Canal** to the canal wharf (now called **Victoria Quays),** or you can walk further along the river to **Rotherham** and on to the huge **Aldwarke steel works,** where you are stopped in your tracks. Obviously **Forgemasters & Aldwarke** can't allow people through their potentially dangerous steel works when even sprained ankles could set off a litigation frenzy, fed by hovering 'no win, no fee' lawyers. If you can ignore the prodigious amounts of litter at the Blonk St./ **Wicker;** the Washford Rd; and the **Tinsley/M1** areas, the riverside walk is surprisingly green & pleasant and, according to the season, you can see coltsfoot & blackberry, swifts & house martins, and butterflies, including small blues & orange tips. There are constant sightings of mallard, heron & kinsfisher; of men at **'Tommy Waards'** and **JE Morrison's** auger bits **forge (Burton Weir)** feeding the dozen, or so white geese, and, for most Sheffielders, the pleasure of hearing the sounds of industry along the river; the hammering of light, and very heavy forges; the clash of steel bars & scrap; the continuous, powerful humming of **Forgemasters, electric arc furnace.**

See also the **Upper Don Walk.**

fizzog face

flatback cheaply-made knife; **Wadsley flatbacks.**

flat hammerman skilled craftsman in the **silver trade** who hammers trays, salvers etc. absolutely flat to a consistent gauge, dissipating any tensions in the metal, using a hammer with a flat, round, chamfered surface, together with a strong, steady arm and keen eye. He gives the tray or salver a rigid, undistorted mirror finish, and his skill is somewhat akin to the circular saw **smither's** , who, it used to be said, 'was paid a **bob** for hitting the steel, and a **quid** for knowing where to hit it.'

flatstick flat piece of ashwood, shaped to fit & cover a knife blade & pressed to the grindstone, aiding the grinder.

flatware spoons & forks, as opposed to **cutlery,** which, strictly speaking, applies to items with a cutting edge, such as knives & **sithers** (scissors**).**

flippin' ; flippin' eck; flippin' Eeley a mild imprecation known nationwide-except the last, which is pure Sheffield (see **Heeley).** Much used by the Poles who settled here after the war, and focussed their lives around 2 clubs on **Ecclesall Road;** a Catholic club & their ex-servicemen's club, **Dom Kombatanta.** One told of his platoon, billeted in a Sheffield church for Christmas 1946, trying to sleep, when one lad took it into his head to play the church organ very loudly, and very badly. The English sergeant bellowed out, "Stop that flippin' racket." The organist bellowed back, "It's not flippin' racket, it's flippin' carol- **Silent flippin' Night!"**

flit to move house; to do a **moonlight flit.**

Wm. Flockton & Sons architects responsible for many fine Sheffield buildings including; **The Mount,** Broomhill, 1830-1832, nicknamed **Flockton's folly** at the time, because it was so far out of town. Occupiers at various times have included **James Montgomery (qv),** and **the United Steel Companies; Wesley College,** Broomhill, which became **King Ted's Grammar School; Ecclesall Union Workhouse,** Nether Edge, opened 1843 for 500 inmates, including 'old & infirm, chronic sick, lunatics & vagrants.' This became the **Nether Edge Hospital,** and has now been converted to apartments. Flockton worked with some of Sheffield's most powerful industrialists, including cutler **Geo. Wostenholm (Kenwood),** and, in the 1860's steelmen **John Brown (Endcliffe Hall) & Mark Firth (Oakbrook).** All the above fine buildings still stand, but an exceptional factory, ca. 1831 for Peter Stubs, Warrington **filemaker**, was demolished in the 1960's. Stubs wanted control of his own steel supplies so had **Warrington Works** built in Rotherham, with an elaborate pillared stone entrance leading to the works where steelmaking comprised of a most impressive bank of 6 **cementation furnaces** and a **crucible melting shop.** If these buildings still stood today they would be listed, & would surely qualify, along with **Abbeydale Works;** the **cementation furnace** on Doncaster street; the **Bessemer converter** at **Kelham;** and the large **Sanderson's crucible shop** at Darnall, for World Heritage status.

flooer floor; **shop flooer: "Thi settin' women on 'flooer; workin' wi 'tongs."** " They're setting women on, on the shop floor; working with the tongs." (Quoted by a woman on **Radio Sheffield,** talking about women doing men's jobs during wartime at **Templeborough Rolling Mills,** Rotherham).

fluff to fart silently; **SBD** (silent, but deadly). If a young lad was unjustly accused; **"Tha's fluffed"**, he might counter: **"Monkeys smell their own muck."** Like French, German & Russian, Sheffield dialect has two words, one for the silent fart, another: **trump (qv)** for the loud one.

fly press machine capable of punching out shapes rapidly in steel.

foggy me first (childrens' games); me first! bags me first!

fon found. **'He looks as though he's lost a bob an' fon a tanner.'**

fooak folk. ' **Thi's** (there's) **nowt so queer as fooak.'**

'Fooarge the forge. Familiar name for the **Park Gate Iron & Steel Co.** Rotherham, which merged with **'Steelos'** upon nationalisation, both firms moving downstream eventually, lock stock & barrel, to **Park Gate's** massive site at **Aldwarke(qv).** Ironically, **Park Gate Iron & Steel Co.** were renowned for rolled, not forged products, their only forge being in a small blacksmiths' shop where implements such as rolling mill tongs were made. There **is** a forge at the district called **Parkgate** in Rotherham, producing rings for the aerospace & oil industries. Once called **Oxley's,** this forge is now part of **Firth Rixson.**

fooerced to used in the sense of **may not** or **might not:** 'He's not **forced to** like it.' 'She's not **forced to** be in.'

fossick to rummage around. Used in Australia to mean to search for gold in abandoned workings, or in rivers.

Sir John Fowler Sheffield engineer, celebrated locally for designing the 1840 **Wicker Arches** & viaduct, & nationally for the **Forth Bridge.**

Samuel Fox another of the great Victorian **Sheffield steelmen;** son of a shuttle maker in **Bradwell;** apprenticed to Samuel Cocker who was a needle, hackle pin, fish hook & piano wire manufacturer of **Hathersage**, he eventually set up on his own producing wire in a former cotton mill at **Stocks' Bridge,** on the Little Don in 1841. Various sources have him moving to the Porter Steel Works, Sheffield with Cocker in 1847, and leasing Upper Coppice Wheel at **Rivelin** as a wire mill, with William Rose in 1854, but it was the little settlement of **Stocksbridge** that developed into a small town, around his ever expanding steel works that came to dominate the valley. He had observed the manufacture of cumbersome umbrella frames in Hathersage, made from whalebone or solid steel wire, and perfected a lighter, folding frame made from **U** shaped ribs. The **Fox frame** was born, forerunner of all modern folding umbrellas, patented in 1852 as the **Paragon,** with its running fox trade mark and covering of alpaca, put on at Titus Salt's works at Saltaire. Fox began to make his own **crucible steel** about 1860 for special wire for crinolines, needles & pianos as well as for his own umbrella frame department. In 1862 he installed one of the first **Bessemer** melting shops to make steel in bulk to feed his rolling mills & forges, installed to meet the railway boom. He built the Stocksbridge Railway in 1877 to link the works with the expanding railway network, transporting tyres, axles & springs made at the works. **Open Hearth** furnaces, installed in 1899, gradually replaced **Bessemer,** and the **Electric Arc** process in the 1960's replaced **Open Hearth.** In 1918 **Fox's** became part of **United Steel Companies,** which, also comprising **Appelby Frodingham** (Scunthorpe-bulk steels) & **Steel Peech & Tozer** (Rotherham-general engineering steels) was then the biggest steel producer in the British Empire. Upon nationalisation in 1967 overall control of these & other proud Sheffield names passed from the Steel City, to government employees in London.

Today, though **Arc melting** has moved to **Aldwarke** and both plants are known as **Corus Engineering Steels**, now owned by Tata of India, the clash of steel still resounds from the sheds in the valley bottom at Stocksbridge, still known locally as **'Sammy Fox's'.** A batch of small **vacuum re-melting furnaces** makes ultra clean steels for the aerospace, defence, power generation & medical industries. Two furnaces have been added recently thanks to an order for the steel for the landing gear of the largest passenger aircraft ever built. When an aircraft weighing hundreds of tons drops on the runway at several hundred miles per hour, the steel cushioning the landing has to be good. The precision strip mill in the valley, now known as

Sheffield Special Strip, producing strip for scalpels & razor blades may be merged into a similar mill at Wincobank (formerly **Arthur Lee's).** A reputation for quality (Gillette U.S.A. ranked the mill far better than competitors in Sweden, Germany & Japan) should ensure continuing production in Sheffield, despite British taxes on industry, Finnish ownership, & closure of British customers (e.g. Gillette U.K. moving production to St. Petersburg).

The modern stainless steel wire plant in Sheephouse wood, above Underbank reservoir is now called **Fox Wire** and is owned by **Bridon,** the Doncaster wire rope manufacturers well known for supplying suspension bridges around the world.

Silver Fox stainless set out to rival **Firth stainless** before Sheffield stainless steel production was rationalised after WW2. Spoons & forks stamped **Silver Fox stainless** are prized by collectors for their rarity.

Fox frames haven't been made in the valley for many years, but are still produced. Yet another enterprise by Samuel Fox (however did he have the energy?) was when he converted an 18th century water powered paper mill into a wire drawing mill in 1866.This was the Eckland Bridge works at Millhouse Green, Barnsley. His work's secretary, William Hoyland, invented the 'Flexus' umbrella frame with spring steel ribs, & set up independently there in 1875. Fox, by then was more involved with the **heavy trades** than the **light** and eventually Hoyland's firm became **Hoyland Fox** taking over **Fox Frames,** then on Valley Road, Heeley (works there previously known as **Empire Rib).** Production continues at Millhouse Green on a site that includes 19th century stone buildings round a courtyard, though this will be redeveloped, inevitably, as housing in 2007, and umbrella manufacture is planned for a new factory elsewhere in Barnsley or Rotherham.

frame thissen get a grip; get organised; **now tha'rt framin'**

fratch argue, quarrel; **feight.** Perhaps more prevalent in Barnsley and Leeds. (Little Leeds girl in the 1940's wanting to be entertained by her argumentative grandparents: **"**When are you going to start **fratching?")**

freecutting steels re-sulphurised, easy machining steels, ideal for the mass production of engineered parts, such as sparking plugs; perfected at **Park Gate Iron & Steel Co.** and still made in great volume in bars or coils, especially for the UK, German & American car market, sometimes with lead or tellurium addition, at the **Aldwarke (qv)** plant of **Corus Engineering Steels.**

Freeman College now being built (2007) on Arundel St. along with the conversion of the former **Sterling Works** of C.W.Fletcher. (This company made hand- forged sterling silver **flatware (qv)** there as well as precision- engineered aerospace parts. Their engineering section has relocated to a new factory in Rotherham, and their world-unique, hand-forged flatware section has been sold to their main New York City customer, who continue production as **Fletcher-Robinson,** on Lambert St.)The college helps young people who are not interested in academic subjects; who 'have learning difficulties'; who may be drop outs from, or disruptive in standard schools, but who may have the brains & skilled eye & hand co-ordination to be good metalworkers. It defies the British Government's view that all manufacturing should go to China, & that industry & a £5 billion per month trade deficit doesn't matter. **Freeman** already has possession of a works on Leadmill Rd., the former home of **Wentworth Pewter** who moved to more modern premises at Darnall in 2005, leaving machinery for students at the new college to use. The college has also bought the ground floor workshops in the newly refurbished **Butcher Wheel** on Arundel St., next to **Sterling Works.** They own, too, **Merlin Theatre,** built 1969 off Union Rd., Nether Edge, together with **Tintagel House,** a Rudolph Steiner centre, & intend also to have a woodland centre in the city.

The College is in **The Ruskin Mill Educational Trust,** founded & directed by **Aonghus Gordon** comprising colleges in Gloucestershire, Stourbridge and now Sheffield, inspired by the ideals of **John Ruskin (qv), Rudolf Steiner** and Sheffielder **Arnold Freeman.** The Gloucestershire college, with a working farm, concentrates on rural crafts; Stourbridge, at the former Royal Doulton glassworks, concentrates on glassmaking; & Sheffield, of course, concentrates on pewter, copper & silversmithing & cutlery manufacture. **Arnold Freeman,** "unkempt & wildly enthusiastic" was, like his more famous friends, keen on education & "the improvement of the working man". He ran an educational settlement in Netherthorpe & at Hollowford, Castleton & was a keen rambler. He "inspired respect, organised lecture courses, & helped Jewish refugees from Germany in the 1930's." His name is now honoured by this college.

freeten; freetened or **frit** to frighten; frightened; **yitten (qv).**

French nail **nail nick** on a pocket knife blade comprising a long straight groove, to enable you open the blade with your nail.

George Fullard (1923-1973) sculptor, born in Darnall, pupil of **Sheffield College of Art,** severely wounded at Casino 1944. See his thin walking man outside the Winter Garden, & the seated woman with child in the yard of the Unitarian Upper Chapel on Norfolk St.

Thomas Fuller wrote in 1662 that most of the working knives used by English country people were made in Sheffield, "the staple town for this commodity...one may justly wonder how a knife may be sold for one penny."

fuller's earth used for fulling cloth, which was made more compact by shrinking & beating it. A national word of course, but commonly heard in Rotherham: **"He dun't know whether he's on this earth or fuller's."**

funnyossity a comic; oddball character. The word, like the oddball character, is not peculiar to Sheffield.

fur far; **It's not fur from here.**

furnaces; he works on'furnaces he works in the **electric arc melting shop;** in the **high frequency melting,** or **vacuum remelting** department; (up to the 1950's; in the **Bessemer** or **Open Hearth shops). Harry Brearley (1871-1948),** inventor of stainless steel, wrote of 'working **in** the (**crucible**) furnace.'

Fusion plate; Fused plate **Sheffield Plate; Old Sheffield Plate, Thomas Boulsover's (qv)** invention ca.1740; silver sheet one eighth of an inch thick fused to a copper ingot ca. one & a half inches thick, rolled into sheet & made into candlesticks, coffee pots etc. A Sheffield silversmith described the copper as being "as thick as 'missus cuts 'bread", and the silver "as thin as she spreads 'butter." Be that as it may, **electro-plating** was a much thinner plate, superseding **Boulsover's** invention a hundred years later, whilst ensuring that pieces made by the old method became highly prized. To distinguish it from electro-plating **Sheffield Plate** became known as **Old Sheffield Plate.**

G

gaffer a national word for factory boss, foreman etc. (Irreverent song sung to the 'International': **"**The working class can kiss my arse, I've got the gaffer's –or foreman's- job at last). But **gaffer** in our region can also mean **the wife.**

gainshire barb, or a notch like a fish-hook; the tang of a knife going right through the handle was sometimes **gainshired=** knocked over where it protudes, securing the blade permanently to the handle.

I'n't it a game! Isn't it a devil!

A game (lame**)** leg is known locally as a **gammy** leg.

gammerouche a 1940's/50's smutty schoolboy or pub word for oral sex. Possibly a national word from the French. The French sound to the word typifies how we regarded our Gallic neighbours. (French author Felix de Grand' Combe, in a 1938 book on English- French attitudes, tells of his disappointment when he asked in a Sheffield bookshop if they had any French books. **"**Yes sir,**"** came the reply, **"**under the counter; that's where we keep the dirty books.**")**

gammerstanging flirting, messing about with girls; (word recalled in the 1990's by former Rotherham steelmen, as used by their grandparents many decades previously, so it is probably now very rare.) Kellet gives West Riding usage of **gammerstang** to mean a 'wanton woman'.

gani; ganni **ganister/ gannister,** a grey, fine grained, highly refractory siliceous rock found beneath coal seams, formerly obtained by **drift mines** into hills at places such as Wadsley Bridge, Ughill, Hutcliffe Wood & **Parkwood Springs (qv).** Examples of local use**: fettling (qv)** Open Hearth furnaces at Park Gate & Steel peech & Tozer; re-sealing the tap hole **(tap oyal)** of the blast furnaces at Park Gate; lining the ladles used to carry molten nickel silver at the **Old Park Silver Mill** on Club Mill Road, near the conflux of the Loxley & the Don. The use of **ganister** was, following America's lead, gradually phased out in favour of less hazardous refractory materials. **Gani** has very high silica content= over 92 per cent Si O2 & the dreadful lung disease, silicosis, was prevalent among miners. My brother-in-law used to say, **"If tha gets that tha'rt booked for a pair o' wings."** He got the disease himself after working in the **Parkwood** mine; at **Pickford & Hollands** refractory brickworks on **Archer Road;** and at **Dyson's** down **Attercliffe,** but he lives a full life and hopefully will live many years before **"getting his wings."**

'garden allotment

six foot an' a gas lamp a very tall person

gash (vulgar) vagina; builders overheard on Sheffield to Rotherham bus, admiring the conductress**: "**Ah bet she's gorra reight gash on her."

gen (hard **g**) gave. **Oogeniter?** Who gave it her? **gie** (hard **g**) give. **Gie it us.** Give it to me. **Gie it mester.** Give it to the man. Can be shortened to **gi: Ah'll gi thi what for gis, giz** (hard **g**) gives. Lad told to stop picking his nose**: It gis me summat to do.**

gennel (soft **g**) passageway- see **jennel** and **eight foot. ginnel** (hard **g**) passageway; narrow alleyway (Barnsley/ Leeds). The **reight** Sheffield word is **jennel (qv).**

gerrit, (hard **g**)**; gerrit etten; gerrit dahn thi.** Get it/ get it eaten/ get it down you (to a fussy eater).

gill (soft **g**) nationally is a quarter pint, but here always means a half pint (of beer), as does **a glass o'bitter.**

gillies (hard **g**) butcher's knives for Scottish trade.

The glass industry in the Sheffield region see **the Turner Museum of Glass**

glaze to give a fine finish to a blade; to polish cutlery on a glazer.

glazer wheel dressed by having its leather or felt rim coated with glue & rolled in abrasive emery powder; person who **glazes** cutlery.

glazing wheels **30 x 2** inch wheels in **double heading** machines comprising of tightly-packed cushions of calico segments inserted under pressure into steel wheels; glue is soaked into the calico & abrasive grit added.

Globe Works classic stone building on Penistone Rd., like a small stately home, built 1820 when steam power was bringing industry into more integrated factories in town. See also **Green Lane Works** & **Sheaf Works.**

Gloops cartoon cat with a **thmile** in the **Star,** 1930's/ 40's/ 50's. There was a **Gloops's Club** with rule book, badges, competitions, outings etc.

glottal stop as pointed out in the book **Orreight mi ol',** the Cockney mid-word **glottal stop** replacing **t** is easy to imitate, and I asked you to imagine the landlady of the Victoria pub, Peggy Mitchell, speaking to Frank Butcher in the T.V. soap, East Enders. (If you don't watch this I don't blame you.): "Fwank, this beer taists like **wo'er**, bwing some more ap; an' while you're dahn there, bwing some **ba'er** fwom the fwidge." An apostrophe indicates the **glottal stop** replacing **t** in the words water & butter.
The Sheffield & other region's **glottal stop** is hard to describe & even harder for outsiders to master. It is the virtual disappearance of the definite article, the word **'the'** before a noun, which is replaced by the briefest closure of the **glottis,** the opening between the vocal cords, (& is replaced in writing by an apostrophe). Sometimes the passage of air is stopped simultaneously by the tip of the tongue too, as though in a vocal belt & braces policy.; **he fell in 'watter. C.f.** South Lancashire & the West Riding where the glottal stop in the same sentence comes **before** the remnant of **'the'** = **'th'** & **'t'**, respectively; **he fell in' thwatter & he fell in' twatter.)** Sheffielders retain the **'t'** in a few sayings; **"T'Wicker weer t'watter runs o'er t'weir." (qv) ; "Put t'wood in t'oyal."** Shut that door!

gob mouth. **Shut thi gob** (rude); **Shut thi gob, an' gi' thi arse a chance** (very rude); **gobby**= loquacious.

hard gob white metal solder; **gobbed on**= soldered on.

gobbing back (mining) When coal or ganister was dug out men would **gob back**= shovel shale, rocks & earth back into the space created by the extraction, rather than just knocking the props out and letting the roof cave in.

gobbo wet cement

goff; goffing hammer **trip hammer;** fast-moving powered hammer, originally worked by water-power; now loosely refers to any power-worked hammer.

goit; goyt sluice; mill race; an artificial cut taking water from the river into a **dam,** or from the **dam** via the water wheel(s) back to the river further downstream. The channel into the dam is the **head goyt,** and the channel out is the **tail goyt.**

gollop to eat fast & greedily. **Don't gollop thi food.**

gooin' , gu going, go. Apprentice mechanic, when asked by his boss what was wrong with a car: **'It wain't gu.'**

Ah don't know whether ah'm cumin' or gooin'.

gooinooam time going home time, in school or factory.

goosegobs; goosegogs gooseberries

gormless, gormy daft, **datal (qv).**

gorra got to. **Sumonemz gorragerroffooam**= some of them have got to go home.

goz (vulgar) spit, to spit.

graining (cutlery trade) using buff with very thin leather wheel for polishing edges of spoons & forks (**'grains'** in 1828 **Hallamshire Glossary** has one meaning= **prongs** of forks); **'heeling & pipping'** handles of spoons & forks.

grand fine, excellent; associated more with Gracie Fields/ George Formby's Lancashire & J. B. Priestley's Bradford than with our region, though it was Rotherham comedian, **Sandy Powell** who used to say, **'I'nt it grand to be daft.'**

A saying; **'Creaking gates last longest'** is used to mean people with many ailments survive longer.

J. G. Graves built up a large cutlery & plate business, and then the **world's first mail order firm.** He was a major benefactor to the city with his **Graves Trust.** The 1934 **Graves Art Gallery & Library,** Egyptian style in startling white limestone, is a prominent city-centre building; **Graves Park,** covering over 200 acres has a rare-breeds farm on part of its invigorating **Norton** heights plus a string of three small dams dropping down through woodland to **Woodseats;** and sections of the **Round Walk** exist thanks to **J.G.Graves. Graves Trust Homes** are found around the city. Most important of all, in 1935, the **Graves Trust** bought an industrial site that is now unique in the world: **Abbeydale Hamlet (qv)** which was eventually restored by what became the **Sheffield Trades Historical Society (qv),** despite efforts by successive City Councils to have it demolished.

greease grease. **Tony Capstick's** nice conundrum heard on **Radio Sheffield: " If oyal is hole, what is oil?.......** (answer:) **"Greease."**

Green Lane Works near **Kelham Island (qv)** with fine, classical gateway leading to a factory round a courtyard & alongside the river **Don,** opposite **Kelham Island** museum. It was built in 1860 for cast iron stove & fireplace manufacturer **Hy. Hoole,** who was already established by then in this expanding Sheffield & Rotherham trade. The factory was, until a few years ago owned by **W.A.Tyzack,** maker of **'horseman'** brand knives between the wars & machine knives after. Unfortunately they were bought by an Austrian firm, renamed Miba Tyzack, & most production will be transferred to a cheap labour country. There are at least a dozen Sheffield-owned manufacturers of machine knives & hopefully they will regain Miba's trade for the city.

'Green 'Un was launched a hundred years ago on 14 September **1907** as the 'Football and Sports Special', and is the world's oldest sports paper. Printed on green paper it soon became known as the **Green 'Un.** A friend who had a newsagent's on Oakbrook Rd. recalls a posh lady who could never bring herself to say **Un',** and would ask **' May I have a Green One, please.'**

grid bicycle (from **gridiron?) 'We're off on'grids to Castleton.'**

grinder along with **buffer girls** ranked high among the heroes of Sheffield skilled labour. See **double shear steel** above for an indication of the **grinder's** skills. Examine hand-forged, hand-ground Victorian table knives made by firms such as **Joseph Rodgers; Mappin & Webb; Walker & Hall** etc.so finely taper- ground from the back to the cutting edge, as well as lengthways from the bolster to the tip, and marvel at the dexterity of their workmen. Hand grinders worked in the **Heavy Trades** but were more prominent in the **Light** and could be found in cutlery, tool & saw factories working on the smallest items such as penknives & open razors to the largest circular saws, up to 6 ft. diameter.

In the days of intensive use of waterpower along the fast-flowing Sheffield rivers- say from 1400 to 1900 A.D., grinders were self-employed independent craftsmen renting a stone & a trough **(trow),** and generally working to suit themselves, often giving themselves **Saint Monday (qv)** off. As well as the waterwheel itself, their workshop too was called the **'Wheel'** as well as **'grinder's hull' (qv).** Walking to & from work along the wooded valleys was pleasant & working in the picturesque stone **hulls** was comparatively healthy, if extremely draughty, & often damp. Lack of glass in the windows & an open door ensured ventilation to offset dust from the grinding to a certain extent. Men would fish in the streams **while** their **'dairy maid' (waterwheel)** picked up speed, or if it stopped because of drought or ice.

The finest **grindstones** or **whetstones** for pocket & table knives & razors were made from quarries at **Wickersley & Brincliffe Edge (qv),** with the **millstone grit** quarries at the **Edges** to the west of Sheffield in the Peak District perhaps more suited for stones to grind scythes, and mill flour. Stones for **scythe grinding** started off as 4 or 5 ft. diameter x up to 1 ft. width. A common size for the table knife grinder was 41 inch diameter x 7 inch width. When he'd worn it down to about 21 inch diameter he'd pass it on to the pocket knife or open razor grinder. These grinders would wear it down to about 15 inch diameter, when it would be a **grindle cowk,** a worn-down grindstone **(cf Grindleford** village near Sheffield).**Grindle cowks** were used as steps **(see Shepherd Wheel),** stepping stones across the five main rivers (cf **Leppings Lane),** pillars holding up outbuildings (see **Abbeydale Hamlet),** seats or receptacles for umbrellas, pokers etc.Some **grindle cowks** were cut in half and used on top of walls (nice examples along with **crozzle** at **Norfolk Park** Granville Rd. entrance**).**

Grindstones occasionally burst when revolving at speed, killing or maiming the grinder. A contemporary wrote: **"** He sits over a tool which at any moment may (break &) send him through the roof with all the suddenness & velocity of dynamite." When a new stone was 'hung' and first worked at speed was a particularly tense time as men wondered whether there were hidden faults in the stone.

Water power began to be superseded by steam in the 1790's and grinders gradually forsook the picturesque stone **hulls** by the rivers for **wheels** in town, freed from 'the fickle power of water.' (They brought the name **'wheel'** for their workshops with them & some quite large steam-driven factories were called **'wheels'- e.g. Butcher's Wheel** on Arundel Street). Their premises in town were less draughty & the power turning the stones more efficient.They could produce much more if they wished, but at the expense of their health. Working hunched over siliceous sandstone **'nose to the grindstone',** throwing the weight of his shoulders into the friction, and, by 'fingering' the blade 'effecting all those dainty touches & delicate graduations which no machine can impart' the grinder gave us those exquisite Victorian knives, but at huge cost. By inhaling dust he contracted silicosis, commonly known as **grinder's asthma** or **grinder's lung** which shortened his life by 10, 20 or even 30 years. Men working on **open razors** and forks were especially threatened, because these were dry ground. They were old men at 30. Other grinders, e,g. table knife grinders, ground wet, the base of the grindstone running through water in the **trow (trough).** They would be saturated with wet wheel swarf (powdered stone & steel forming a sludge-see **crozzle**) which dyed them a deep saffron colour from head to toe- hence their nickname **'yaller bellies'(qv).** In 'The conditions of the working class in England, 1845', drawing on reports at the time, Engels gives the average life expectancy of a dry grinder as barely 35 while a wet grinder might live 10 more years, so it was worthwhile being a **'yaller belly'.**

Though in general steam engines were more reliable, a mechanical fault could lead tc a reversing engine, resulting in a reversing grindstone wobbling off its axle, & sometimes breaking.

Grinding was inevitably, therefore, a young man's trade with a young man's scorn for the future. Many grinders were fiercely independent, self employed, well-paid, heavy drinkers who believed in a short life & a merry one, ignoring safety measures, even dust extractors, as though challenging disease & death to do their worst. Engels, commenting further on official reports on Sheffield in 1844 says grinders even destroyed dust extractors 'since they fear that if their trade becomes safer, it will attract more workers & so lead to a fall in wages'. Their numbers included quite a few roisterous, boisterous roughnecks, much feared in the town. If they lived today they would be showered with 'asbos'. They were sometimes even regarded as sub-human: **'Who's that at 'dooer?',** a woman asked. **' Two men and a groinder',** her son replied. (Dialect poems & anecdotes of the day spell **groinder** thus, showing either that Derbyshire- born men dominated the trade, or that our dialect is as much North Midlands as Yorkshire). Whatever the grinders' faults it is hard not to be moved by the words of **Ebeneezer Elliot (1781-1849):**
“There draws the Grinder his laborious breath,
There, coughing at his deadly trade he bends
Born to die young, he fears nor man nor death
Scorning the future, what he earns he spends
Debauch and Riot are his bosom friends.”

Look at the grindstones under **Stanage, Burbage & Millstone Edges,** some with faults, & imagine the chagrin of the stone craftsman chiselling one out, in situ & in all weathers, only to find it defective. Most, however, look perfect- you can see several hundred lined up alongside a grass track below the **Surprise View,** for all the world as if they are awaiting depatch. Why did the trade stop, seemingly so abruptly? Some blame America for periodically doubling duty on the Sheffield trades, in order to protect their infant cutlery, steel & tool trades. Some blame France for sending over their high quality stones at a lower price, but the millstone's demise was assured most of all by Sheffielder **George Jowitt's** manufacture of artificial, bonded, abrasive wheels, based on work he'd seen in America. These emery wheels of the early twentieth century lasted longer, burst extremely rarely, and most important, didn't contain deadly silica. Grinders began to live much longer and more satisfying lives, and gradually lost their reputation for being violent roughnecks. Two of the most refined men with a lifelong zest for knowledge died within the last decade after both working over 50 years in their respective trades: **Billy Hukin,** open razor grinder (he hated the term **cut throat razor**), was the last in this trade in Sheffield and died aged 92, fortunately having years previously listed the 36 different processes in razor grinding, & having had his work videoed by **Ken Hawley. Ed Chapman,** pocket knife grinder from Heeley lived 10 years longer, dying in 2003 aged 102. Both men had spent all their working lives using what they called **patent wheels** (artificial stones).

There are still specialist hand grinders around Sheffield, some quite young- see film made by bevel-edge chisel grinder **Barry Gribbin** at **Weston Park.** (And back in the early 1900's the demise of hand grinding was forecast due to mechanisation. It's a long time a-dying!)

rough grinding grinding all over the surface of a job to remove hammer marks & scale. A grinder specialising in this is called a **rougher.**

A saying: **To charm the heart of a grindstone.**

Gripple a unique wire joining & tensioning device, invented by **Hugh Facey** and sold throughout the world: over 150 million of them in ten years. Millions of these Sheffield products can be seen on Australian farms & on tree-top walkways in the rainforests, as well as in French vineyards.(It is the only British product ever to receive a major French award for industrial innovation & design). It is made in an award-winning, Prince Charles approved factory converted from **Thos. Firth's West Gun Works** on Savile Street. This has Canadian Redwood timber roofing, and a history of making guns for the defence of the British Empire, from the cannon for Lord Napier's Abyssinian campaign to big naval guns for WW1 &2.

Guest & Chrimes a fine 1857 building in Rotherham housed their brass & iron foundry. Cast iron covers all over Britain keep their name alive. Ed. Chrimes invented the modern high pressure screw-down tap in 1845.

gullies gutters (in Rotherham).

H

hack hammer adze-shaped hand tool used to dress the face of a grindstone, removing irregularities; **'truing it up'.**

Sir Robert Abbott Hadfield (1858-1940) His diary 18th May 1876 read,"Had my furnace going, melted steel". This was a lad who'd refused the chance to go to Oxford or Cambridge, preferring an apprenticeship with steelmaker **Jonas & Colver** as well as tuition in chemistry from leading steel analyst **A.H.Allen. Allen** persuaded **Hadfield's** father to let the teenager build a furnace in the cellar of the family home, Ashdell Mount! **Michael Faraday** had utilised Sheffield steelmen's skills in a quest to artificially improve cutting edges, and decrease corrosion by adding elements to steel. **Robert Mushet** had improved performances of cutting tools by adding tungsten, using the expertise of steel firm **Samuel Osborn.** Towering above these **Hadfield** was indefatigable in inventing **alloy steels,** manufacturing them & finding uses for them, involving extensive travels both in Britain & the U.S.A. He is the real **father of alloy steels.** His own father, tired of being a local rate collector, had recruited a steel moulder from **Vickers** to manufacture castings at Newhall Road, Attercliffe. The son developed **Hadfield's Steel Foundry** into the biggest in the world towards the end of the Victorian era with two huge factories, **Hecla Works** and further down the Don, **East Hecla Works** (where Meadowhall shopping centre is now.) This was thanks to his invention of **Manganese Steel** in 1882, an alloy with 1% carbon and manganese 12/14% , having the remarkable properties of both **work hardening** and being immensely hard wearing. The more it was worked, the harder & tougher it became. Its best-known use is for railway & tramway points. A manganese steel **'frog'** at Brooklyn N.Y. at a spot where trams passed every 27 seconds was found to last 25 times longer than ordinary carbon steel. Points at **Fitzalan Square** installed in 1907 lasted 12 years = 48 times longer than carbon steel. Excavator/dredger buckets could be made massively bigger thanks to teeth made from the steel. Tank treads & soldiers' helmets were made from **Hadfield's** steel & during WW2 many German as well as British troops' lives were saved thanks to the steel –some of which was exported to Germany in the 1930's. (It has been said that thousands of finished helmets made by **Hadfield's** & destined for the Wehrmacht were stranded at the works at the outbreak of war, but this may be what is now called 'urban myth').

Hadfield then went on to invent **Silicon Steel,** patented 1883/4; low hysteresis , more magnetic than iron & hard with it, suitable for magnetic cores of electric transformers & for electric motors & generators.An American engineer ('History of Electric Light & Power 1982'), calculated that the total world saving in the 17 years following Hadfield's 1903 U.S. patent for **Si Steel** amounted to $340 million, enough then to fund the building of the Panama Canal.

On top of his frantic business life **Hadfield** developed **Parkhead House** (now called **Parkhead Hall**) into a family home, where he lived from 1898 to 1939; he was **Master Cutler** in 1899 & was knighted in 1908.

In the world wars Sheffield metalworking firms were obliged to do war work & **Hadfield's Foundry** specialised in heavy shells. See a picture of thousands of them stacked up awaiting despatch in Dalton's book, 'Sheffield, Armourer to the British Empire.' This was very profitable at the time but disastrous at the end of the wars, when work for the hugely increased workforce & the new machinery was abruptly ended, at the same time as their pre-war peacetime orders had been taken by steel firms in non-combatant countries.

The firm never really recovered; were taken over by a City financier with little knowledge of steel; merged with a smaller firm; bullied by mass-picketing into the 1980 **British Steel Co.** v government strike, and closed down not long afterwards.

haft; hafter handle; cutler who makes handles of ivory, stag & buffalo horn, bone; **xylo;** wood etc. and fixes them to knives. Old saying: **'Sheffield made, haft and blade; London, for your life, show me such a knife'.** Doggerel stemming from the days when the two cutlery centres competed, with London having the reputation for more expensive knives, and Sheffield for the sharper. New steelmaking expertise, concentration of craftsmen in the region, water, then steam power ensured Sheffield's supremacy in the 1800's and the capital faded away as a cutlery centre. See also, **Scarlett & Whiting, horn cutters.**

hagg; hollin stand of holly trees/bushes; holly. Holly was used as winter feed for cattle- perhaps the upper leaves which are not prickly. **Hunter's 'Hallamshire Glossary'** gives 'a Hag of Hollin' as holly trees sold or leased by the Lord of the Manor 'by the hag'. C.f. names at both sides of Rivelin valley: **Hollins Lane. Bellhagg Road, the Hagg, Hagg Hill.**

Hallam an early mention is in the Domesday Book 1086 which describes **Ateclive & Escafeld 'said to be inland in Hallun.'**

When the last **Shrewsbury,** lord of the manor & protector of the 300+ years old cutlery industry died , the cutlers banded together & **The Company of Cutlers in Hallamshire (qv)** was incorporated by an act of parliament in **1624**. The need to unite was shown in the long fight against the iniquitous hearth tax levied twice yearly between 1662 and 1689. Most people in

Sheffield depended on the trade in those days and many suffered double taxation- on their home fire & forge.(In 1672 the tax collectors recorded 224 smithies to 494 houses in the township, and a further 372 smithies in the outlying areas). The **Company's** jurisdiction was over cutlers alone, then later over scythe & edge-tool makers, but when Sheffield became the world's steel capital, the power, influence & wealth of the steelmen forced a reconsideration, & eventually all the metal trades within Sheffield & 6 miles beyond its boundaries were admitted. Many thousands of poor agricultural labourers flooded in from Lincolnshire, Notts. & Derbyshire etc. aiming to enrich themselves at **Vickers** & other giant firms. John Betjeman captured the results of this succinctly with a line in his poem on Broomhill: **'Strange Hallamshire, county of dearth and of bounty.'**

Hallam now refers only to the well-wooded, well-heeled parliamentary constituency west of Sheffield which rises from about 200 feet near the town centre to 1500 feet at **High Neb** on **Stanage Edge** and includes such gems as the Victorian stone houses of Fulwood, the farms of the **Mayfield Valley** & **Hallam Moor.** Unfortunately there is great pressure by developers on owners of grand stone houses to sell up, & have their beautiful & extensive gardens crammed with expensive houses.

Hallam and **Hallamshire,** once the southern boundary shire of Anglo-Saxon Northumbria, separating Northumbria from Mercia, the namelives on in the names of many important organisations:

Hallam Cathedral whose Victorian spire poses a Roman Catholic challenge to the venerable Anglican cathedral. **John Rawsthorne** is **Bishop of Hallam,** and the **Diocese of Hallam** contains no less than 53 excellent schools. **Hallam F.C.** the world's second oldest football team (after **Sheffield F.C.)** and still playing on their original ground in Hallam.

Hallam FM radio station & Arena. **Hallam University** has climbed the academic & popularity league to be a worthy competitor of **the University of Sheffield.**

Royal Hallamshire the huge monolithic grey hospital building on the Broomhill skyline. Merged with **The Northern General** in one huge N.H.S. Trust, there are centres of excellence on both sites, in various fields, that match any in the world.

to play Hamlet to give someone a scolding. **"Thi mother 'll play 'Amlet when she gets 'ooam"**

hammers; he works on'hammers he works in a forge; he's a forgeman. (the **hammers** can have a falling weight, a **tup,** of up to 25 tons.)

Joseph Hancock a pioneer of the **Sheffield Plate (qv)** industry who brought the manufacture of holloware to the city. (**Boulsover,** the inventor, concentrated on small items, especially buttons.) **Hancock** then established the **Old Park Silver Rolling Mills** ca. 1770 to supply the burgeoning industry with copper, nickel silver & sterling silver sheet & wire. The remains of these mills can be seen by the river Don on Club Mill Road.

hand forger man forging heated steel to shape with a hammer on an anvil, without mechanical help.

happen perhaps.

hardening/ quenching heat treatment of steel bars, coils, wire, strip etc. or of steel products by heating to a set temperature, then **quenching** suddenly in oil (e.g. steel bars); oil or a mixture of oil & water (e.g. table knives); water (e.g. leaf springs); iced brine (e.g. cook's knives) & once upon a time, whale oil (e.g pocket knife blades). Some processes are obviously more severe than others, some are cheaper e.g. water than oil but all the steels & steel products have then to be **tempered (qv)** to avoid brittleness. Today hardening is automated, except by the **Little Mesters,** but previously the hardener/forger would need a keen eye to distinguish the changing colours of the steel. Colours when heating in gradations of roughly 50 degrees centigrade from 600 degrees up to 1200 degrees would be, in turn, brown red/ blood red/ dark cherry/ cherry/ light cherry/ light red/ light orange/ yellow/ light yellow & white. There are tales of men keeping fruit by the furnace to help them judge the right temperature- an orange might indicate ca. 980 degrees.

Hardwick Hall 'more glass than wall' completed for **Bess of Hardwick (qv)** in 1597. We claim her as a Sheffielder since she married the **6th Earl of Shrewsbury (qv)** and lived with him at his **Sheffield Castle** & **Sheffield Manor,** during those tumultuous Elizabethan years when they held **Mary Queen of Scots** captive. Her initials, in stone, **E S; Elizabeth Shrewsbury,** stand proud on the battlements.

Harrison Brothers & Howson a fine old cutlery firm absorbed into **Viners** in 1959. Their impressive red brick building on Carver Street now houses non-manufacturing businesses but see the stone entrance with beautifully carved date 1900, and their trade mark Alpha under a crown.

Dr. Wm. H Hatfield (1882-1943) after employment in the labs. at **Hy. Bessemer** from 1899 & evening studies at **Firth College,** he became one of the first Doctors of Metallurgy at **the University of Sheffield** in 1913. He followed **Harry Brearley (qv)** as head of **Brown-Firth Research** in 1916. **Brearley's** 12/13% Cr. Ferritic stainless steel was ideal for knife blades, capable of being hardened & tempered, but was not malleable enough for pressings, nor stainless enough for e.g. containers holding aggressive chemicals. Krupp of Essen, the steel & armaments dynasty, whose founder had visited Sheffield in the late18th century to try to steal the secret of **crucible**

steel making, had experimented with low carbon, chromium/ nickel steels & in 1923 **Firth Brearley** granted them use of their 13% chromium cutlery patent in exchange for use of the Krupp patent. **Hatfield** didn't find Krupp's 20/7 chromium/nickel entirely satisfactory, since it did not invariably provide a soft, non-magnetic steel. After further research he found that low carbon steel with 18% chromium, 8% nickel, an austenitic stainless, was ideal, when rolled into sheet, for pressings for the chemical & food processing industries. It could be welded, brazed & rivetted and when polished was highly resistant to corrosion. Eventually the largest Sheffield firms combined their stainless interests to form **Firth Vickers Stainless Steels,** and the famous **Firth's 18/8 Staybrite** was born.

Hathersage a fine stone-built village just over the high moors from **Dore** & from **Ringinglow,** and below **Millstone Edge** & **Stanage Edge** with their evidence of gritstone quarries & grindstone manufacture. In the 19th century it was a centre for needle manufacture with five mills to rival Redditch. One firm, **Stead,** eventually moved to Sheffield and changed from the manufacture of needles, including gramophone needles, to superb hand tools, specialising in trimming knives, hacksaws and above all, screwdrivers. Their demise came in the 1980's when even engineers & joiners put cheapness before quality. The **Cockers** ran two mills, Dale Mill & Atlas Mill, this latter changing from water power to steam ca. 1830. **Samuel Cocker** employed a young lad from Bradwell, **Samuel Fox (qv),** destined to invent the folding umbrella & own the huge steelworks in Stocksbridge. **Cocker** moved to start a new mill at **Porter Steel Works** in Sheffield in 1847 and the same family are believed to be the **Cocker Brothers** that made springs for the motor trade in **Attercliffe** into the 1970's. **Robert Cook(e)** moved to Hathersage from the Midlands in 1811 building the **Barnfield Works** powered by a huge waterwheel and, like **John Darvell (Darvell's Mill)** and **Tobias Child (Victoria Mill)** made needles, hackle pins, tenter hooks etc. **Cook(e)** was a wire drawer too, for the needle as well as the crinoline trade, and also had a works at **Ringinglow (qv).**

Charlotte Bronte stayed at **North Lees Hall** several times in 1845,and was friends with the Eyre's who owned it. The much earlier **Robert Eyre** lived at **Highlow Hall** across the valley and is said to have built a hall, including North Lees, for each of his seven sons, all within view of Highlow. Charlotte based her 'Yorkshire' novel, Jane Eyre, very much on Hathersage, with the heroine's name, plus description of the hall matching North Lees, plus reference to needle makers and needle factory in the valley, all indicating the Derbyshire village connection.

Hathersage's best known inhabitant, apart from the remains of **Little John** in an extra long grave, is “the heroic figure of **David Mellor**”**(qv)**, world renowned designer of a huge variety of industrial products from traffic lights & tubular steel lighting to pillar box, & hand tools. More importantly, designer & **manufacturer** of fine silverware which is found in churches, embassies & design centres & museums worldwide.Most important of all, he has continued Sheffield's 700+ years tradition of cutlery manufacture, bringing production from **Broom Hall** to the **Round House,** based on the site of the former village gasometer. Visit the shop, museum & café or, if you can't get to Hathersage, see his beautiful cutlery at **the Famous Sheffield Shop** on **Ecclesall Road.**

the Hawley Collection the world's largest collection of Sheffield-made tools, with also knives, razors, old machinery & catalogues, housed in the University of Sheffield **Hawley Building** on Mappin Street. This building, given by the University was once part of steelmaker **S.&C. Wardlow's** Portobello works, and stores, rather than displays the collection. Room should have been made at the **Millennium Galleries** or at **Weston Park Museum** for a permanent, revolving display. The collection is of international importance, especially to Americans since, at the time of the greatest expansion of the Unted States westward in the 18th & 19th centuries, most of the tools they used to build the new America**:** saws, hammers, adzes, axes, chisels, augers, anvils etc. were made in Sheffield. If Americans of those times thought of English towns & cities Sheffield would readily come to mind. **Huckleberry Finn (qv),** in one of his adventures down the Mississippi claims to be a Sheffielder! American enthusiasts of U.S.history and of old tools- and there are plenty of collecctors of the latter-would cross 'the Pond'to see the **Hawley Collection,** but they wouldn't be drawn by, say, an Austrian modern jewellery display at the **Millennium Galleries** featuring necklaces made from tomato plant stems. No Sirree!

I'll leave the above invective in though **Ken** has given me the excellent news (April 2007) that the collection will be housed in a building on **Kelham Island,** near the **Brooklyn Bridge** to be built from the **Island** across the **Don** to the **Brooklyn Works (**now flats).

Lt.Col. & Ethel Haythornthwaite gave much of their lives towards preserving Sheffield's **“Golden Frame”** & the Peak District. Excepting **Firth Rixson's** forging press at Darley Dale on the edge of the Peak, Sheffield industry has only a small presence in the National Park; **Carbolite,** furnace manufacturer and **David Mellor's** famous round building cutlery factory. Had it not been from pressure from the Haythornthwaites **Firth-Brown** would have built a rolling mill in the Hope Valley to meet WW11 needs. Their home on Endcliffe Crescent became the Sheffield & Peak District Branch of the Council for the Preservation (now Protection) of Rural England.

'eeadache headache - said of a defect in a pen or pocket knife if the blade wobbles from side to side.

Heavy Trades steel & engineering - see **Sheffield Trades**

Heeley district of Sheffield; parliamentary constituency, once Conservative. Has its own city farm on **Richards Rd**.

flippin' 'Eeley; blinkin' 'Eeley, or, more vulgar, **bleedin' 'Eeley** a unique Sheffield curse.
he lives top o' Heeley bottom Heeley duffers or **duffems** petty criminals that **duffed** the Sheffield police by committing crimes in Sheffield & escaping over the **Meersbrook** boundary into Derbyshire. The little brook running from the hills, mostly culverted, into the Sheaf was formerly the county boundary. **Heeley duffems** also applied to people dodging the rent man.

helve hammer **tilt** hammer; forging hammer, where the blows to the item forged are delivered by the **tilting** action of the **helve (**= the 'handle' of the hammer; the main beam= oak trunk ringed with iron to stop splitting). Depending upon the point of the pivot, there are **tail helves (Abbeydale Hamlet); nose helves** or **belly helves (**for heavier work e.g. **Wortley Forge** which made railway axles).

Henderson's Relish; Hendo's made in Sheffield for over 100 years, beloved by ex-pats. There was a local rival up to the 1950's called **Waterhouses**.

hiddy hiding (child's game). **I've 'iddidit.**

high frequency melting furnace more than any other process this replaced the **crucible** furnace for small scale, high quality steel production. A prominent notice on a steelfirm's gate on **Stevenson Road** warns people with pacemakers not to enter.

Hillfoot area of Neepsend at the foot of **Parkwood Springs**

Hillfoot County School one of many built about 1880 characteristically comprised of classrooms round a central assembly hall. Now demolished, only the perimeter wall remains, with entrance marked 'Girls' on one side of the schoolyard, and another entrance at the other side of the yard marked 'Boys'.

Hillsborough a lively area of Sheffield 6

Hillsborough stadium home of **Sheffield Wednesday F.C.(qv).**

Hillsborough barracks originally built to keep rebellious Sheffielders, with their republican tendencies, in check, it eventually housed at various times,fine British Regiments; Dragoon Guards, KOYLI, Yorks. & Lancs. etc. King Edward V11 & Queen Alexandra presented the Colours on 12th July 1905 after opening buildings for the new University of Sheffield. The Army retreated in 1930 and the fine stone buildings have housed various firms since then, notably; **Burdall's Gravy Salts, Chadburn-Chantrey,** furnace builders, the **Stainless Steel Wire Co.** with currently, Morrison's supermarket & **Sheffield Insulations** the most prominent.

Hillsborough Park a compact park with running track, small lake, walled garden built in commemoration of the **Hillsborough disaster,** and a splendid library in what used to be **Hillsborough Hall.** The Hall, built 1779, housed two generations of the **Dixon's** silversmithing family; James Willis Dixon (1814-1876) & son James Willis Dixon (1838-1917).

Joseph Beeston Himsworth owner of two fine cutlery companies; **B.Worth & Sons** and **Beeston & Co.** with their **Mazeppa** trademark, also author of **The Story of Cutlery from Flint to Stainless Steel (1953).** (Stokes Paint on Little London Road have **Mazeppa** atop their factory with effigy of the Ukranian strapped to his horse). **Himsworth's** daughter **Joyce** was a designer-silversmith and examples of her exquisite work is in the **Millenium Galleries.**

hire work work done on behalf of other firms, usually in **the Heavy Trades-** e.g. **hire-rolling** steel. **The Light Trades** would normally call work done on their behalf **outwork.**

hit or miss, run two if there is a disputed decision in a boys' cricket match, the batsman, to stay in, has to run two, whether he hits the next ball or not.

Samuel Holberry (1814-1842) a Chartist seeking parliamentary reform but by foul means, rather than fair. He planned to seize the town hall & Tontine inn, and kill a few big-wigs; got caught and jailed 4 years in York, he died in prison, & was given a hero's funeral in Sheffield.

G. Calvert Holland a physician who published vital statistics of Sheffield in 1843 including number of workers, ages, level of literacy, & occupational diseases across the huge range of trades (Sheffield-made articles covered 12,000 square feet of the 1851 Great Exhibition at Crystal Palace). With such a variety of products there was a high degree of hand work; of job satisfaction; of self reliance, with the **Little Mester** tradition commanding good wages, and in comparing our trades with those in other industrial cities concluded that in Sheffield the " labouring classes are higher in intelligence, morality & physical condition, than where machinery is extensively used, as in Manchester, Leeds, Nottinham & Stockport."

In contrast to this rosy picture **Ebenezer Elliott (qv)** had told an earlier enquiry (1841)**:** "Let any stranger, who happens to have formed a high opinion of the intelligence and morality of the workmen of Sheffield, take a walk on a Sunday morning through the Old Park Wood, or visit the lanes and footpaths adjoining the town, and he will be surprised to meet group after group of boys and young men playing at pitch-penny, or fighting their bulldogs, and insulting every decently dressed passenger." (source; **David Hey: A History of Sheffield).**

hollin holly, see **hagg**

holloware teapots, trays, jugs, etc. in silver, E.P.N.S. or stainless steel.

Honolulu penny infant schoolboy smut for the earlier Victorian penny featuring Britannia holding a lance at an angle between her legs.

Robin Hood was he a Sheffielder? Do we want him as a Sheffielder? Well, he was Robin of **Loxley,** and the **Robin Hood** pub overlooks Loxley valley; **Little John** is buried nearby at Hathersage; and now **Robin** even has **Doncaster Sheffield airport** named after him.

hooks; feeling off 'ooks feeling poorly; feeling **badly (qv);** this meaning is now rare outside the Sheffield region, though if someone were to say: **Tek thi 'ook,** (clear off) he would be understood everywhere.

hop a national, if archaic word for a dance; popular name for university dances, Sheffield had its **Pyjama Hop,** or **Jump** which became too exuberant for the older generations & was banned. **Hunter's Hallamshire Glossary, 1828:** "A meeting of the lowest order, for this species of amusement, is called the **penny-hop**."

Hope pleasant **Peak District** village with squat church with spire, overshadowed by Lose Hill & Lafarge cement works. Overshadowed too by neighbouring **Castleton,** but **Hope** hits back with the saying: You can live in **Hope;** you can live in **Castleton** - that's beyond **Hope.**

horse muck , use of by **hand forgers**- see **'dropped wrist'.**

horse suet used with water to lubricate machinery in rolling mills. Ordinary **greease** wouldn't mix with water.

horsin'; 'orsin wooden saddle, the **grinder's** seat, usually a thick block of oak, shod with iron back & front, plus hooks fore & aft to hold it down by chains.

house living room; front room.

housing framework of a machine, esp. for **rolling mills**- see **Davy.** These can be massive castings of up to 300 tons involving 400 tons of molten steel at **River Don Castings,** part of **Sheffield Forgemasters** on Brightside Lane. They then trundle overnight on 72-wheeler trailers to **Davy-Markham,** Darnall to be machined, then despatched to Goole for shipment.

Huckleberry Finn Mark Twain's immortal character (1885) could be said, along with **Robin Hood** & **Florence Nightingale,** to be the world's best known Sheffielder. At least he claimed to be from Sheffield during his adventures along the Mississippi, though he was almost caught out by a bright girl with a hare-lip: " The hare-lip she got to pumping me about England, and blest if I didn't think the ice was getting mighty thin, sometimes." Huck says he sees the King, 'William Fourth' ('I knowed he was dead years ago, but I never let on') at his church regular – his 'pew's right over opposite ourn.' The girl says she thought the King lived in London: "Well, he does. Where **would** he live?" "But I thought **you** lived in Sheffield?" I see I was up a stump. I had to let on to get choked with a chicken-bone, so as to get time to think how to get down again. Then I says: "I mean he goes to our church regular when he's in Sheffield. That's only in the summer-time, when he comes there to take the sea baths." "Why, how you talk - Sheffield ain't on the sea." Huck gets out of this by saying that sea water is brought to Sheffield in barrels: "There in the palace at Sheffield they've got furnaces, and he wants his water hot. They can't bile that amount of water away off there at the sea. They haven't got no conveniences for it." Huck naturally equates Sheffield with furnaces in his young mind. He also mentions **Barlow knives (qv)** a couple of times in the story.

Look at the **Hawley Collection** on Mappin Street to see the importance of Sheffield edge tools, saws, files, knives & steel in the early development of the United States.

Billy Hukin see **grinder. Billy** was the last of Sheffield's **open razor grinders** (don't call them **cut-throats),** dying at a ripe old age in 1991.He had worked for 50 or 60 years as a grinder, sometimes on kitchen knives with a **jimped (qv)** edge but mainly on razors, and always with **'patent'** (artificial) stones, never with the deadly silica-bearing **millstone grit.** His job required much skill; speed to ensure earning power; and a steady hand involving 36 grinding and polishing operations. He tested the fineness of the edges by pushing the back of his thumbnail against them. Boffins from **Sheffield Hallam** university magnified four smooth-edged knives from **The Hawley Collection** x 154 under the electron microscope & found the edges to be jagged. One of **Billy's** razors was magnified 6000 times and it was still "too smooth to focus on." (**Star** article 15/6/95).

hull a **grinder's** workshop; a **grinder's hull** in a **wheel(qv)** (=works with grindstones turned by water power, later by steam). **Hull** was also used to mean **pigsty**, perhaps showing what some of our ancestors thought of **grinders,** many of whom indulged in 'debauch & riot' before the dreaded silicosis settled in their lungs. See **grinder.**

Rev. Joseph Hunter (1783-1861) son of a cutler **Michael Hunter** (see below), he became a Presbyterian minister in Bath at the age of 26. While in the spa town he must have felt the pull of his home town, since he wrote **Hallamshire(1819),** a major historical study of the Sheffield region, as well as **South Yorkshire** (2 volumes **1828 & 1831**) and a small gem on the Sheffield dialect: **The Hallamshire Glossary (1828)** - reprinted thanks to the **Centre for English Cultural Tradition and Language** at the **University of Sheffield.** The handbook of the British Association for the Advancement of Science 1910 meeting in Sheffield refers back to the reasons **Hunter** gave for the development of the world's foremost steel industry here:

"The industrial development of Sheffield appears to have been due, not so much to the presence of coal in the neighbourhood, as to the existence of beds of ironstone (argillacerous ferrous carbonate) in the coal measures above & below the Parkgate seam; the proximity of beds of easily reducible iron ore; of plenty of timber from which charcoal for smelting could be made; of beds of fireclay & ganister; of gritstone for grinding; of limestone to act as a flux, and of water power supplied by the various streams are the causes to which **Hunter** ascribes the pre-eminence of the town & the surrounding district in the manufacture of steel."

He should have added the inventive genius of men such as **Huntsman,** and the unique & often exquisite skills of the Sheffield workmen passed down the generations.

He married Mary Hayward in Bath and they had 6 children. They moved to London in 1833 when he got a post at the Public Records Office. His widespread interests were shown in the huge personal library he built up, which took four days to sell by auction at Sotheby's upon his death. The **Hunter Archeological Society** lives on to this day.

Michael Hunter & Son made beautiful pocket knives & scissors with their hunting horn trade mark, which was granted by the **Cutlers' Company** in 1760. Three **Michael Hunters** ran the firm , with the second one **(1800-1886)** overseeing substantial expansion, as well as finding time to be mayor, alderman, JP, **Master Cutler (1852 & 1860),** and doing good works at the Unitarian church on Norfolk Street. (There is a plaque on the wall in the church commemorating him). See the superb Victorian **1851** Exhibition scissors in the **Millennium Galleries.** The company was eventually bought by **Needham, Veall & Tyzack,** who in turn were eventually absorbed by **Harrison Fisher/ Taylor's Eye Witness (qv).**

Hunters Bar the original gritstone pillars with replica white-painted wooden bar stand on the rounabout at **'Bar.** They once stood alongside a toll bar cottage forbidding traffic out of town until a toll was paid. Tolls were abolished in 1884, and a large sandstone block on the heights of **Stoney Ridge** before the road drops down to **Fox House,** commemorates this date and a toll house that stood there too. Back down to **'Bar,** the area is a pleasant mixture of stone and brick grey-slated houses in the valley between **Broomhill** and **Sharrow/Nether Edge,** and leading to **Greystones.** The little **river Porter** with relics of water-powered industry in **Endcliffe Park,** at the **Lescar, Stalker Lees** and **Wilson's** wonderful Georgian **snuff mill (qv),** gurgles its way to meet the **Sheaf** in town. Kingfisher, heron and dipper are seen townwards as far as **Waard's brewery** flats. Parents are pleased to get their little children into **Hunters Bar** school, and students from all over Britain and beyond bring zest to the shops & bars & cafes of **Sharrow Vale Road** and **Ecclesall Road,** & litter & gunge to the small adjoining streets.

Hunters Bar, more than any other part of Britain, is home to rock & mountain climbers, who cut their teeth, and sometimes break their legs, on our local **gritstone edges,** especially **Stanage (qv).**

Benjamin Huntsman (1704-1776) there were already a few **cementation furnaces (qv)** in Sheffield producing several hundred tons of **blister steel** a year, which was mainly forged into **shear steel** for knives, and **Huntsman,** a clock & watchmaker, was drawn to the town to attempt to find a more reliable steel for his springs. A Quaker, born in the North Lincolnshire village of **Epworth,** and a contemporary of the **Wesleys (qv)**, he became an established clock & watchmaker there, then in Doncaster, before moving to Handsworth, Sheffield to work on improved steels. A superb **Huntsman Sheffield** grandfather clock now at **Kelham Island Industrial Museum** shows he continued clockmaking after his move to the steel town. (This clock was for many years at **Hadfield's (qv),** who took over **Huntsman's** works). See **crucible steel** for more details, but essentially **Huntsman** thought that if he could melt some pieces of the inconsistent **blister steel** in clay pots, or **crucibles,** the impurities would rise to the top in a slag, which could be **slagged off.** This sounds simple but there were immense problems. He probably knew of the glass works at **Catcliffe,** a couple of miles from **Handsworth,** where glass was melted in small clay pots. However, glass, like cast iron, melts at 1100 degrees centigrade, whereas the temperature has to be raised right up to 1600 degrees, and then held at that temperature for about 4 hours to melt and refine steel. This had never been done before anywhere in the world, but **Huntsman** did it and **crucible steel** and the world's steel industry was born here ca. 1740. The clay crucibles had to be pure enough to avoid contaminating the steel, and strong enough to withstand the molten metal at such a high temperature for such a long time. A major problem that **Huntsman** had to overcome was that when steel is poured into a mould, it solidifies & contracts from the walls of the mould inwards, and from the bottom of the mould upwards, leaving a central cavity towards the top centre of the ingot. This would become a central defect known as **pipe** if the ingot was knocked out at this stage, and the defect elongated by subsequent forging or rolling. **Huntsman** solved this by borrowing a section of clay pipe from nearby builders, and fixing this on top of the mould. This acted as a reservoir which would fill the central cavity as it formed in the steel below it, giving a **sound**

ingot. This clay **"hot top"** became known as a **dozzle.** Nice words you've learned**; dozzle** and **crozzle-** you can't get more Sheffield than that!

Thanks to **Benjamin Huntsman** Sheffield became the world's largest steel producer; in 1840 making 40,000 tons of **crucible steel = 90%** of British production & **50%** of European. It led to industrial heroes such as **Jessop; John Brown; the Vickers Bros.; Cammell; Bessemer; Hadfield** and many more thriving here, and to today's 2 million plus tons p.a. of special steel production. It led to Sheffield developing from a small town to England's 4th biggest city. See 1/ **Britannia Inn,** Attercliffe, where he moved to after Handsworth.The large numbers **1772** on the gable wall are said to be made of **crucible steel.** 2/ his grave at Hilltop cemetery, Attercliffe. 3/ the superb small **crucible melting shop** at **Abbeydale (qv),** which is the only complete shop in the world similar in layout to **Huntsman's** original. (A surviving example of a large Victorian **crucible melting shop, Sanderson's,** Wilfrid Rd., Darnall, has been listed by English Heritage, and saved by current owners, **Mayflower Engineering,** who operate a laser cutting & engineering service in an adjacent building.)

Husband & Co. They were consulting engineers based in a seven storey brick building below the **Octagon building.** Projects they were involved with included the Jodrell Bank Radio Telescope, completed thanks to Sheffield brain & brawn, since **United Steel Co.** did the superstructure & **Tommy Waard** the rail trackwork. Another notable achievement was the stout wooden bridge for the film ' Bridge on the River Kwai.' This had to be strong enough for a loaded train to run over it, yet made so that it would collapse dramatically when sabotaged.

husky idle**; he's dead 'usky.**

Wm. Hutton originally from Brum **Wm. Carr Hutton (1803-1865)** moved to Sheffield in **1832** and built up a fine, solid, bustling silversmithing firm. After his death the firm took over a London firm, and then the famous Sheffield firm of **Creswick** in **1902**, with their **crossed arrows** trade mark. See the imposing 1900 **Hutton's Buildings** on **West Street,** built, typically, round a large courtyard, vacated in the 1920's when Hutton's business was transferred to **James Dixon.**

I

Ibberson their **violin** trade mark was granted by the **Cutlers' Company** in **1700**, and has been the sign of best quality pen & pocket knives ever since. They are now owned by **Eggington,** sharpening steels manufacturer on Allen Street, as are other top quality firms, **Joseph Rodgers & George Wostenholm.**

ice creeam old ditties: **I screeam; tha screeams; we all screeam for ice creeam. "Ice creeam penny a lump, the more you eat the more you trump. Ice creeam penny a part, the more you eat the more you….."** don't want to hear such childish 1940's ditties. Local manufacturers today include: **Bradwell's,** 'flavour in a tub' made in the Peak & now owned by Sheffielder, **Lawrence Wosskow; Cuneo's; Granelli,** obtainable from vans or from their sweet shop on Broad Street with its sign: **"**Old fashioned **spice (qv)** at an old fashioned price.**"; Smith's of Chesterfield.** Old favourites include **Taggy's.**

Icky; "Icky wi' his eye cut." A flippant answer to a child's constant questioning; "Who's that mam?"

inch **10 / 12 / 18 / 24 inch rolling mills** at **Park Gate Iron & Steel Co.,** for example, were **hand mills** with bars man-handled by **tongs,** the men catching the hot steel as it emerged from a groove & guiding it into another groove in the **rolls.** The inch sizes refer to the diameter of the grooved rolls, the larger sizes rolling larger sized bars. These particular mills are now just a memory, the Parkgate site a retail park, and even the **11 inch continuous bar mill** at nearby **Roundwood** has been superseded by an expanded **Thrybergh mill** on the massive **Aldwarke** site further down the **River Don.** This mill, operated round the clock, is a **continuous mill** operating a series of **rolls** in a **train,** with hot billet entering at one end and emerging at the end of the **train** at varying speeds depending upon the finished size required, small sizes being coiled; larger ones run out onto bar **cooling beds.** Production is held up if there is a **cobble (qv).**

inside downstairs of bus or tram. **"Inside only!",** the conductor would shout if the top deck was full. It stems from the days when the top deck was "outside"= open to the elements.

insider in the cutlery trade the **spoon & fork insider** buffs inside spoon bowls, and between fork prongs. When working on the latter it is called **'graining'** and very narrow buffs covered with molten resin are used. **Insiding buffs** can be small circular pieces of leather, say, 4 inches diameter x half inch width, for buffing inside table spoons, down to button-sized **buffs** for inside salt & mustard spoons.

Irishman silver trade term for a conical mandrel, a solid steel forging or casting, rather like a traffic cone without the skirt, standing up to 5 feet high.It is used, for example, for shaping & sizing strips of copper, nickel silver or silver for various sizes of gallery trays.

Kinder Scout

Pot preparation area, Crucible melting shop, Abbeydale Hamlet

Stan Shaw with exhibition knife

Stan Shaw's former workshop, Garden street

Water wheel at Pro-Roll Ltd, Loxley

Little Mesters workshops, it's humble but it's home!

"What tha lookin' at?" Man relaxing on barrow off London Road

Stoup at Moscar

Bottom mill Sharrow Snuff Mill

Five Weirs Walk, Spider Bridge

Jessop's Tilt Hammer, Abbeydale Hamlet

Gripples, walker & Higger Tor

Grindstones at Stanage Edge

Crozzle, Mary Street by the river Porter

Used grindstones (cowks) at Abbeydale Hamlet

Cammell's former home, Norton

Magna, formerly Steelo's melting shop

Cast iron railings at Redmires

Tapping, high frequency melting furnace, Ecclesfield

Brightside 5 ton hammer - ex Firth Brown

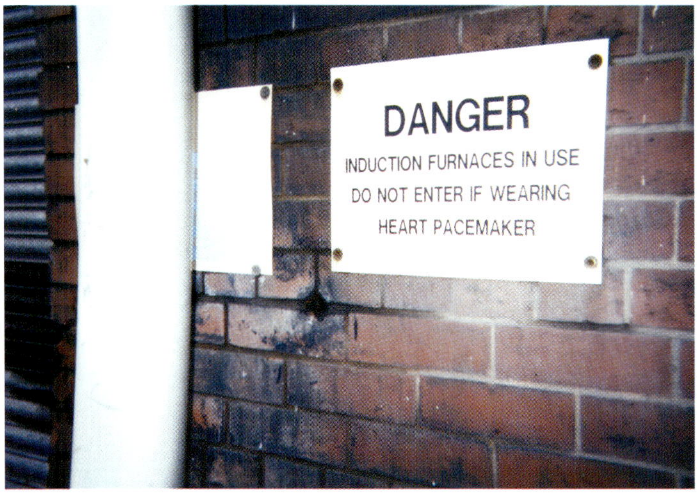

Steelworks sign

Buffer girl from steel & plants, Sheffield

Mary Alexander at St Mary's Garrison, Isles of Scilly with canon produced by Walkers, Rotherham

More grindstones, Stanage Edge

This way to the Kop. Up the Owls

iron Dr. Johnson said; **"The use of iron constitutes much of the difference between savage and polished life,"** and the Sheffield region has played a large part in producing the metal. In earlier times we have to thank the monks, such as those at **Beauchief Abbey (qv),** aristocrats such as the **Fitzwilliams** & the **Shrewsburys (qv),** leading up to early self-made industrialists such as the **Walkers,** whose cannon played a major role in the victories on land & sea against Napoleon. Cast iron at 4% carbon is brittle but very hard wearing, and in Victorian times numerous Rotherham & Sheffield firms set up, making ornate fireplaces, staircases, ornamental gates down to small items such as door-stops etc. **Yates Bros. & Harwood** of Rotherham, and **Hy. Hoole** of **Green Lane Works (qv)** were just two prominent manufacturers whose work can be seen at the **Metalwork Gallery,** and **Kelham Island Industrial Museum** in Sheffield, and at the **Clifton Park Museum** in Rotherham. **Newton Chambers** at Chapeltown made such items, but their two blast furnaces produced iron mainly for steelworks and gasworks heavy plant. **Crosslands Foundry Ltd.** formerly of **Parkgate**, now in the **East End,** who recently cast the 'wheel pattern' gates at the **General Cemetery,** and **H. & H.** at **Durham Foundry,** Harleston St., who make cast iron fireplaces to order, carry on the ornamental tradition, though the old street grates seen all around made by local foundries such as; **Blakes, Charlton, Ecclesfield, Allen, Robinson** & **Guest & Chrimes** give way on new sites to crudely-finished, but cheap Indian versions. Large items were made in cast iron for the steel industry, such as **ingot moulds (Renishaw Foundry); rolling mill housings, rolls** & **drop forging machines (Davy & Brightside-** see the black-painted, powerful 5 ton **drop forge** gracingthe corner of Sutherland St. & Savile St. made by **Brightside,** and far more impressive than any modern sculpture). The last **blast furnaces** for making **iron** to be converted into **steel** by the **Bessemer** or **Open Hearth** processes in our region were at **Park Gate Iron & Steel Co.,** Rotherham. Two funaces produced about 2000 tons of iron a week which was either cast into **pigs, (**the sand moulds into which iron was poured were shaped like a legless sow leading off to piglets under her; some imagination needed), or poured into a ladle & transferred to a 400 ton holding **mixer** furnace, to be processed into steel in the **Open Hearth** furnaces.

Sheffield & Rotherham, being at the centre of a huge metalworking area at the heart of Britain, are ideal for **electric arc** steel making plants, these relying upon **graded scrap** for the base raw material. Bulk steel production is now dependent upon imported **iron ore** & **coking coal** and nearby **Scunthorpe** has **blast furnaces** producing 10,000 tons of **iron** a day, for converting to steel in 300 ton **L.D. oxygen blown furnaces. (**The old blast furnaces at **Park Gate** used low grade **ore** from their own Lincolnshire opencast mines & **coke** from their own **ovens,** produced from locally-mined coal.)

Cast iron is too brittle to be forged, rolled or drawn, and before steel held sway with its myriad analyses & properties **wrought iron,** made by removing the carbon content in **reverbatory** or **puddling furnaces,** was made locally at **Park Gate; John Brown's** & other firms, and rolled into armour plate & railway lines. Gates and similar ornamental items were made from **wrought iron** rolled into strips or bars, though if you see **wrought iron gates** advertised today they are, in fact, **mild steel.**

Sheffield's **Ironbridge** built across the Don at **Bridgehouses** in **1795**, was destroyed in the **Sheffield flood** of **1864 (qv).** It was possibly built by **Walkers' Ironworks,** Rotherham to a design by **Thomas Paine** of 'Right's of Man' fame, who worked for them.

the **Irons** **Scunthorpe United** football club

Ivan a lumbering giant of a man, a grave-digger at **Wardsend cemetery** in the 1940's/50's; a Wednesdayite who would chase lads who shouted out 'Up the Blades' in his vicinity.

ivory was so important to the cutlery trade in Victorian times that the **Cutlers' Company** chose an **elephant's head** on top of their coat of arms- see the two coats of arms above the **Cutlers' Hall;** note too the fine stainless steel door with elephant's head door knob. The best knives had ivory handles, most plain but some with exquisite carvings. Pictures of the ivory warehouse at **Joseph Rodgers (qv)** in the 1890's showing huge stacks of tusks might shock today, especially when we learn that in one year alone- 1878- **Rodgers** used 26 tons, comprising 2561 tusks with average weight 22 lbs. each. **Rodgers** were, however, the largest cutlery manufacturer in the world, had the Royal Warrant, and exported to every major country in the world. Most ivory used came from Africa, though cutlers also used **mastodon/mammoth** tusks retrieved from the ice in Russia.

Izal no Briton over the age of 50 can fail to remember the bottle of blackish brown **San Izal** disinfectant with the green cross & distinctive smell, lurking under the sink. Discovered by a chemist, **J.H. Worrall** at **Newton Chambers (qv), Thorncliffe, Chapeltown** and first used as a sheep dip, it was a product distilled from the oil, which came from the gas from the beehive coke ovens, which in turn used coal mined from the company's local collieries. The trademark **Izal** was registered in **1893** and a year later a dilution 1 in 200 was claimed to kill off germs that spread such diseases as smallpox, cholera & typhus. Hospital wards & corridors always had a faint odour of **San Izal** and one wonders, if it was in widespread use today, would those cunning little MRSA bugs be around? It spawned a host of other products from soap to toilet paper to throat lozenges- see the display at **Kelham Island Museum,** with an advertisement for its use on poultry farms.

J

jackaleg a type of **spring knife** attributed by Dyson to legendary cutler, **Jacques o' Liege** who came to Sheffield in the 16th century to escape religious persecution. Perhaps **jackknife** derives from him, or from **Jack Tar?**

jennel; gennel urban passageway often between walls and buildings, sometimes through buildings, usually cobbled or paved, sometimes trodden earth. (Not the short passage through terraced houses leading to a back yard, which is called an **entry.)** See also **ginnel; eight foot** & **snicket.**

Jerry; jerry German; chamber pot, piss-pot, pail, po or **guz-under** (=goes under the bed). Not just a local word but it led to a feeble double-entendre joke about a couple in bed during the **Sheffield Blitz:** Woman: **"** Jerry's o'er.**"** Man: **"** Ne'er mind. Mop it up in' mornin'.**"**

William Jessop & Sons Ltd founded in 1774 by William who was an expert **crucible steel melter,** under his sons it became the biggest steelworks in the world in the early Victorian era, with its **Brightside Works** covering thirty acres on both sides of the **Don,** with three miles of railway lines, and to power the works, six water wheels & twenty eight steam boilers. **Thomas Jessop (1804- 1887)** was the most dynamic son, with trips to America for the burgeoning U.S. trade, and nearer home, to Birmingham where **Jessops** supplied 700 tons a year of **crucible steel** for the Brum pen trade. He called himself the "Brummagen traveller" and one of the biggest customers was a cousin, **Joseph Gillott.** (One of the Gillotts later established himself in a fine big stone built house near the top of Woodseats Rd. and made his own steel in Sheffield, latterly by the canal side at Kilnhurst). As well as looking after his huge works **Thomas** was a police commissioner; a Liberal town councillor; a Unitarian at Upper Chapel involved in founding Congregational schools at Brightside; helped found **The Sheffield Technical School** in 1884; & founded a hospital for women- see below. At various times he was borough magistrate, Mayor, and **Master Cutler.** He wasn't the imagined earnest Victorian benefactor though, having enjoyed a beer at the King's Head, Change Alley for 50 years, revelling in the banter & racy, humorous tales of the Sheffield workers of his youth. When journalists asked him for the story of his life he replied, "There's nowt about missen worth telling." Other Sheffield steelmen such as **Cammell, Vickers, Firth, Brown** & **Hadfield (qv)** overtook **Jessop** and Birmingham Small Arms (B.S.A.) took them over in 1919. It became known nonetheless under the **Jessop-Savile** name for beautiful, exotic steels for aerospace & other demanding industries, eventually coming under **Sheffield Forgemasters'** wing.

Jessop Hospital for Women every Sheffielder knows the imposing red-brick building at Brook Hill, and has family or friends who were born there. The **University of Sheffield** is now redeveloping the site, though happily keeping the Victorian part, and the hospital is now at the new **Jessop wing** of the **Hallamshire Hospital.** In his book **'Giants of Sheffield Steel',** Geoffrey Tweedale tells of **Thomas Jessop** buying **Brooklyn House** and its grounds in 1875 for a Hospital for Women, which , with 35 beds, was opened on 22 July, **1878**.

Jewel Razor the first stainless steel razor blades, made by Wilkinson Sword in the 1960's, with much technical expertise from **Samuel Fox** precision strip metallurgists, created a huge demand world wide. Two engineers from Wilkinson, a Canadian & an Indian , who had developed the blades, set up on their own in Sheffield making them as good, but cheaper, from **Fox** strip. They built up a healthy trade, purely on word of mouth, and eventually branched out into making scalpel blades too. Their firm on Penistone Road is now part of the **Swann Morton (qv)** group whose factory opposite **Owlerton Stadium,** with production at one & a half **million** scalpel blades **a day,** is the largest producer in the world.

jigged bone pocket knife scales, coloured & scored to imitate stag horn.

jiggered tired out; knackered

jimped edge; jimping milled, finely serrated knife edge; e.g.: **'Friaredge'kitchen** knives; ornamental back edge of a hunting knife. **Billy Hukin (qv)** said when the **open razor** trade slackened he worked doing **'fine jimps'** on **Friaredge** knives.

job, jobbie childish word for **bobar;** pooh. Vulgar, boyish doggerel sung, out of teacher's earshot, by 7 to 10 year olds as they marched in twos from the infants school to the swimming baths: **"Left, left, I had a good job and I left it in my trousers."**

Joe Plug poltergeist; nick name for Dr. Eker, French master at **Firth Park Grammar School 1940's/50's.**

Amy Johnson (1903-1941) Hull born, University of Sheffield trained in Arts, then Engineering. She achieved worldwide fame as a flier, and was even the subject of a popular song. Amongst several long distance flight records her most notable achievement was being the first woman to fly solo to Australia. Perhaps inevitably, she died young, crashing into a misty Thames estuary as a war time pilot in 1941.

Jonas & Colver steelmakers, they became part of the **Neepsend** group. The founder, **Sir Joseph Jonas,** was born in Germany, naturalised British, became Lord Mayor in 1905 and was proud to carry on the Sheffield tradition of fine steelmaking. Unfortunately British propaganda in WW1 which had German troops throwing Belgian babies in the air & catching them on their bayonets, induced wild anti-German feeling leading to butchers with German names, such as Friedrich's on the Wicker, getting their windows smashed, and eventually in 1918 to the arrest of **Jonas.** It was alleged that business letters he wrote in 1913 to a long established German customer, who bought his Sheffield steel before the war, constituted a misdemeanour, if not a felony. He was fined & stripped of his knighthood and this man, who had become more English than the English; who had married an English girl and raised a family in Sheffield; who had produced steel for the British war effort in the "war to end all wars"; who was a great benefactor locally, helping build the university and giving his home, Endcliffe House to the university, (it became a hall of residence); now found his reputation in tatters, and within three years he was dead. His grave is in Ecclesall cemetery.

George Jowitt was a pocket knife grinder in late Victorian times **on Joseph Rodgers,** Norfolk Street, then, in view of the dangers associated with **sandstone wheels** he pioneered **emery grinding wheels** in Sheffield. (See **grinder** above).His own improved wheel for the wet or dry grinding cutlery trades was capable of faster production; greater precision; cleaner, safer operation; requiring less pressure than sandstone wheels. A remarkable man, at 83 years old in 1949 he rode tandem with a 63 year old from Land's End to John o'Groats =870 miles averaging 60 miles a day. His firm were on **Sharrow Vale Road**, with many workers from nearby company houses, and when his successors moved production to **Dronfield** they sold the men the houses at a very low price.

Jubilee stout **Sheffield stout;** black beer- see **breweries.**

jungle juice **Stooanses (Stones)** bitter beer- see **breweries.**

K

kale a gem of a Sheffield word meaning turn (in a queue): **get in thi kale; I'm out o' mi kale; Tha'll loise thi kale.**

It' s my kale...quoted in the **Hallamshire Directory, 1828.** **Somebody's kaled me...** jumped the queue ahead of me. (Said by ex-**grinder, Billy Hukin,** when his N.H.S. operation was delayed.) I've kept a nice little poem from the **Star,** 1st April 1959 from someone who signed himself **Harry Hadenough** of Sheffield 12, whose pet gripes to the **Star & Green 'Un** were **Wednesday's** constant relegations after being promoted (= the **yo-yo teeam),** and the state of the windswept, uncovered **Kop: Ah went t'barbers Sat'day, so's he could cut mi hair. An' when it came to my kale, ah sat missen in 'chair. "How's tha want it cuttin'?" said kiddin' barber Ken, "How abaht 'new Wednesday style - straight up & dahn again?"** (after some lines on falling gates- blamed on'telly)

Ah've gorran idea," said my oppo 'Mousey "Why not run, three nights a week, a game of housey-housey?" "Wi 'cash comin' in, we'll have 'Kop covered in, then tha'll see 'spectators really roll in."

katey-cornered out of true, askew, skew whiff; Collins gives **cater-cornered** to mean diagonal in U.S. & Canada.

kaylied drunk

Karl Wilhelm Kayser (1841-1906) a scissor forger from Solingen he came here in 1860 to study 'the Sheffield manufacture' and seek his fortune, since in Solingen 'there was only one party who kept a carriage & pair.' Naturalised in 1864, with name now Charles William, **Kayser** worked with great energy for cutlers **Wilson, Hawksworth, Ellison & Co.** When U.S. tariffs threatened to bankrupt the firm he got them to turn to **crucible steelmaking** with such success that, by 1888, the firm was under his control & renamed **Kayser Ellison, & Co. Ltd.** In the early years of the 20th century he backed a local lad, **Herbert Austin,** who had started a motor car manufacturing business in Oxford, supplying him with finance as well as special steels, such as oil-hardening nickel-chrome molybdenum steels for gearboxes. **Kayser's** son, Frank, became a director of the Austin Motor Co.

Harry Brearley (qv) worked as a chemist for **Kayser Ellison** for a time, and appreciated being allowed to do private analytical work on steels, and write his first book; "Analysis of Steelworks' Materials." He was impressed by **Kayser's** practical skills: he cast round ingots because scale fell off more easily, and turned ingots before forging, to give a cleaner steel. He was less impressed, though amused, by **Kayser's** meanness when, for example he took back one of two pencils on **Brearley's** bench, with the observation that 'only one could be used at a time.'

Kayser Ellison supplied most of the Solingen & Hamburg **open razor** manufacturers, and **Billy Hukin (qv),** the last of Sheffield's **razor grinders** described **Kayser's,** as well as another Sheffield steel maker,

Vessey's, as "a beautiful steel." **Kayser Ellison** were merged with **Sanderson Bros. & Newbould,** another fine steelmaker in 1960, and renamed **Sanderson Kayser (qv).**

kecks trousers

Kelham Island Industrial Museum The Penny magazine in 1844 described Sheffield as one great workshop "which scatters its separate departments in different parts of the town, but still retains them all, like so many links in a chain." **Kelham** is a superb museum celebrating Sheffield products in all their diversity, and if you visited every week for a year you'd have a job to take it all in. There's cutlery, tools, pewter & silverware, of course, but also a bewildering variety of other items from **Henderson's relish** to a ten ton 'grand slam' bomb; from liquorice allsorts to todays **gripples;** from **San Izal** to a Victorian Penny Farthing bike; from Rolls Royce Merlin crankshaft to an early **Bramah** hydraulic press; from ice skates to a grandfather clock made by **Benjamin Huntsman.** There's a realistic looking forge; a **James Dixon** buffing shop, and die-sinking shop; a gallery containing early Sheffield cars, including a **Sheffield Simplex;** the history of steelmaking, from **blister steel (qv)** to **electric arc.** A monster 12,000 horse power steam engine is periodically set in motion. Made by **Davy** in 1905 when British power, underpinned by the Royal Navy, was at its height, it powered a massive plate **rolling mill** capable of rolling steel plate up to 15 inches thick from 50 ton **ingots.** (See **Davy** who are still building rolling mills for world markets, including China & India).

Best of all, at Kelham there are **Little Mester** workshops, where, if you are lucky, you can see knives being ground, and surgical instruments being forged.

Outside there's a **Bessemer converter;** a large hollow forging by **Sheffield Forgemasters,** and a **ganister** grinding machine.

The museum will soon be connected to the **Five Weirs Walk** by a new 1/10th size Brooklyn bridge over the **River Don.**

Kelham Island brewery round the corner from the **museum** & next to the **Fat Cat** pub this brewery opened in 1990 and regularly wins awards for its **Pale Rider; Easy Rider** & **Kelham** real ales. See also **breweries.**

kelterment trinkets, trash, **rammel,** rubbish, truck, tack left lying about a workshop.

key, keyse pronounced as in **ey up,** not as in **ee by gum.** Cf. **cheyse** & **peyse.** Practice the sentence: **Ee's allus loisin' 'is keyse.... Thi theer sithee, on'table, near'cheyse & peyse.**

kick tiny protrusion on a clasp knife blade by the **shoulder,** serving to keep the blade's edge from hitting the spring when snapped shut.

kiddo child, kid, old son, mate. **Nah then kiddo; Orreight kiddo** = hello; how are you? **Our kid** =brother or, less common; sister.

Kimberworth, Rotherham in the British Association 1910 Sheffield handbook **J.O. Arnold,** Prof. of Metallurgy at the **University of Sheffield** tells us that in 1160 the monks of **Kirkstead Abbey,** in Lincolnshire, had two works for smelting iron ore, and two more for forging iron into bars at **Kimberworth. Valerie Answer** pinpoints the site as the hillsides of **Thundercliffe Grange, Ecclesfield,** (which is, in fact, today in **Rotherham,** opposite **Lower Shiregreen,** a couple of miles or so from **Kimberworth.)**

kings a standstill or truce as respite from being chased in a game of **tiggy,** possibly crossing your fingers for emphasis.(See Harpo Marx in "A Night at the Opera.") Shouting "**Queens**" allowed you to set off again.

Kiveton Park the colliery, 1867-1994, is now just a memory, but **Kiveton Park Steel Ltd.** march on, hopefully profitably, into the 21st century. Founded 1922 they specialise in precision heat treated, drawn & ground carbon, free-cutting, alloy and spring steel coil or bar & wire, in rounds, hexagons, squares & flats.

knackers; "tell 'em to knackers" Rotherham steelman's advice to salesman when faced with unreasonable customer complaint.

knee polisher in cutlery trade = blade polishing where knee is used as a lever.

high knees when a marble is flicked by thumb nail against index forefinger from knee or mid thigh height

knife board wooden tray in factory for carrying pocket knife parts, part-finished knives etc. from one department, or works to another.

knocker up man who went around the streets knocking workers up for the early shift, by tapping upstairs' windows with a long pole.

knur & spell now largely forgotten game where a round piece of wood, a **knur,** was sprung in the air and clobbered with a wooden club, a **spell,** for as far as it would go. It was played by miners and steelworkers in the dreadful depressions of the 1920's and 30's, though its origins are much older. Hunter mentions the game in **The Hallamshire Glossary,** 1828, adding that **knur** derives from the Teutonic **knorr,** "used for the globular excrescences sometimes found on trees," and that "Peak miners use it for the globular pieces of ore."

Bobby Knutt; Knutty Popular comedian, especially in pantomime. The book **Orreight mi ol',** is prefaced by his comment that **"God must have been a Sheffielder - look at all that theein' and thouin' in'Bible."**

Kop the popular side of a football ground known around the country, but especially in hotbeds of the game such as Anfield, **'Lane** and **Hillsborough.** The **Wednesday** ground is unusual in that they use the words **Spion Kop** in full on direction boards outside the ground. (As you all know **Spion Kop** was a hill fought for in the Boer War, 1898-1902.)

L

lad boy; **so & so's lad**= son or apprentice.

t' owd lad father; formerly also meant the devil: In a 'catechism' at **Ringinglow Church Mission** on **Sheephill Road** in 1864, the preacher asked a rough little lad; **"Who's the devil?"**
(lad) - **"T'owd lad."**
(preacher) - **"What's he do?"**
(lad) - **"Teks bad lads."**

laddo used when you don't know, or have forgotten someone's name. Heard, for e.g. on a **Radio Sheffield** phone-in, when a man had momentarily forgotten the Prime Minister's name: **'laddo, er, ...Tony Blair.'**

ladle in a steelworks a huge 'bucket' made from **refractory brick-lined** steel plates for holding & transferring **srap, molten slag** or **steel.**

lag **he's gone for a lag** = pee, **wazz.** To **point Percy at the porcelain.**

laik to play, or to shirk, skive.The late, great **Tony Capstick** on **Radio Sheffield: '** I'm off till Monday, but I'm not **laiking,'** (= shirking) well I **am** laiking (= playing a policeman in an episode of "Last of the Summer Wine.") **Doncaster La(i)kers** rugby league team. **Ah tha laikin' terneet?** Corny play on words: **Astha bin laikin** = a Barnsley terrorist.

lambfoot pocket knife with straight blade tapering to a sharp point.

lampin' sport especially popular in mining districts of hunting rabbits at night with the help of lamp, gun and lurcher dog. A lady in **Dinnington** out walking her lurcher didn't know what the lad meant when she was asked **"Is it any good wi 'lamp?"**

'Lane the Lane = **Bramall Lane (qv)** football ground.

lap in cutlery trade a **glazer** (wheel) with lead surface to give an extra fine polish. per **Ed. Chapman,** ex **grinder (qv),** aged over 100 in 2002.

a 'appy Larry a miserable bloke.

lass girl; **our lass** = my daughter, or wife; **our old lass** = my wife, or mother; **t'owd lass** = mother, old lady.

lasses can also mean 'lasts': **" When I get 'eeadache it lasses all day."**

latt lath; a thin strip of wood; **'thin as a latt.'** (c.f. **latten**= a thin sheet of brass).

G.H.Lawrence 'Laurel' brand razor blades were made in a factory on **Nursery Street** from the 1930's to the 1960's. Just one of the countless thousands of small metalworking firms that have come & gone in Sheffield's long & continuing manufacturing history, yet **George Lawrence** deserves a mention. Having seen the devastation in France caused by the First World War, he helped to revive a small French town where Sheffield soldiers had perished. Like so many other Sheffield manufacturers, who knew the job inside out, he was at one with his workforce, and typically, at the height of the **Blitz (qv),** he drove from his Hathersage home, via the **Millstone** pub, to the factory to make sure those on the late shift were alright. Friends playing dominos at the pub must have found being there nerve-racking enough, with the sound of bombing & the red glow in the sky over the burning Steel City, but he insisted he had to go. (See **An Accessible Wilderness - Life at Stanage & the North Lees Estate).** He made it to the factory, but unfortunately the Luftwaffe hadn't finished; Nursery Street was bombed & he was killed alongside several of his staff.

Laycock unlike the above , this firm's management were not at one with their workforce, which was led by diehard communist union men (as was fellow G.K.N. plant, **Shardlow's**). This shouldn't detract from the fine engineering work done at the works, from its early days as a **railway carriage** & **motor car** manufacturer, to its concentration on automotive parts after WW2, especially on **clutch assemblies.** Some of us remember with nostalgia the sound of **clutch discs** being stamped out through the night, from **Brinsworth strip,** from the works on Archer Road behind their impressive 1902 red brick , three storey office building, (all now demolished in favour of supermarket sheds). **Brinsworth Mill,** opposite the former **Templeborough Melting Shop,** also supply **Lamellungs und Kuplungsbau,** who were a leading competitor of **Laycock's,** and this selfsame **LUK** eventually took over the firm from G.K.N., & opened a new factory at **Wales Bar**, **Kiveton Park**. **Laycock's** sports club, with tennis courts & bowling greens, survives on Archer Road.

Leadmill Road a water powered white lead mill was on a site opposite a 19th century steam powered flour mill. This latter building now houses the

Leadmill, an innovative nightclub & arts centre, which nurtures new musical talent. (Originally the **Esquire club,** it competed with **Peter Stringfellow's Mojo** club. Further along **Leadmill Rd. Wentworth Pewter (qv)** - which no longer contains **lead** - moved production to Darnall in 2006, leaving their town factory to **Freeman College,** together with machinery for the students to use.

leather (cutlery trade) a wheel made from solid leather, originally **buffalo hide** (see **buff/ buffer girls), bull neck** or **walrus hide** (in Sheffield called **sea horse hide).**

leet light; **"Turn 'leet off when tha guz aht, will tha."**

leg (crown green bowls) used in the phrases; **'not enough leg',** if ball rolls too short of the jack; & **'too much leg',** if ball overshoots the green.

Wm. Leng (1824-1902) took over the **Sheffield Daily Telegraph** in 1864, and investigated the collapse of **Dale Dike** reservoir in that year. See - **Sheffield Flood.** A son, **Christopher D. Leng** succeeded his father as editor/ joint owner, & built the **Towers,** an impressive 'Scottish baronial' house off Sandygate Road.

leppings leapings; stepping stones across a shallow part of a river. Often the stones were used **grindstones = cowks,** but as the metal trades began to use artificial stone = **patent wheels,** old millstones became desirable & were stolen for garden ornaments, or built into walls. Cf.**Leppings Lane,** and **S.W.F.C. Leppings Lane End** near the little river **Loxley.**

Letsby Avenue When the Ordnance Survey rang South Yorkshire Police Operations at Sheffield City Airport for the name of the new road outside their complex, a quick-witted copper replied **'Letsby Avenue.'** So **Letsby Avenue** it now is in the Sheffield A-Z. (Mind you, the Ordnance Survey people, down at Southampton aren't the brightest of map makers - on the O.S. indexes of over a hundred towns and cities shown on an outline of Great Britain, Sheffield, England's 4th city, doesn't appear. When the boss at O.S. came to **Sheffield Hallam University** how did she find her way here?)

lig lie down; (heard in north Sheffield, Barnsley, Wakefield, Pontefract). Was in common use in Sheffield: **to lig on** = to lay on much pressure in filing or grinding; the **Hallamshire Glossary,** 1828, quotes an old Sheffield rhyme:

"Lady Cow, (lady bird), Lady Cow, fly thy way
home, Thy house is on fire, thy children all gone:
All but one that **ligs** under a stone,
Fly thee home, Lady Cow, ere it be gone."

The verb is used nationally in earlier English literature: Shakespeare- a Scots captain in Henry V: **"....**ay'll **lig** i' the grund." Chaucer's Canterbury Tales: ".. and foond thee **ligging** by (= with) his wife."

'Light Trades the cutlery, tool, pewter & silverware trades - see **Sheffield Trades.**

lillilo a (pretty) light. (Mother to child).

limestone this calcium carbonate rock gives us the **White Peak;** the dales caves & grey stone walls, contrasting with the **Dark Peak,** which has gritstone edges & walls, heather clad moors, with different bird & plant life. Quarried extensively near Buxton, Stoney Middleton, Matlock, Longstone etc., controversially for roadstone, less so, along with veins of **fluorspar** (calcium fluoride) as a flux in steel production. A quarry near **Hope (qv)** supplies the cement works, and is expanding production to meet increased demand in the South East, following the closure of a works there, and in anticipation of orders leading up to the London Olympics in 1012. New sidings are being built and railway wagons ordered, to take loads transported by rail to over one million tons p.a. See **Anston** re. **magnesium limestone**

line shafting pulleys & leather belting which transferred power from the water wheel, or steam engine to the grindstones, or other machinery. Sometimes they ran up through the ceiling in multi storey factories.

liquorice allsorts originally sold in bags containing one type only, a salesman from the Sheffield factory over a hundred years ago, dropped a trayload of different samples onto the floor in a customer's shop, and the shopkeeper said he would take a mixture of **allsorts. Bertie Bassett's liquorice allsorts** were born.

little **tl** is often pronounced as **kl** in Sheffield, so 'little' becomes **likkl :** similarly **dl** is often pronounced **gl,** so 'saddle' becomes **saggl. "**The child was sittin' on 'is 'orse on a **likkl saggl." ....** I owe this information to life-long friend and linguist, **Jack Sullivan,** who points out the same phenomenon is found in the Pskov dialect of Russian!

little Mesters self employed cutlery craftsman- see **Mester.**

livener a drink before going to work.

loadhog reusable pallet-securing device with plastic lid, invented by **Hugh Facey,** who also invented the **gripple (qv).** It will hopefully replace thousands of tons of plastic sheeting currently discarded after one delivery. Produced in a striking new factory alongside the **River Don** in the **East End,** it had a big stainless steel heron overlooking the river, but this being Sheffield, a paradise for metal thieves, it was soon stolen.

Joseph Locke (1805-1860) a railway engineer of exceptional talent, he could survey the lie of the land, choosing the best way over difficult terrain, whilst "embracing as many towns as possible, and engineering the railway according to the traffic potential." **" The name of Locke will be associated with the triumphs of the locomotive and the marvels of the Steam Revolution for all coming time."** Thus said the Provost of Greenock in 1841, and certainly, **Locke** should rank alongside his contemporaries Robert Stephenson & Isambard Kingdom Brunel in any railway roll of honour. He is, however, largely forgotten, even in Crewe, which he founded, and in Sheffield, where he was born. His family moved from **Attercliffe** to **Barnsley** when he was 5, and, thankfully, **Barnsley** has kept his memory alive. **Barnsley Grammar School** which **Locke** attended from 7 to 13 years old is now the **Cooper Gallery,** and well worth a visit. The town organised a whole series of lectures & events to celebrate **Locke's bicentenary** in 2005. His wife **Phoebe** had given **Barnsley "**The People's Park", after his death, which was later named **Locke Park,** with his statue & the **Phoebe Locke Memorial Tower,** and this was spruced up in 2005.

His works, of course, are his enduring legacy. He met his lifelong friend Robert Stevenson when apprenticed, aged 14, at a Durham colliery, later working at Stevenson's locomotive factory and then, in 1826, becoming sole executive engineer to the **Liverpool & Manchester Railway Company.** He was engineer for both the **Dutton Viaduct** across the river Weaver in Cheshire, and the whole of the **Grand Junction,** the world's first long –distance railway, which opened in 1837**.** In France, 1843, he was decorated with the Cross of the Legion of Honour at the opening of his Paris-Rouen, **Barantin Viaduct.** He worked on two more French railways & a Dutch line before coming back to become president of the Institution of Civil Engineers in 1857, and, back home to work on the **Manchester, Sheffield and Lincolnshire railway,** the **Woodhead** line.

loise to lose; **th'i loisin=** they are losing (usually in answer to **Ah's Wednesday/ United gooin' on?) 'Pigs are loisin'**- see **Pigs**.

loisin' former coming of age ceremony in the cutlery trade.

loppy lairy, manky, dirty.

Ludlum's dog used in the phrase; **"As idle as Ludlum's dog (that leeans its 'eead ageeanst 'wall to bark)."** Ludlum was said to be a pub landlord on **Scotland Street**.

Loxley see **Sheffield Rivers. Robin of Loxley** = Robin Hood.

lug; lug oyal ear; ear hole

lugs tangled knots in hair.

lump short round walk- especially a circuit from home, round several terraced streets, & back. **To walk round 'lump.**

luv friendly term of address in the Sheffield region, especially by men & women working in factories, or on the trams & buses. Sheffielders even use it man to man, which can be disconcerting to male newcomers to the city. Pin back your **lug oyals** in the markets, at the match, on the buses, & in neighbourhood pubs & you may be greeted**; "Orreight (mi ol') luv."**

M

mabs marbles. **He rattles like a can o' mabs** = he's gobby; he goes on & on.

She's got all her mabs about her = she's got all her marbles = she's all there (often said about an old woman with a keen brain).

Magna Science Adventure Centre based in the massive black steel sheds of the former **Steel Peech & Tozer Ltd. (qv), Templeborough Melting Shop,** built in 1919 on the site of a Roman fort & ironworking site. A well known photograph shows the works, filling the background with its 14 tall chimneys serving 14 **open hearth** furnaces, whilst a tractor works in a field of wheat in the foreground. The foreground became the site for **Brinsworth Strip Mills (qv)** after WW2; the 14 **open hearth** furnaces became 6 **electric arc** in the 1960's - the chimneys went and orange smoke **puthered** out of the roof, before the Clean Air Act obliged steel companies to collect the dust, fumes & smoke in the roof, and recycle it. Steel production moved to the 800 acre **Aldwarke** site, where 2 x 200 ton **electric arc furnaces** can now produce as much steel in a year = one million tons as ever **Templeborough** could hope to achieve.

Magna, one of the most successful millennium projects, with its themes of air, water, fire & earth, and its realistic impression of an **arc furnace** in action,(with genuine **Rotherham** voices) honours **Templeborough's** steelmaking history.

magnets **Thomas Swift Levick (1845-1926)** founded a steel & file works in Attercliffe in 1891, & pioneered **magnet steels** prior to 1914, challenging the then German dominance of the market. His firm changed from **crucible** to **high frequency melting** in 1932 to meet the demand for magnets within loudspeakers, phones, electric meters, car magnetos etc. **Swift Levick's** modern plant at **Barlborough** was taken over by an American company –a kiss of death- since the Yanks took the technology & the order book to China, closing the factory in **2007.** Sheffield, remains the centre of the U.K. magnet trade, with a number of firms**: Anchor magnets,** producer of a retractable magnetic retriever for **Footprint Tools; E magnets; Eclipse magnetics (James Neill); Magnaquench; Precision Magnetics; Rotary-Burnand; H.Shaw.** These firms between them produce a wide range- from tiny compass needles, & the smallest of magnets for educational & industrial use, to big electromagnets up to7 ft. wide for steelworks & scrapyards.

makker forger; a **hand forger** employing a **striker** when doing two handed work (on large blades when work needs to be done fast while the steel is hot).To see two men hitting and shaping a hot blade at speed with alternate blows of their hammer is poetry in motion, and, fortunately there is a film in the **Hawley Collection,** showing **Harry Drabble** & his **striker** in action. There were **blade makkers & sither makkers,** the latter working onbig **shears**. (In the North East, Sunderland people are known as Makkems, or Maccams, supposedly from the boast that 'we make 'em'= ships, whilst Newcastle merely sold them).

mam mother

mankin' boy playing around with a girl

Mappin Brothers/ Mappin & Webb **Joseph Mappin** set up in Norfolk St./ Mulberry St. making pen & pocket knives,razors & table knives in 1810 with trade mark, the sun. (His brother, **John Newton Mappin** became a brewer in Rotherham, and gave his art collection to found the **Mappin Art Gallery-** see **Breweries).**

Joseph's son **Sir Frederick Mappin (1821-1910)** ran the firm until 1859 when he moved to the steel industry, acquiring **Thos. Turton's Sheaf works,** at the canal basin (now **Ant Marketing).** He became rich, adding to his uncle's collection given to the city, became Liberal M.P. for **Hallam,** was knighted and died in 1910 leaving a massive one million pound fortune together with his big Fulwood house**, Thornbury,** now a hospital. Meanwhile, his younger brother, another **John Newton Mappin (1835-1913)** had built up an electroplating & cutlery business which became known as **Mappin & Webb.** This company expanded into the famous **Royal Works** on **Norfolk Street,** near the current Peace Gardens, and their beautiful silverware was valued worldwide. After WW2 they were bought by a financier, merged with **Walker & Hall** and **Elkington** under the title of **British Silverware Ltd,** production was consolidated in a factory on **Queen's Road-** and then they were closed down. Silverware is still made for **Mappin & Webb** shops by various Sheffield firms, some by men who set up on their own when the **Queen's Road** factory closed. Another **British Silverware** has arisen, this time in sound Sheffield hands- see **James Dixon.**

mardy a cry baby; someone who **wain't** join in, is tearful or moody. **Mardy arse,** or less vulgar, **mardy bum** is the insult thrown at such a person. The word is known across a swathe of middle England (becoming **mard** in Manchester), & **High Green** group, the **Arctic Monkeys,** with their hit song **Mardy Bum,** have spread the word around the world. Infant school chant**: Mardy bum, mardy bum, tell thi mother to smack thi bum.**

mark steel stamp to impress names, trade marks, made in Sheffield, coats of arms etc. on cutlery & tools. When you see the, sometimes intricate, patterns cut by hand at the end of a piece of steel bar, for stamping on a blade etc., bearing in mind that all letters & numbers etc. have to be done as in a mirror, you realise the skill of the **mark maker.** Best known firms are **Pryor; Davidson; Eyre & Baxter: Wright & Simpson,** but though there are a small number of craftsmen left, most **trade marks, hallmarks,** etc. are now **laser etched** on

mark side side of a knife blade showing the trade mark, company name etc. The opposite side is the **pile side (qv).**

Mary Ann in the mid 19th century **Sheffield Outrages (qv)** anonymous letters, threatening employers of non-union labour, were signed **Mary Ann.**

Mary Stuart, Queen of Scots (1542-1587) Intrigue, plots, international political & religious fears & hatreds, war, murder & romance swirled around the tragic Queen, from the moment she was crowned **Queen of Scots** in Stirling, when she was only 9 months old to the day of her execution at Fotheringhay, when she was 44. **Queen Elizabeth** entrusted **Mary's** captivity for most of the time she was in England to Sheffielder, **George Talbot, 6th Earl of Shrewsbury (qv),** with his formidable wife **Elizabeth, Countess of Shrewsbury,** better known as **Bess of Hardwick (qv).** They held her for short periods at Tutbury Castle, Wingfield Manor & Chatsworth, before bringing her on the 28th November 1570 to the **Shrewsburys** main domicile, the massive, secure **Sheffield Castle (qv)** at the junction of the **Don** & the **Sheaf.** Historians & novelists gloss over her stay here, partly because little is known about the great castle, demolished in 1648, but she was a Sheffielder, albeit reuctantly, for 14 years, the longest time she spent in any one place during her lifetime. A book by J. Keith Cheetham; **Mary Queen of Scots - The Captive Years** highlights her days here, both at the **Castle** and the nearby **Sheffield Manor (qv)** with its surviving **Turret House,** nicely restored in 1873. The **Manor** was at the centre of an extensive deer park, the existing **Norfolk Park** covering just a small part of this.

When **Samuel Roberts,** one of the greatest silversmiths & **Old Sheffield Platers (qv)** built a turreted home in 1837 in blocks of local stone, in what was once part of the lower end of the deer park, he named it **Queen's Tower**, in honour of **Mary.**

Karl Marx A proposal by a government Commission that children under 18 shouldn't work night shifts, inspired the mid-Victorian prophet of world Communism to write a whole chapter of **Kapital** inveighing against Sheffield steel firms. These included **Sanderson; Cammell & John Brown,** and he informed us, for example, that the last-named employed 3000, including 500 boys under 18, of whom 170 were under 13. (**Brown's** would perhaps have employed more, but boys couldn't handle the heaviest work). Responding to the Commission's proposal **Mr.J. Ellis, John Brown's** managing director, said that "boys who work in the day sets must take their turn in the night sets also........Our objections to not allowing boys under 18 to work at night, would be on account of the increase of expense..." (= to the firm having to employ men instead.) How cynical, we might think today from our lofty heights, even as we wallow in a tide of goods made by 7 year olds in China, India etc. The Victorian steelmen were less hypocritical, and most young lads were eager to finish with school, certainly at 12 years old, and begin work with their father, brothers and friends in the mills. **Crucible steel melters,** aristocrats of the steel trade, along with **first hand rollers** in the **rolling mills,** often took on their young sons –see **Harry Brearley.** Working class lads, made good, such as **Brown; Cammell; Firth; Vickers; Hadfield** etc., forged our modern world, while **Marx's** theories led to Lenin, Stalin (and, indirectly, to Hitler), Mao & Pol Pot.

mash to make, brew tea in a teapot. **Ah tha mashin'?**

mashing in **Barnsley** can also mean snogging.

Master Cutler except for some years in the 1850's – 1870's & at times of national crisis, such as WW1 &WW2, a new **Master Cutler** has been appointed every year since 1624 to be head of **The Company of Cutlers in Hallamshire (qv).** Along with the **Lord Mayor** he is Sheffield's most prominent citizen with a full diary of duties, and a responsibility to look after the interests of the metal trades. For over 200 years the **Master Cutler** was almost always a **cutler** or owner of a cutlery manufacturing company, but the honour carries with it huge expense, and from the 1860's owners of edge tool factories, steelworks, and engineering workshops were allowed to become **Masters.** See also: **Cutler's Hall.**

maungy surly, sulky, grumbling or **mardy: 'he's a maungy beggar.'** "What tha **maungin'** abaht?... Has tha gorra **spell** in thi finger, or summat?"

Meadowhall huge shopping mall in the **East End,** opened 1990, which attracts the highest retail rents in Yorkshire, and which is one of the most successful malls in Britain. Built on the site of **Hadfield's (qv) East Hecla** works, some critics call it Meadow**hell,** especially those who remember the power & the glory of hot steel being worked, and the hard men, who'd given their working lives to the firm, shedding tears when it closed in the 1980's. An excellent, larger than life, sculpture in bronze of an earlier steel making process is prominent in the mall: three men, the **melter;** the **teemer,** holding a **crucible** with a long pair of tongs & pouring the molten steel into a mould, while biting onto his silk **sweat scarf** to protect his lips from burning; & the young **slagger-off,** holding back the slag with a steel rod to prevent it entering the mould & contaminating the steel.

The River Don runs by **Meadowhall** having passed through **Sheffield Forgemasters** and, if you stand outside on a still summer's evening, you can often hear the distant thumping of a very large **open die drop hammer,** emanating either from the brooding sheds of **Forgemasters,** or **Firth Rixson's** further downstream, cocking a snook at the retail emporium.

meight; meyt meat (pronunciation as in **eight**= eat; **feight**=fight; **reight**=right, but note that night is pronounced **neet,** and light **leet.)** He's a vegetarian, he **dunt eight meight.**

potted meight a Sheffield speciality, sold in small jars, plastic tubs or on open sale in butcher's shops. Best known were the two **Sutherland** firms, one of which was taken over by Quaker Oats, the other still prospers; **Hartley's,** who were in the red brick building now housing **The Famous Sheffield Shop** among others, & **Bingham's,** who also, we trust, still prosper.

David Mellor has been justly described as 'Britain's greatest, designer-maker-manufacturer' and 'the heroic figure' towering over post-war design. Best known for his beautiful cutlery, which he didn't only design; he involved himself in the nitty gritty of production in the hallowed Sheffield tradition, together with his wife, author **Fiona MacCarthy,** converting the part-Elizabethan semi-derelict **Broom Hall** into half-home, half-factory. **Pride** pattern cutlery, which **Mellor** developed initially in his teens in the 1940's at **Sheffield College of Art (qv);** then had manufactured by **Walker & Hall,** remains popular today, & along with more recent patterns such as **Paris, City, English,** plus a range of kitchen knives, is made in his factory, **The Round Building, Hathersage,** built in 1990. His **Embassy** silver **holloware,** made by himself, and **flatware** hand forged to his design at **C.W. Fletcher,** grace British Embassies around the world. His **silverware** is found in churches & cathedrals, in private homes & public museums/ art galleries; in the City of London as well as in the **Cutler's Hall;** the **Assay Office** & the **Millennium Galleries** in Sheffield.

Apart from cutlery & silverware, he has designed so many items found in modern life that it is difficult to know where to begin: Tools for **James Neill (Eclipse);**

Spear & Jackson; John Guy, & Tyzack..... Stainless holloware for **Bramah.....**Solid fuel heater for **Grahamstown Foundries.....**Tubular steel lighting columns, bus shelters,outdoor seats, stainless litter-bins for **Abacus.....**Teleprinter & square shaped, easy-emptying pillar box for the **Post Office....**Traffic lights for the **Ministry of Transport** that are now standard throughout the country..... Push-button phone, revolutionary in 1968, for **Standard Telephone & Cable.......**Gear cutting machine for **Goulder** of Huddersfield. etc. etc. **Mellor** kitchen knives and cutlery can be found at the **Famous Sheffield Shop** on **Ecclesall Road,** and kitchen knives at the shop in the **Millennium Galleries,** but, if you can, go to his factory, shop, mueum & café in **Hathersage,** all now ably run by **Fiona,** daughter **Clare,** & son **Corin.**

mend 'fire will tha? Please put some more coal; **nutty slack; cowk;** wood on the fire.

mer, mur (childish) so there! **My dad's bigger than tha dad - so mer!** Sometimes followed by pulling tongue out.

Mester; Little Mester Master; Master Cutler; self-employed craftsman

gie it 'mester (to a child) Give it to the gentleman

bad mester the devil; **t'owd lad**

Mestrawley, Mestrardy Mr. Hawley, Mr. Hardy. Elided for ease & speed of diction.... or through laziness

metal; hot metal usually refers to molten steel, but can apply to silver, pewter, brass, copper, or even, in the local glass industry, molten glass.

Metros **Metropolitan Vickers,** electric traction manufacturers on **Attercliffe Common, & Greenland Road.**

midden earth closet; outside toilet (not flushed), cleared by **night soil men;** rubbish heap. **Cock o'midden**= a little Hitler.

Middlewood big, fearsome red brick Victorian lunatic asylum, now converted to flats; it also used to be referred to as **Wadsley.** There were countless stories regarding the patients, most showing that they weren't all that daft. E.g. Mr. Preston's dad, a builder, seeing a patient wheeling a barrow upside down: "Tha wants to turn it 'reight way up." Patient: "I don't. They'll fill it then, won't they."

Millers **Rotherham United F.C.** probably named after the large flour mill, on the **Rother,** near the junction with the **Don.**

Millennium Galleries see the **Ruskin Gallery** and, best of all, the **Metalwork Gallery,** showing the skills in manipulating steel, silver & pewter that brought Sheffield fame & fortune.

mimi-mokin' gesticulating behind someone's back.

mind aht watch out; move please. Sometimes said rudely: **Mind aht o' rooad** = get out of the way.

mint rock another Sheffield speciality found in old-fashioned **spice (qv)** shops. It is a transparent yellow rock with round, white rings running through, broken into pieces, & sold from large glass bottles. Currently made by **Maxon's/ Dixon's** on Bradbury St., off Valley Rd., and formerly by other firms too, such as **Batty's,** and **Butler's** of **Snig Hill.**

mirror polish usually refers to a highly reflective finish on stainless steel imparted when sheet is rolled through polished rolls. **Clair** polishing machines are used for knives, taking over a lot of the hard graft. Two of the last self-employed **mirror polishers/ buffers, Edna Stone & Ethel Grayson** retired in 1993, aged 80 & 82, having starred in book & film hard at work, in their shop on **Beehive Works.** When **Stephen McClarence** interviewed them (**Star 9.7.1993)** he described lads in overalls bounding up the steps with parcels of knives "wrapped in old **Stars,** for them to glaze, felt & dolly at £1 per dozen."

missus buffer woman in charge of **buffer girls (qv).**

mite, widely used in the phrase **'poor little mites'** when describing the lot of little children, brought up in WW2 with little food, and no luxuries, especially during the **Blitz (qv).** (Actually the **poor little mites** rather enjoyed life, playing in the street, in the woodyard, on the **blitzed ruins,** and even **gooin' up Rivelin.)**

mithered or **moithered** irritated; harassed. To **mither** = to moan; get on someone's nerves; to **whittle (qv).**

modge hash without the meat

mog off to clear off; go away

moit, moyt **mote;** steel or stone grit,sometimes hot, sometimes red hot, in the grinder's eye. Usually there was an expert in the grinders' **hull** who could remove it with a wet handkerchief, or even with the tip of a pocket knife blade that would have a degree of magnetism. In his book **Houseley** tells of the bloke at his **wheel** who made a magnetic lance which got the steel **moits** out. **Peter Gribbon,** a modern **grinder** shown on film at **Weston Park Museum** says a fellow grinder used the tip of his tongue to relieve him of a painful **moit.** Middle Dutch **mot** = grit & Norwegian **mutt**= speck, but, of course, **mote** goes back at least to the time of the "most dread Sovereign" James' version of the Bible: **And why beholdest thou the mote that is in thy brother's eye, but considerest not the beam that is in thine own eye?**

Dyson gives **moits** to mean, also, childrens' size knives & forks.

Mojo club in **Pitsmoor** run in the 1950's/60's by **Peter Stringfellow** who is now Britain's night club king.

Saint Monday; God sent Monday Most **cutlers, grinders** etc. were self-employed,even when gathered together in big factories such as **Wostenholm's Washington** works, and often didn't work Monday, after a roisterous day off on the Lord's day. **Houseley** tells us that much of Monday was spent in a local boozer with cards, chats & sing-alongs. In mitigation, we should remember that they worked hard Tuesday to Saturday, and having Monday off wasn't confined to the cutlery trade. My cousin recalls **"that Tuesday morning feeling"** heading to work underground at **Smithy Wood,** then later at **Manton colliery.**

to have **'monk** on to sulk; be **mardy (qv).**

mon't , pronounced **moan't** must not; **tha mon't laddie**= admonition to a small child, or large one, come to that. **Tha mun** is the opposite. C.f Robbie Burns "To a Mouse"**: Poor beastie, thou maun live.**

James Montgomery (1771-1854) hymn writer, essayist, editor of the **Iris** newspaper, he campaigned on such issues as the abolition of the slave trade, and the welfare of chimney sweeps. Scots born, he should have been mentioned in the list of **bloody minded (qv)** Sheffielders, since he was accused of supporting revolutionary France, and served two prison sentences; for libel, and for publishing seditious ballads. Before he retired to the **Mount, Broomhill,** he was active in the Sunday School movement, and **Montgomery Hall** opposite the **Town Hall** is his legacy. His statue stands in the **Cathedral** grounds.

mood basic stamped or forged **blank** in cutlery & tool trades

mooer same pronunciation for both **more & moor. The Mooer (Moor)** used to be Sheffield's main shopping street with locally owned **Atkinson's & Roberts Brothers,** as well as Debenhams, Marks & Spencers, and **Woolies.** Heavily bombed in the **Blitz,** those of us who lived through those times remember the heady days of the 1950's when rebuilding started, all with the obligatory Portland stone frontages. The indoor markets are being shifted from **Castlegate** to **'Mooer** which should revitalise the area.

mooer hen is, of course, a moorhen, but a **mooer cock** is a grouse.

mop (cutlery trade)- a wheel made from a number of textile discs rivetted between fibre, or similar washers.

silent morn someone who is not open; doesn't talk much. (Perhaps from the hymn 'Hail Silent Morn')

on **mornins** working on the morning shift; usually **6 while 2.** **cf; on afters = 2 while 10; on neets = 10 while 6.**

Mosborough **William Cobbet, 1830,** after visiting what is now an outer suburb of Sheffield wrote: **" The whole of the people.....are employed in the making of sickles & scythes....they are very well off even in these times. A prodigious quantity....go to the United States of America."**

R.F.Mosley cutlers in the **Portland Works** from 1878 to 1968 who were first to forge **Harry Brearley's (qv) stainless steel** into knives in 1914. WW1 meant that the revolutionary metal was diverted to the new aeroplane industry, but from the 1920's onward **Mosley's** knives, with trademark **Rustnorstain,** appeared in the shops.

Portland Works, built round a courtyard, and with frontages on Hill St. and Randall St., now houses several workshops, including **Stuart Mitchell,** sword & Bowie knife maker.

Moss.........see **Sheffield Rivers.**

mothers dee mothers die; hedge parsley; **mothers dee steps** were near **Old Park Silver Mills,** on **Club Mill Road,** by the **River Don.** Superstitious children from nearby **Hillfoot County School** feared that if they walked up the steps their mothers would die.

Mount Pleasant red brick 1777 mansion, which **McClarence** tells us was once home to the **Sitwells (see Renishaw);** served as a lunatic asylum; a school for foundling girls; a driving school and a Social Security office.It is now a community centre.

Mousehole Forge a 17th century forge near the junction of the **Loxley** and the **Rivelin** rivers, it was famous from 1827 to 1933 for the manufacture of anvils. **M. & H. Armitage** were the most prominent maker in Britain, with their trade mark of a **mouse** & a **hole**. Hundreds are to be found in Britain with at least 25 in the **Hawley Collection,** An excellent book has been written on the forge by an American, **Richard A. Postman** (available from him on the internet) with the help of **John & Julia Hatfield,** who heroically saved it from dereliction, and converted it into a home.

mousin' **glazing** down bone, wood, ivory etc. on a wheel for knife handles. **Glazing** bone gave off an unpleasant mouse-like smell.s

muck can also mean poor **coyal,** and the man who dealt with this **dahn'pit** was a **mucker** (which throughout Britain also means a friend).

muck or nettles all or nowt e.g. a do or die tackle on a rugby pitch.

muck joints **Himsworth (1953)** writes of **"shut knives"** (pen or pocket knives) with round, square & **muck joints.** It came to mean a multi-bladed pocket knife & I last heard it used by **Margaret Oversby,** a manager at **Taylor's Eye Witness** works.

mutton suet used as a lubricant for e.g. axle bearings of grindstones.

Mylnhurst big house at **Ecclesall** once owned by the **Blakes** of **Stephenson Blake,** the last of the British **type founders. (Stephensons** then owned nearby **Banner Cross Hall).** A **Walsh** of the **John Walsh** department store (now **T.J.Hughes)** later bought **Mylnhurst** and lived there before selling to the **Sisters of Mercy,** who converted it to the present Catholic school.

N

na(h) denn, orreight now then, how are you? **nah denn dee,** or as newly arrived West Indians said , working on Heeley Sidings & learning the language, **now denn dee.**

nails **Mapplewell & Staincross** were a centre of the hand made nail industry with 55 nailshops in 1870. A shop at **Hoylandswain** was preserved by the **Sheffield Trades Historical Assn.** and is looked after by their successors. The last hand made nail & gimlet manufacturer retired from his **Ecclesfield** shop in the 1970's.

nailing furnace corruption of **annealing furnace.**

nail nick small nick stamped in the blade of a pocket knife, to allow you to open it with your nail.

French nail straight grooved **nail nick,** running right along the top edge of a pocket knife

a **namer** a steam train having a name- not just a number. Trainspotters on the bridge at **Neepsend** station would shout excitedly " A **namer;** a **namer!"** They would be even more excited if it was a **streak**= a streamlined **namer,** such as the **Mallard.**

neb, nebby nosc; noscy. **High Neb** on **Stanage Edge** at 1502 feet is the second highest point in the city of Sheffield.

neb tang wooden-handled knife with flat **through tang** that curves round to a beak at the end. Also scythe tang knocked over at the end to secure it to the wooden handle.

ne'er pronounced **near** = never.
ne'er mind eh?

ne'er mind 'playin' fields of Eton - 'Battle o' Watterloo wer won in 'Walker's cannon foundry in Rotherham.

neet night. **Sithee terneet.**

neets; on neets working on the night shift: **10 while 6.**

Nelson knife a broad bladed knife with three, flat prongs curved round at the end of the blade, like a cheese knife. A one handed person can use it to cut, hold & eat food.

James Neill High quality Sheffield tool firm which used to be in a multi-storey red brick & glass building on **Napier Street.** Best known for **Eclipse** brand **hacksaw blades**, an Argentinian customer of **The Famous Sheffield Shop** on **Ecclesall Road** said **Eclipse** was the generic word for the blades in Argentina. Their adjacent red brick **magnet** factory on **Napier St.** was patterned by darker 'Staffordshire blue' bricks shaped as magnets. Now merged with **Spear & Jackson,** both tool & magnet factories are in single storey factories in the **East End. Spear & Jackson,** established in the 18th century, surged ahead after moving to their **Aetna works,** one of the first steel & tool plants to develop in the **East End.** They made steel, rolled it in hand mills to sheet, and made **saws,** hand and circular, for which they were, and still are, famous, though they now buy in the sheet. They are famous too for **garden tools;** took over **C.T.Skelton (qv)** of **Heeley** then merged with **Elwell's** in the Midlands. Production of garden tools became centred at Wednesbury but is due to return to Sheffield in 2008 to their **machine knife** factory off **Brightside Lane.**

nesh a Sheffield classic- even if it is known elsewhere in Britain- meaning feeling the cold**;** unable to stand cold or face an unpleasant situation. E.g young lads in the Life Boys who wouldn't swim in the cold North Sea & stood on the edge shivering, were **nesh,** or had **neshed it. .....** Heard at **Hillsborough** when a **Wednesday** player wouldn't get stuck into a tackle: **'he's neshed it sithee!'** A venerable word, the Old English is **hnesce.**

Newton Chambers, Thorncliffe, Chapeltown much respected conglomerate operating coal mines, foundries, engineering workshops, etc. with a wide product range that encompassed coke; iron castings for ornamental staircases, stoves **(Redfyre)** gas lamps; gasworks and steelworks plant; excavators and Churchill tanks (WW2); not forgetting **Izal (qv)** toilet rolls to disinfectants, & **Ronseal,** that still "does" today, under U.S. ownership, "exactly what it says on the tin." (This jingle has now come into the language to mean someone or something you can take at face value**).**

The conglomerate started when **Thomas Chambers** & **George Newton** of the **Phoenix Foundry,** Sheffield, leased the Thorncliffe site from **Earl Fitzwilliam** in 1793, and ended soon after the firm was bought by asset strippers in 1973. With **NCK** excavators, taken over by Ransomes, & **Izal** taken over by Jeyes, the everlasting flame on top of a chimney, burning waste gases, & visible night and day from the M1 was extinguished, and an industrial empire was no more. As with most Sheffield firms there was fierce company loyalty, though there were darker days in Victorian times, especially at the coal mines, with lockout & riot, so soon after the **Sheffield Outrages (qv)** in the neighbouring **light (metal) trades,** cofirming national opinion of the town as a rum sort of place. Even the threatening letters to the bosses in local industry were similar, with **Mr. Chambers** being warned by a striking miner in 1870, that " if thou means to let us **clam** & starve. We mean to have it out of you you bugger as thy Days are numbered. so prepare to meet thy God." See **"...A Most Enterprising Thing..."** a most entertaining history of the firm by **Joan & Mel Jones.** The **Chapeltown** site is now a thriving industrial area again including, as well as **Ronseal,** hi-tech surgical instrument manufacturers, & the **British Glass Industry Research Association.**

nickel silver spoons & forks for the mass market were made in this yellowish/white metal before the invention of **18/8 stainless steel.** It is an alloy of **zinc, copper** and **approx. 10% nickel.** It doesn't contain **silver,** but best quality silver plated cutlery is **E.P.N.S. = electro plated nickel silver,** with silver plating ca. 35 microns.

Florence Nightingale ranks with **Bess of Hardwick** as the most famous woman who ever lived in Sheffield. Celebrated for her work in the 1854-56 Crimean war & for establishing nursing as a respectable profession for women, she was born in Florence to wealthy Sheffielders Edward & Frances Nightingale. Her father had changed his name in 1815 from **Shore** to **Nightingale** to secure an inheritance. Her grandparents lived at **Tapton Hill** and a statue of **Florence** was found at the University **Tapton** hall of residence when it was refurbished. Grandad **Shore** was a banker as well as being involved in the steel & cutlery trades. For most of **Florence's** childhood & youth up to 19 years of age the **Nightingales** lived in Sheffield, though spending summers at Holloway, near Matlock. In her book **Notes on Nursing** she wrote about the importance of good food**;** about the proper airing & cleaning of wards, & stressing simple things like washing hands. If she was around today, perhaps with the help of a few bottles of **Izal,** she would send MRSA & other 'superbugs' scurrying for their little lives.

After the war she set up a training school for nurses at St. Thomas' Hospital, and locally, became a life governor of the Sheffield Infirmary. She & her family donated money for the 1856 war memorial that stood, latterly, in the Botanical Gardens. Declining an offer to lay the first stone, she wrote**: "** I believe I shall best honour the cause of those brave dead by abstaining from appearing to court that publicity which I consider to have been my greatest impediment in the work I have been engaged in for their sakes, impeding it by arousing in some minds care for worldly distinction."

nithered cold. See **clemmed; starved; nesh.**

no in Sheffield can be pronounced**: 1/** as a sharp **now -** say it like **nowt** without the **t. 2/** as a dismissive **naeow-** a longer drawn out sound, almost as an Essex girl pronounces no. **3/** as **nay (neigh)-** often used comically**: Nay lad, tha mon't do that** – and Frankie Howard's**: Nay, nay, thrice nay.** (Dutch **nee).**

nooase nose. **Keep thi nooase artnit=** mind your own business **Get thi nooase art o'trough=** don't be greedy.

Nora a gaunt, angular, eccentric woman with loud, aggressive voice, who used to frequent Pond Street bus station in the 1960's and 70's. Sudden shouts of, for e.g., **"Roll yer dollar down"** would echo around the main hall.

Norfolk, duke of now based in Arundel, he had extensive Sheffield interests, including what is now **Norfolk Park,** and large tracts of **Parkwood Springs.** There are **Norfolk Arms** pubs at **Ringinglow** and **Rivelin** and **Norfolk Street** by the **Crucible theatre.** To have a face **'as long as Norfolk Street'** is to be a **misery guts**. See **(Earls of) Shrewsbury.**

No 6 Norfolk St. was formerly the main factory, H.Q., and showroom of **Joseph Rodgers & Co.,** the world's leading cutlers employing ca. 5000 workers in 1900. Pocket knives stamped with their name, trade mark **star & Maltese cross, (**granted **1682** by the **Cutlers' Company),** & address **No.6 Norfolk St., Sheffield** are highly sought after by collectors around the world.

the **Norfolk Knife** Big & beautiful Victorian spring knife made by **Joseph Rodgers,** with 75 blades finely etched with various scenes such as **Chatsworth House,** Crystal Palace- built for the 1851 Great Exhibition, & the White House, Washington. This can be seen along with the **Year Knife (qv)** at the **Cutlers' Hall.**

normalising steel heat treatment process, similar to **annealing** but the steel is cooled in still air. The aim is to modify the **grain size,** render the structure more uniform, and to improve the mechanical properties.

Northern the **Northern General** hospital.

nowt nothing, naught. What have we got, **owt** or **nowt?** We're short o'**nowt** we've got. **We sell nowt but tools** sign in **Ken Hawley's** tool shop 1950's – 1990's.

a **nowter** a ne'er do well

nurks chips; **fish n'nurks**

nutter national slang for a crackpot, but an interesting reference to an 1809 notice in **Lady Spring Wood** on the **Round Walk (qv)** tells us that people "who style themselves as **nutters"** are damaging trees & fences and if caught will be shot at dawn. (I might have got this last bit wrong- perhaps it just says 'will be prosecuted.).

nutty slack 1940's mixture of open cast slack and poor quality coal manufactured into cobbles, when coal was rationed by the Ministry of Fuel & Power, known locally as the **Ministry of Fools in Power**.

O

Oakbrook House built off **Fulwood Road** for **Mark Firth** when the giants of Victorian steel vied with each other, with their vast works in the **East End,** and palatial homes in the **West End.** Now **Notre Dame** school. See **Mark Firth/ Firth Park.**

oatcakes once common- sellers used to tramp the streets of Neepsend & other areas shouting **'oatcakes, pikelets'** which they carried, covered by a linen cloth, in a wicker basket strapped before them. Still made in Sheffield- e.g. for **Lily's,** the Hillsborough bakers, and nearby in Derbyshire, as well as Staffordshire.

obstrocolous obstreporous

o'er, oo'er over. **workin' o'er** =working overtime. **"He does nowt all day an' works o'er to finish it."** (unkind description of a labourer at **Laycock Engineering,** Archer Road).

o'er laid overslept

o'er ageean over against; **purrit o'er ageean 'wall will tha.**

o'er shot wheel **over shot waterwheel** where the stream of water runs from the **dam** via a **pen trough** over the top of the wheel into **'buckets'** fitted against each slat, thus turning the wheel. See also **ovver**

of can mean **on; of** a Tuesday. A reply by someone hard of hearing to the question; What did he **dee** of? **"He deed of a Tuesday."**

okker watter earth containing **ochr e**= ferric oxide, seeps into the local fast moving streams at various points, giving them an orangey, yellowish, reddish hue. There is an **Ochre dike** at **Beighton** with **Ochre Dike Lane** by **Crystal Peaks** shopping centre. **Ochre Dike Walk** at **Rockingham, Rotherham** is near nicely named Squirrel Castle Plantation; Dog Kennel Pond and Handkerchief Piece. If you go on the **Round Walk** see the **okker watter** in parts of **Limb Brook** in **Ecclesall Woods.**

Old Park Silver Rolling Mill now in ruins on **Club Mill Road** where the **Loxley** meets the **Don,** it was founded ca. 1760 by **Joseph Hancock** who took **Boulsover's** invention of **Sheffield Plate** into both production and pieces of larger scale than the inventor's **buttons** & **snuff boxes. Hancock** rolled ingots of copper **fused** with **silver** into sheets out of which his skilled men fashioned a wide variety of items from tea & coffee pots to humble saucepans. (One of these is shown at the **Metalwork Gallery** in town). The Sheffield Directory of 1797 describes **"Mr. Joseph Hancock** (as) an ingenious mechanic (who has) brought wealth and population to the town.**"**

Old Park eventually concentrated on rolling silver and **nickel silver** for the trade, in wire, bar, and especially in sheet form. **Davy (qv)** built them a waterwheel in 1858/9 which was subsequently badly damaged along with the mills in the 1864 **Sheffield flood**. Water power worked alongside steam when, in 1875, a steam engine was installed to power **Old Park's** largest mill which cold rolled wide sheet. The water wheel was taken out in 1920 & replaced by an electric motor drive free of charge by **Sheffield Corporation,** since the water rights were required for the cooling towers of **Neepsend Power Station. Davy** put in a 500h.p. electric drive in 1928, replacing the steam engine.

The firm struggled after WW2 with a decline in the silver trade, and the replacement of nickel silver by stainless steel in the cutlery & holloware trades, & finally closed in the 1960's.

oliver a small tilt hammer operated by a foot treadle.

snotty Oliver a stuck up persson.

on 'Cliffe ; on 'Cross (he lives) down **Attercliffe;** on Parson Cross. **on 'Manor** on the Manor estate, built on the grounds of **Sheffield Manor** which, together with the huge **Sheffield Castle,** housed **Mary Queen of Scots,** held captive for

14 years in those tumultuous Eizabethan days.

on can mean **at** a firm; or **in** a department: **"**I went to work **on Brookes & Crookes,** on St. Phillips road.**"- George Watts, hand forger.** **"** I had a little (work)**shop on Pinder Brothers". Stephen Giffard, spinner,** now owner of **Camelot Silverware.**

He works **on 'hammers; on 'furnaces**

on 'Labour out of work

got 'onk on; got horn on; got a bar on to have an erection (schoolboy slang).

'ooam home. Who's he when he's at **'ooam?** Sometimes pronounced **'om** as in the Buddhist chant: **He's off 'om** or **'ooam; She's gone 'om** or **'ooam- well I'm gooinooam then.**

ooo (pronounced as unaspirated, elongated **who)** oh; oh dear. **ooo that's luvly** Rotherham parrot's comment after sipping from a bowl of water, expertly mimicking its lady-owner's voice. This came as it was being interviewed on local T.V. news, after its escape, then recapture thanks to a twix chocolate bar.

Ooslams or **Oosnams** familiar names for the world-famous **I XL** cutlery firm **George Wostenholm & Co. (qv).**

Ooterbridge Oughtibridge, a well-wooded settlement by the **Don,** still with a few metalworkers & the paper mill (formerly **Peter Dixon's,** now U.S. owned).

oowashiwee? washiwee ersen? visitors to Sheffield thought two women on a bus were speaking Chinese, but in fact the beautiful sounds translate as; **" Who was she with? Was she on her own?**

Open Hearth (Siemens-Martin) steelmaking process invented by Wm. Siemens in 1861 & using Pierre Martin's method, 1867, of making carbon steel by diluting **pig iron** with **wrought iron** scrap. Unusually for advances in steelmaking the men had little connection with Sheffield, but the ten hour process giving time to adjust additions, temperatures etc. suited Sheffielders better than the frantic **Bessemer** process. The best known local **Open Hearth melting shops** were **Firth Brown's (**their **Siemens Dept.** stone archway still stands, leading to new factory sheds), **Steelos & Park Gate (qv).**

As it became less economical to make bulk steels in Sheffield & Rotherham, at the heart of Britain far from the docks, the region consolidated its role as a world leader in electrically melted special engineering & stainless steels, highly alloyed steels, & finished products for the aerospace, defence, medical, power & motor industries.

oppen razor open razor. **Bill Hukin,** Sheffield's last **open razor grinder,** got annoyed if you called them **cut-throats.**

oppner; tin oppner; weer's tin oppner?

Orgreave coking plant at **Catcliffe** was, in 1984, scene of mass picketing by miners attempting to stop lorry loads of coke heading from the plant to **blast furnaces** at Scunthorpe & Teeside. Such was the struggle between police, many brought in from other forces including the Met., and miners,many from other U.K. coalfields, with images of mounted police charging, and baseball-hatted **Arthur Scargill** clutching a megaphone & struggling to avoid arrest, that the whole scenario became known as **the Battle of Orgreave.** Subject of articles, books, T.V. documentaries & films it still stirs passions, ranging from rage to comical amusement & scorn.

Samuel Osborn= Sammy Osborn's an impressive stone built building on the **Wicker** with carved date 1853, name **Shortridge Howell & Co,** trademark **hand,** and brooding heads looking down on the thoroughfare, became the headquarters of **Osborn's Clyde** works. The firm eventually had factories around Sheffield, as well as in Manchester & Low Moor, Bradford, and were best known for tool steel & **high speed** cutting tools for industry. Their tall brick-built **Regent works** with name & **red hand** trademark, which housed **sheet mills** stands on Rutland Rd. by the river **Don,** opposite the **Rutland knife Co.** & the **Gardeners Rest** real ale pub.

Robert F. Mushet in the Forest of Dean invented a 7% **tungsten self-hardening =air hardening** steel which could cut twice as fast as standard carbon steels. His trials came to a blank end & he gave **Samuel Osborn** sole manufacturing rights at his works on the **Wicker.** Half the world's self-hardening tool steel trade was in **Osborn's** hands up to the 1890's even though other Sheffield firms such as **Seebohm & Dieckstahl** (a nieghbouring firm on the **Wicker), Sanderson Bros., Edgar Allen, Swift Levick & Huntsman** developed similar steels

Other countries such as Germany, France, the U.S.& Austria built up strong tool steel industries in the 20th century, and after WW2, even though **Osborn's** rationalised with a fine new plant at **Ecclesfield,** they, along with most other Sheffield steel firms, were outside the Labour government's nationalised net, so got neither support, nor protection from subsidised foreign manufacturers.

Firth Rixson (qv)/ Barworth Flockton now carry the flag for Sheffield tool steel production at **Ecclesfield,** but the **Osborn** mini-empire is no more. A large white multi-storey building I saw rise in 1944, as a boy in Neepsend, for **Osborn Mushet Tools**, still produces cutting tools under Chinese ownership.

orreight? Are you alright? - a typical greeting: **orreight mi ol' (luv)** = are you alright my old (love). Usually a man to man greeting.

outworker independent cutler or other metalworker contracted to do work for a larger firm.

ovver less common than **o'er** for over: **ovver yonder; ovverlaid; ovvereead crane** (in steel & engineering works); **ovveralls.** In the days when the M1 was newly built & garages advertised 'last petrol before M1' a workers' boots & clothing store on **Attercliffe Common** had a big sign in the window proclaiming, **'Last ovveralls before M1.'**

owd can mean hold as in, **owd thi osses**= hold your horses; hold on a minute, but usually= old: **tell thi this much owd lad (ahr kid; squire** etc.)

owd Queen's 'eead Old Queen's Head, Elizabethan pub by **Pond Street bus station.**

t'owd lass; ahr owd lass usually = wife, but can mean mother.

t'owd lad father, or the devil- see **lad**

t'owd walk old footpath/ **jennel** from the river **Sheaf,** steeply up by the side of **the General Cemetery** to **Sharrow Head.** Now corrupted to **Toad Walk,** especially since it meets **Frog Walk,** which runs alonside the **Sheaf** then by the grounds of **Wilson's snuff mill** to **Sharrow Vale Road.**

Owlerton usually pronounced **O-lerton** (as in **oh** dear), not **Owl-erton** (as in too whit too woo), this area of Sheffield 6 makes products of special steels & exotic metals of the very highest quality. E.g. **Swann-Morton scalpel blades-** they are the world's biggest producer at one and a half **million** a **day; Doncaster's precision forge-aerofoils; Independent Forge & Alloy- forgings** for **aerospace, power generation** etc.; **Thorntons-** precision **cast & forged medical implants; Hy. Taylor- wood carving tools.** We have to hope that **Bassett's** continue production by the **Don,** and that Cadbury will not follow the trend to shift production to cheap labour countries that are not weighed down by our taxes & red tape. This industrial area at the conflux of the **Loxley** and the **Don** was badly affected by the great flood of June 2007 with the bridge joining Livesey Street & Club Mill Road destroyed.

Just by **Owlerton church** stands a branch of **Napoleon's casino** and **Owlerton greyhound & speedway track,** rescued & revived by **Dave Allen,** owner of **Sheffield Wednesday.**

A large new college has been built whose staff and pupils hopefully won't complain if the nearby battery of **forging hammers** and **drop stamps** rattles their windows. They should rather have pride in their city's world class industry.

the Owls the bird of prey symbolises **Sheffield Wednesday F.C.** perhaps since they moved to **Hillsborough** in 1899, the **Kop** end being just up the road from what we think of as **Owlerton. (**In fact both **Hillsborough Park** & the **Wednesday** ground are as much **Owlerton** as **Hillsborough** and many older supporters still talk of going to the match at **Owlerton).** **The Wednesday** were formed, predominantly by cutlers, in **1820** as a cricket club playing on Wednesdays. To keep the men together over winter the **Wednesday Football Club** was established in **1867,&** 20 years later were playing on a new ground at **Olive Grove** on **Queen's Road**, almost within sight of **Bramall Lane!** When they moved from **Olive Grove** their mascot, a monkey, died and the **owl** was adopted. Ironically, their nickname up to the move was the **Blades,** which United then adopted in 1899. **The Wedneday** won the F.A. Cup in 1895 and the league in 1903 then hit a purple patch between the wars, being champions in 1928,1929,1933 & 1934 as well as cup winners in 1935. Most Sheffielders long for glory days to return to either **Wednesday** or **United,** and some of us would even like both teams to do well. The only Sheffield success since WW2 **; Wednesday** winning the **Carling Cup,** beating Manchester United 1-0 in 1991. (I think it was called the Carling Cup or League Cup at the time, or what a **Blades** fan dismissively called **'that faffin' about cup.')**

Wednesday were generally regarded as the biggest Sheffield **teeam** with a record crowd of over 72,000 before the war, compared to **United's** 68,000, and current seating capacity of about 40,000 compared to 32,000 at **Bramall Lane.** Even a midweek 'County Cup' final at **Hillsborough** in the late 1940's between **Wednesday & Doncaster Rovers** attracted 52,000. With **Kevin McCabe & Neil Warnock** at the helm, premiership football at **'Lane** in 2006-2007, ground improvements plus a new hotel, the **Hillsborough** hegemony was threatened, so **Wednesdayites** were relieved at **United's** immediate relegation. **Wednesday** were also regarded as having, generally speaking, a rougher, more working class, type of supporter- or am I too much influenced by my father's attitude, & my likening **Wednesdayites** flooding down from the big pre-war **estates** through the **Five Arches** to the Mongol hordes! At any rate, **Heap,** the brilliant caricaturist & cartoonist for the **Green 'Un** always drew the **Wednesday** supporter in a cloth cap & the **United** supporter in a bowler. More recently the picture has been reversed and **United** have been called the inner-city team, with implication that it sits among the poor & needy & multi-racial. (With city centre apartments now rising all around will the wheel turn again and **United** revert to being the poshest team?)

Music at both grounds in the 1940's, 50's & 60's was usually provided by military or police bands playing Sousa or Alford marches, before the match or at half time, accompanied by mass whistling (many of the crowd had been in the Forces). **Owls** fans would sing to the tune of 'Covered Wagon':

Roll along Sheffield Wednesday, roll along, to the top of the league, where you belong. If Daley (later **Quigley,** then **Dooley) gets the ball, he's sure to score a goal, roll along Sheffield Wednesday, roll along.**

Blades fans would substitute **United** for **Wednesday,** and **Hagan** for **Daley** etc. or would keep **Wednesday** and **Daley** etc.but would substitute **bottom** for **top,** and **slip & fall,** for **score a goal.**

Dooley, a gangly red head was such a hero, with 47 goals in one season, that fans altered the words of a pop song 'Truly, truly fair' to **'Dooley, Dooley fair'.** Had it not been for a tragic accident in a game, leading to him losing a leg, he would surely have gone on to play for England. He's too tough a Sheffielder to let a tragedy spoil his life though, crossing the city divide when he was pushed from **Hillsborough,** to become chairman at the **Lane.**

owt anything. **What tha doin'; owt or nowt?** Yorkshireman's motto:

'ear all, see all, say **nowt; eight** (eat) all, sup all, pay **nowt;** an' if **tha** ever does **owt** for **nowt,** allus do it fer **thissen.** (Of course this meanness of spirit doesn't apply to the Sheffield region, the generous heart of Britain). An insistent request: **"What's for tea?,** can be met by; **"Owt tha can catch, wi' salt on."** A nurse at the **Hallamshire** was heard giving an old bloke, lets call him **Sheff,** a list of healthy options for his dinner, all of which he countered with, 'rubbish; can't eat that; never heard of it' until she asked in exasperation; **'Well Mr. Sheff,** what **do** you want?' **'Owt',** he replied. 'Use your initiative.'

owt like promising (of weather). **If weather's owt like, we'll walk up Kinder.**

oyal hole. Much used: for outbuildings, usually in the **back yard; bin oyal=** bricked recess holding the bin; **coyal oyal=** coal house, usually next to the **bin oyal; dog oyal**=kennel, and to be **in 'dog oyal** is to be in trouble, in the doghouse, usually with the wife. The **dooer oyal** is the door frame, and **put 'wood in' oyal** means shut that door. Parts of the body: **arse oyal; lug oyal; cake oyal** (U.S. pie hole). **Chip oyal** or **chip og** are used for the fish & chip shop (chippie would never pass **Old Sheff's** lips, neither would **p- -s oyal** or **s- -t oyal** for urinal or toilet).

tap oyal tap hole in blast furnace= hole that is drilled at the base of the furnace to release = **tap** molten iron.

P

Thomas Paine (1737-1809) we can't claim him as a local man, but the author of "Rights of Man" invented a new type of **iron bridge** and worked for the manufacturers, **Walkers (qv)** of **Masborough, Rotherham, ironfounders,** (who also saved Britain with their **cannons** for Nelson's fleet & Wellington's army). A Sheffield filecutter, **Joseph Mather,** wrote a song, "God Save Great Thomas Paine" set to the National Anthem, following the publication in 1792, by **Joseph Gale,** proprietor of the **Sheffield Register,** of a sixpenny pamphlet edition of "Rights of Man," which sold 1400 copies. (See **Sheffield Newspapers).** Another, smaller connection: Lafayette gave **Paine** the key of the Bastille to send to George Washington as a symbol of French friendship towards the U.S.A. & **Paine** added to the gift by including half a dozen **cast steel Sheffield razors**.(= hot forged from **crucible cast steel).**

panshion; pancheon big earthenware bowl for mixing dough & baking bread with **barm** (=yeast). Bread was **sad** if it didn't rise.

pappap child's word for a motor car.

Paradise Square a fine Georgian square built 1736-1770 on a slope behind the **Cathedral.** It was a meeting place & local lad, **John Wesley** (well, he was from **Epworth,** north Lincs.) preached before the largest congregation he had ever known on a weekday. (Perhaps it was a **Saint Monday). Chantrey (qv),** the famous Victorian sculptor had a studio in the square. Today cars spoil the atmosphere..... If only room could be found for them elsewhere!

Park working class area of Sheffield 2 built on part of the site of **Shrewsbury's (qv)** former deer park. An old delineation of trade skills read, **"melters from Hillsborough, grinders from Heeley, and buffers off 'Park."**

Park Gate Iron & Steel Co. formed by two Sheffield ironmasters in 1823 at **Parkgate, Rotherham;** taken over by a Brummie syndicate in 1832; then by **Samuel Beale, chairman of the** Midland Railway, in 1842. Along with a partner he installed a **rail mill,** rolling 2000 tons of rails per month. **Blast furnaces** were leased at **Holmes** (original site of **Walkers, Masborough** works), and at **Chapeltown.** In 1849 they began rolling **plate** for the Navy, & between 1856-1861 they were the only works in the world rolling plate up to four and a half inches thick for warships. The large plates for Brunel's **Great Eastern,** launched 1858, were rolled at **Park Gate.**

In 1888, with customers demanding **steel** instead of **iron, 3 x 25 ton Siemens Open Hearth (qv) furnaces** were installed with new **cogging** & **slabbing** mills. Production was eventually concentrated on bars in carbon, low alloy and **freecutting (qv)** qualities made with steel from **10 x 60/100 ton Open Hearth** furnaces.

1951 brought the first nationalisation of steel , one of 'the commanding heights of the economy'; 1956 brought de-nationalisation and purchase by **Tube Investments** of **Park Gate & Renishaw Iron Co.** together with a massive thousand acres of land further down the **Don** which has become the **Roundwood/ Thrybergh** & **Aldwarke (qv)** sites of the former **British Steel,** then Anglo- Dutch **Corus,** now **Tata Steel** of India. This last ownership shouldn't mean ta-ta to steelmaking here at the heart of Britain. The plant is ultra-modern and, thanks to the huge number of steel using factories & scrap gathering & sorting facilities in the Sheffield region, its main raw material; graded scrap, is right at hand. Together with **Stocksbridge (**for the more precious steels), **Aldwarke** should be the jewel in the crown for **Tata's** English Empire.

Park Hill flats in 1961 John Betjeman visited Sheffield and praised its woods, gardens, parks, open moors & tumbling streams along with its leafy western suburbs- **Broomhill** being for him "the prettiest suburb in England." He then went to see **"**the new blocks of flats rising near the city centre. The first sight of them was terrifying and inhuman, tier on tier of concrete with ugly **contemprikit** detail rising on a steep slope called **Park Hill.** When you start to walk about among them and see the flats inside, you become acclimatised.

The City Architect has, as it were, taken the old two-storey streets and raised them one on top of the other**.......**High up here the living room windows look out on to the magnificent moorland and if you cannot make out which dot in the area below is your child, you are at least centrally heated and with hot water and proper sanitation.The planning is thoughtful and ingenious and people do not much miss the gardens they never had."

Mr. Womersley, the City Architect in question was compared to Le Corbusier & feted with awards, but cynics said he never had to live in the flats. Similar groupings at **Kelvin** & **Hyde Park** – these last rising even higher to 18 stories on the **Sky Edge** ridge- were demolished within 30 years. Amid much controversy **Park Hill** has been grade II listed by English Heritage, and Manchester firm Urban Splash have the contract for their renovation.

(single) **parsa, parser, parsey** ingenious drill used by **pocket knife cutlers** to cut **pattrens** into stag, wooden, buffalo, ivory, pearl or xylo **coverings** (handles), into which is inserted a silver, nickel silver or brass **shield,** or name plate. A **double parsa, split parsa, two-legged parsa, parser** or **parsey** has twin steel cutters capable of forming more intricate **shields.** The drill is fitted into a **bobbin** with a steel point at the other end. The cutler cuts the **shield** shape required into a steel **template;** wears a metal breastplate, presses the pointed end of the **parsa** into the **breastplate** and the drill through the **template** onto the **covering,** and with a stick & cord, called a **boring stick** works this like a violin bow on the bobbin, thus working the drill & cutting the pattern. The technology of this is said to be ancient Egyptian!

Parkwood Springs a large hill stretching from the **Five Arches** over **Herries Road** in the west to **Rutland Road** in the east, best known now for a **ski slope** and a huge landfill site excavated into the hillside overlooking **Owlerton Stadium.** There were quarries and the **Sheffield Brick Company** fronting **Rutland Road,** and a **ganister drift mine (qv)** near the top of **Parkwood Road.** My brother in law, **Cyril Boswell,** was a miner there and he said that **coyal seeams** (ancient vegetation) lie over **gani seeams** (ancient roots) and which was most valuable would depend on quality, & demand at the time. Coal was sold to **Neepsend Power Station,** by the **Don** below the mine, & **gani** to the iron and steel industry, as well as to the **Old Park Silver Mill** on **Club Mill Road. Gani** with a bluish tint was most valued (just as **sandstone= millstone grit** with similar tint was best for **grindstones-** see **Brincliffe blue.)** Conditions in the mine were poor for men & ponies alike, with the bottom seam knee deep in water, Silicosis was a constant danger and this was made more of a threat by some miners who drilled into the rock dry to speed the process up, rather than turn on the water through the drill to damp down dust. **Wardsend cemetery** remains, overlooking **Bassett's,** but **Parkwood Springs, '**the forgotten village' overlooking **Neepsend** is no more. All that remains of the busy railway line, first steam then electric, **Sheffield Victoria** to **Woodhead** to **Manchester** is a night service moving steel between **Aldwarke** and **Stocksbridge.** From '**Springs** you can occasionally hear the sound of motor bikes from **Owlerton Stadium** far below, as well as the sound of off-road bikers on paths around the old quarries above. Far more evocative sounds though, come from the **forges** & **drop stamps** around **Owlerton.** Good old Sheffield- still at it.

parky park keeper

pattrens patterns (e.g. wooden ones by **a pattern maker** for steel castings).

Charlie Peace infamous Victorian criminal, born 1832 to a one-legged former miner who became noted as a wild animal tamer with "Wombwell's Wild Beast Show." **Peace** was a slight man, 5 ft. 4 inches tall, who walked with a limp following an accident in a rolling mill when a hot steel bar smashed into his leg. He had pronounced bow legs, possibly as a result of rickets, which illness was common right up to WW2.

These disabilities did not hinder him in his chosen career, which was as a 'portico thief' or, as we now say, a cat burglar. By day he was a picture framer but at night he broke into houses across the length and breadth of the country, certainly Sheffield to London, and Manchester to Sheffield to Hull, using the new railway networks. His skill at disguise and ability to contort his features "in such a way as to change altogether the character of his face" captured the Victorian imagination, especially when, upon being caught he leapt from a speeding London-Sheffield train. Once, his own wife failed to recognise him when he turned up dressed in middle class clothes, with a fox terrier on a lead.

Another woman was his downfall though; a woman called Dyson, who lived with her 6 ft. 5 inches husband, Arthur, at 959 **Ecclesall Road,** now part of the **Banner Cross** pub. His fixation with her led him to murder Arthur, claiming later that she was his mistress. She strongly denied this, calling him a demon, "beyond the power of even a Shakespeare to paint." After shooting Dyson dead, **Peace** fled to Hull, shaved his beard, dyed his hair, put on spectacles, and distorted his features. To hide a missing finger, shot off, he said, in an argument, he made himself a false arm with a hook at the end.

With a £100 bounty on his head he was caught eventually, brought to Armley gaol, Leeds, and hanged in February 1879. A few days before his execution he was visited by the Reverend Littlewood, vicar of **Darnall,** and with retribution looming, confessed to shooting a Manchester policeman as well. A man held for this crime, was released and given £800 compensation

Sir Arthur Conan Doyle, in "The Adventure of the Illustrious Client" gave **Charlie Peace** a mention, when Holmes discusses how those most dedicated to a life of crime, may sometimes have other talents. "A complex mind," said Holmes, "all great criminals have that. My old friend **Charlie Peace** was a violin virtuoso." **.......** A virtuoso he may have been, and I've lost count of the people, like my mother, who claimed to have distant relatives who made violins for the rogue, but he carried a gun in his pocket, and tools of his burgling trade in his violin case. A lawyer had the last word, as they so often do when there's a bob or two in it: the Earl of Birkenhead, former solicitor general, describing **Peace** in a biography as "a curious mixture of sordid villainy and artistic tastes."

peff to cough

peggy tub dolly tub; wash tub

penknife slim, usually two-bladed folding knife with slim blades opening at each end. Originally for cutting & shaping feather quill pens.

"First therefore be the choice of your **penknife;** a **right Sheffield** knife is best." – who are we to argue with Peter Bayles, in his "The Writing Schoolmaster" of 1590.

scrap pens steel industry term for partitions made of strong steel sheet & bar for holding various grades of scrap for the **melting shop. C.f.** sheep or cattle **pens.**

pen trough wooden tank at the head of a **dam** for constricting & channelling water from the **dam** over a **watter-wheel** (usually an **overshot wheel).** A sluice gate at the front of the trough was raised or lowered, regulating the flow, & therefore the speed of the **wheel,** by an ingenious lever control inside the **forge, rolling mill** or **grinding hull** where the machinery was powered by the turning of the **wheel.**

peyse peas. At **skoyal, peyse** were as hard as **mabs.** Similarly, **pleyse** is heard for please (and **cheyse** for cheese); He listens to me **then does as he pleyses.**

petty closet; outside toilet; **gooin' across 'yard** or **ter 'top o 'yard. Petty** indicates the influence of Derbyshire & Nottinghamshire on the boundary city's dialect. Note that familiar French has **petit** besoin for **number one,** (and gros besoin for number two) – so did **petty** come from **petit** via the troops in WW1?

Pickerings 200 year old firm, formerly makers of **Blanco (qv)** for H.M. Forces, now cardboard box makers on **Little London Road.**

pictures; gooin'ter 'pictures going to the cinema; to the **Unity;** the **Roscoe ('bug 'ut);** the **Oxford** at **Upperthorpe;** the **Hillsborough Kinema;** the **Paragon** at **Firth Park;** the **Essoldo** at **'Lane Top;** the **Forum** at **Parson Cross** (little kids after the Saturday cowboy serial, were silhouetted on the **Parkwood Springs** hills slapping their backsides as they ran back down to **Neepsend,** in imitation of both hero **Roy Rodgers,** and his horse **Trigger).** Cheers at the cinema when the **big picture** was announced; boos, I'm afraid, if it was preceded by a British film. There were such cinemas all over the region of course, and there **is still** the **Penistone Paramount.**

pie-can idiot, you stupid boy, **pob 'eead**

tha couldn't stop a pig in a passage; a pig in a entry (qv); a pig in a jennel (qv) ......said of a poor goalkeeper or wicketkeeper.

pig iron cast iron with high carbon content of 3 to 5%. **Molten iron** could be seen run into **pigs** = a series of **small castings** off a channel ressembling suckling piglets at the **Park Gate Iron & Steel (qv) blast furnaces** up to the 1960's. Most iron from the two **blast furnaces** was poured into a ladle then transferred into a 400ton capacity **mixer furnace** in the **Open Hearth melting shop** until it was needed for steel making. Steel making, further down the river **Don** at **Aldwarke** now is all electric and the basic raw material, as for all special steel production in the Sheffield region is graded steel scrap.

Pigeon City area at **Darnall,** near **High Hazels Park,** home to many pigeon fanciers' lofts.

Pigs Sheffield Wednesday according to Unitedites; Sheffield United according to Wednesdayites. **'Pigs are loisin'** = delighted cry from a United supporter at a Fulham v Sheffield United match, on hearing via his mobile phone that Wednesday were **loisin'** at **Hillsborough. "We will also need Onyx"** (waste disposal firm) **"to follow them to collect all the pig muck." -** E-mail from **Wednesdayite** Councillor Peter Price re **Sheffield United's** planned parade in 2006 following their promotion to the Premiership.

Up 'pigs arse on 'second shelf a vulgar schoolboy's answer to "where is it?"

'piggery familiar name for workers' canteen at **Phoenix Rooms, Steelo's (Steel Peech & Tozer).** In British fashion, staff & workers were segregated, but staff preferred the workers' canteen with plentiful, tasty meals, such as the 'full English'. Once, an office worker rang and asked, "Is that the piggery." "Yes", replied a woman, "And your trough awaits you."

pikelet flat round soft yeast cake, full of holes, usually 5 or 6inches diameter; wrongly described in the rest of the country as a crumpet. **Oatcake (qv),** a somewhat similar local delicacy, but usually wider=10 inch diameter, is now less common here than in Derbyshire & Staffordshire.

piking peeping

pile side A Sheffield classic=the side of a knife opposite to that carrying the mark; the reverse side. Though, when seen on a box of unfinished blades it is/was perhaps an instruction to put the mark **on** the reverse side, as was the fashion at one time. c.f. French **pile ou face** = heads or tails, when tossing a coin. A knife was tossed similarly, the **Hallamshire Glossary** (1824) telling us: **"Mark & pile are used of a knife as head & tail of a coin."** In his book on Sheffield trade terms, 1936, **Dyson** writes that the **pile side** "is ...where the **iron** of the **tang is piled up on the steel of the blade."** The tang & bolster, made of wrought iron, were hot forged onto the shear steel blade- see **shear steel & thumb mark.** This applied to most knives made before the 1920's, & though **stainless steel** then became the norm, the term **pile side** continued to be used.

'pillock o'parish local crackpot

pins more usual name for rivets in the **cutlery trade.** Note, in the same trade, rivets are pronounced **revits.**

pippoes chips (when addressing small children); don't confuse with **poppoes** = horses (when addressing small children).

piss-bed dandelion; probably a national word (French pissenlit) as is the vulgar phrase said locally about politicians, lawyers and other professional people when looking after their own; high fees, perks etc: **they all piss in 'same pot.**

pistol pattern knife handle resembling the butt of an old-fashioned pistol.

Samuel Plimsoll (1824-1898) from the age of 14 he lived at 50 **Regent Street, Portobello,** and at 7 **Sheaf Gardens,** and his mother later lived at 45 **Wilkinson Street.** He worked at lawyers **Hy. Waterfall** and then for 10 years at **Thos. Rawson,** brewers. His marriage at **Ecclesfield Church** to Eliza Railton, step daughter of a mine owner perhaps led to his later job selling local **coyal** to London, using the new GNR railway line to Kings Cross. Mining disasters such as the **Lund Hill** explosion & fire in which 189 men perished led him to raise funds, and agitate for pit safety, to such an extent that he became known as **'the miner's friend.'**

In 1864 he bought **Whiteley Wood Hall,** off **Common Lane,** near **Ringinglow Road**; a hall that had one belonged to **Thomas Boulsover,** inventor of **Sheffield Plate (qv).** From loss of lives down the mines he turned his attention to another national outrage that was the loss of lives at sea, caused by overloaded and unseaworthy ships. His book "Our Seamen: An Appeal" sold 600,000 copies and this, together with meetings he held around the country, stirred public opinion & the press. While living at **Whiteley Wood Hall** he became, in 1868, M.P. for Derby and tried to pass a merchant shipping bill to address the scandal of hundreds of unnecessary deaths every year at sea. This was opposed by M.P.s, ship owners and the Board of Trade and when Disraeli dropped the bill, seemingly because of these powerful vested interests, **Plimsoll** shook his fist in the Speaker's face. Huge nationwide demonstrations for **Plimsoll** and maritime safety ensued forcing Disraeli to pass an act which, among other things, introduced markings on ships showing laden limits, markings which became known as **the Plimsoll Line.**

Samuel Plimsoll was a national hero, with novels, plays, music hall songs and even sports shoes produced in his honour. (These **plimsolls,** being rubber below and canvas on top, should, like ships, only be submerged in water to a set point.) Unfortunately, being a hero doesn't pay bills, and, oppressed by legal fees, he had to sell**Whiteley Wood Hall.** (One source gives this in 1873, another in 1876.)

plodgin' ; splodgin' **coarse** fishing. Canal and riverside fishing is immensely popular in Sheffield, and was even more so when every works of any size had their own angling club. There were said to be 50,000 anglers in the city, equalling the total number who followed football at **Hillsborough & Bramall Lane.** When **Fred James, bowie knife** maker worked **on Christopher Johnson's** at **Portobello** he said 9 out of ten men were anglers. For the men who worked in the heat, noise & dust of the steel industry, relaxation **plodgin'** along, say, the quaintly-named **South Forty Foot Drain** in deepest Lincolnshire was especially welcome- even if they were **watter-licked** (=didn't catch **owt.)**

pob; pob 'eead a mild insult

pobs bread soaked in hot milk for children or old folk who are **badly (qv).**

pocket knife usually a folding knife, or clasp knife with blade(s) opening from one end only. Normally bulkier than a **pen knife**, though this can have a **pen blade** at one end and a **pocket blade** at the other.

pog a place in a pub, café, cinema etc. **"Save us a pog."**

polly head (said of child).

Porter once home to about 20 water mills along its length, now only **Shepherd Wheel (qv)** & **Wilson's Snuff Mill** wheel remain and from **Hunter's Bar** upstream through the **Mayfield Valley** to its source on the moor above **Ringinglow,** it passes through scenes of incredible beauty. See **Sheffield Rivers.**

posser; posher wooden handled copper plunger, used on **wesh days.** See **dolly posh,** which, as well as having a **wesh day** meaning, is also used, uniquely in the Steel City to mean **left-handed.**

pot 1/ clay **crucible** for steel making; **pot makker. 2/** plaster for broken arm, leg etc. **Got 'pot on.**

up to press was a common schoolboy saying in the 1940's=up to now (perhaps national; perhaps American?)

pressed scales **horn scales pressed** into handle shape, usually for cheaper knives from **cow horn,** softened by boiling. **(Dyson).**

prints **dies** for producing **bolsters** by hot hammering to shape.

Pryor on **Egerton St**. are one of the world's leading **marking equipment** manufacturers- see **mark.** Tiny 12mm & even 6mm stainless steel discs having the Lord's Prayer stamped on in full, in English, German or Italian, or the Marsellaise in full in French are produced to show their skills, and can be seen at the **Famous Sheffield Shop.**

pubs as well as there being many named after local gentry or royalty: **Devonshire Arms, Norfolk Arms, Fitzwilliam Arms, Effingham Arms, Earl of Arundel & Surrey, Old Queen's Head** (Elizabeth 1), **Victoria, Prince of Wales** etc. there are, and sometimes were, those following the trades: **Cutler(s), Cutler's Arms, Little Mesters, Foundry, Moulder's Rest, the Steel Melters, Rail Mill Inn, Nailmakers' Arms, Anvil Arms, Filesmith's Arms, Blacksmith's Arms, the Jolly Buffer, Hammer & Pincers, Miners'Arms** and, to end with one in Leeds, **the Crooked Billet ....** (well, I like the name and they were next to **re-rollers, Coghlan's** who bought their **billets-** usually straight ones- from **Park Gate Iron & Steel Company.)**

Some pubs are/were known by their nicknames: **the Victoria** on Parkwood Road was known as **the Monkey,** and the building, today known as **the Monkey Works,** now houses an engineering firm. **Lord Nelson** off the **Moor** is known as **Fanny's,** after a landlady there. **Fagan's** on Broad Street adopted the name of this well-known landlord.

The trend towards silly names died off: e.g. John Thomas reverted to **Bell Hagg** (before being converted to flats), and the Real Macaw reverted to **the Prince of Wales.**

puddin' ; Tha wants to get some puddin' dahn thi= said to thin little lad by fat steelworker, playing football together on the cobbled streets in the 1940's.

puddled daft

puffabilly a steam train (when addressing a small child).

puffler a boss; deputy dahn **'pit-** especially around **Barnsley.**

pulpit control room high above the **shop flooer** in steelworks' **melting shop** or **rolling mill.**

purremineer put them in here

push; to be allus on'last push to be always last minute

put; to make a put to make an effort, start something (at last), get something done. **I'll have to mek a put an' gerrit done wee.** (Collins gives **puten** as 12th century for **push).**

puther to billow out, of smoke. Before the clean air act you would see from the number 69 bus between Sheffield & Rotherham orange-red clouds of smoke **puthering** out from **Steelos' melting shop** roof. This was from the **electric arc furnaces,** and was progress of sorts since previous furnaces here and elsewhere in the region had been **Open Hearth** which **puthered** out black smoke. With smoke from a thousand works and a hundred thousand houses right up to the 1950's- that's when pollution **was** pollution.

Q

Queens! In children's game means you can run off again after a standstill **(Kings!)** from being chased at **tiggy.**

quench to cool rapidly by plunging glowing hot blades, bars of steel, cutting tools etc. into oil or water, or even iced brine if **quenching** has to be severe. **Quenched** steel is intensely hard and brittle and is followed by **stress relieving** or **tempering** in order to recover some of the **ductility & toughness,** without drastically reducing the **hardness & strength.** A wonderful material, steel when it is treated right & doesn't lose its temper.

R

race to true up irregularities on a **grindstone; racin 'stooan** =racing the stone using a **racing tool** or **iron.** The tool is passed over the surface of the revolving wheel to remove embedded dust & true up the wheel surface. **John Watts** have patented a tool with small serrated wheels set in a metal handle for truing up abrasive grinding wheels.

raddle tool used in **puddled iron** trade to stir up molten metal.

rag an' booan man see **booan** and **donkey stooan.**

rag an' tag the old open **Sheaf** market known by some, unkindly, as **rag an' louse.**

Ragg well known for their **tuning forks,** of which they are the only manufacturers in Britain. Now in the **Granton Knife group** they can trace their ancestry as knife & razor makers to 1601.

rammel rubbish, **kelterment.**

rattening wilful damage of machinery, or cutting or removal of leather belting that drove machinery by strikers or agitators, hitting at non-union workers, or non-union workshops. See **Sheffield Outrages.**

J. B. Rawlins, Hope Works, were at 137, **Harvey Clough Rd.,** off **Derbyshire Lane,** built ca. 1869, just one of untold thousands of small metalworking firms in Sheffield and outlying areas such as this in **Norton,** then in Derbyshire. They deserve a mention though, because of their exquisite hand forged corkscrews and ladies' tweezers, glove hooks, pins, nail files etc. with hand carved ivory, mother of pearl, tortoiseshell, & stag as well as silver handles. Their heyday was the late Victorian/ Edwardian era and two world wars meant lost trade and men in such luxury trades as theirs. When **Jack Hawksworth,** joint owner in 1973, who had worked at the firm for 50 years, showed me round in July of that year, the firm were making scissors (including blunt ended ones for H.M. Prisons); nickel-plated brass nit combs for Derpac; letter openers for H.M.S.O.; eyelet hooks for the Post Office; and, latching on to a vogue at the time, stainless steel tiles. **Jack** had started with the firm as a lad collecting horse muck from the roads and lanes around the works, which was left until tinder dry, then put in the recess in sandstone **stocks** under the **stiddies (qv)**= anvils used by the hand forgers. The horse muck acted as a shock absorber preventing, or delaying an arthritic condition known as **dropped wrist (qv).** Like so many firms in the **Light Trades** they survived thanks to their versatility- Mr. Murphin, the other director, made the machinery, e.g. one with three cutting heads for the nit comb job, though eventually they closed the firm down and the old red brick factory was demolished ih the 1980's.

razors even as late as the 1950's John Betjeman called Sheffield "this hill-shadowed city of **razors** and knives", but the days are long gone when every man in the Royal Navy was issued with a Sheffield-made **open razor (qv)…** (don't call them **cut-throats-** see **Billy Hukin). Open razors** of superb artistry were made especially in Victorian times by **Cadman's Bengal Razor; Wostenholm True Pipe; Rodgers Star & Maltese Cross; John Heiffor; Thomas Turner** etc.etc. The American King Gillette largely put paid to the **open razor** with his patented safety razor, and it wasn't until the patent ran out in the 1930's that a further batch of Sheffield manufacturers came on the scene: **James Neill, Thomas Ward (Wardonia Works** off **Bramall Lane), G.H. Lawrence (Laurel blades, Nursery Street), Swann-Morton, Durham-Duplex** etc. All these used carbon steel cold rolled precision strip made principally by **Samuel Fox** or **Arthur Lee.** A final Sheffield name in the razor trade, **Jewel Razor (qv)** came on the scene in the 1960's with stainless blades & now no longer make these, but it is worth noting, all you Sheffielders with the "it's all gone thi's nowt left" mentality that **1/** The world's best razor blades made around the world by such as Gillette, are still made from Sheffield precision stainless strip. **2/** The above local firms might no longer make **open** or **safety razors** but **Swann-Morton & Jewel** make one and a half **million** scalpel & industrial blades a **day; Durham-Duplex** make industrial blades; **James Neill** makes tools; **Rodgers & Wostenholm** make beautiful pocket knives. **3/** A new firm, **Edwin Jagger,** make metal, reuseable safety razor holders as a reaction against throwaway plastic.

John Read (1744-1805) founded the **Sheffield Smelting Co.** ca. **1765**, originally extracting silver from scrap **Sheffield Plate.** He moved from **Green Lane** to **Royds Mill** (then a farm cum-cutler's wheel cum-corn mill owned by a family called **Rhodes**- hence **Royds)** in **1787,** where the firm still are today, and you can walk alongside it by the river **Don** during daylight hours as part of the **Five Weirs Walk.** Now the firm is known by its initials **Thessco,** in the city based **Solpro Group,** rolling, drawing & supplying silver sheet, bar & wire to the trade as well as producing coin blanks in precious metals- see their coins & commemorative medals as well as a silver ingot in the **Millennium Galleries. British Silverware Limited,** inheritor of famous names such as **James Dixon (qv)** & **Cooper Cobb** and formerly in the **Solpro Group,** is now trading separately.

rec recreation ground. The one serving **Parkwood Springs** was surfaced with ash & fine clinker from the nearby **Neepsend Power Station,** resulting in scraped & bloodied knees when playing football there. **Neepsend** lads preferred playing with **rolling mill** workers on cobbled streets, judging cobbles and steelworkers' clogs less hazardous than clinker and the unknown wild hill tribes **on'Springs**.

reight right. **Orreight (mi ol')** Are you alright (my old (love)) Title of a best selling book on Sheffield dialect- well, a few thousand copies.... **Ee's a reight un'; a reight lad.** Sometimes spelt **reyt,** and there is a local band called, in text message speak, **OR8.** Note that in our region **reight** is **never reet. Reight** may be **reet** in Lancashire but here **reet** is **wrong. Orreight?** (Though, confusingly night is **neet..qv).**

reight Sheffield good quality: a phrase known nationally in the 16th/17th centuries, though, of course, pronounced elsewhere as **right Sheffield: "First therefore be the choice of your penknife. A right Sheffield knife is best." – Peter Bayles 1590** in his book "The Writing Schoolmaster."

Renishaw Hall & Gardens Italianate gardens, bluebell woods, laburnum tunnel, lake, stone stables with nice stainless steel nymphs central fountain, art gallery, museum, café & shop. The hall is lived in, home to the **Sitwells**, and is not normally open to the public. It is a pity more is not made of the coal, steel and iron foundation to their wealth. Cannon balls for Nelson's Navy were made at **Renishaw Foundry** (to be fired in anger from **Walkers, Rotherham-made** cannon) and latterly the foundry, part of **British Steel Corporation,** cast ingot moulds etc. before closure.

The **Sitwells** also built **Mount Pleasant (qv)** at **Highfield**.

revits rivets- see also **pins.**

Richards established by **Gebrueder Richartz** in Solingen, one of the family set up on Broomhall Street in 1932 making, as did the German factory, cheap pocket knives under the **lamppost** brand. By 1940 they employed 400 in Sheffield at two factories and during the war had to switch to military production, including spanners. Ironically, both factories were bombed in the **blitz** but in 1945 they built a huge three storey factory on **Moore St.** mass producing diecast scissors, chrome vanadium kitchen knives & **pocket knives,** these with celluloid **coverings** sold carded in volume, especially in seaside towns, with **coverings** showing views of Cleethorpes, **Skeggy,** etc. etc. etc. Young boys; Scouts, Cubs, Boys Brigade etc. were major buyers in those far off days when boys and their parents behaved, could be trusted with knives, and teachers had authority in schools. Employment peaked in 1960 at 800 but when the three Germans involved in the firm died or retired in that decade, and Far Eastern competition appeared at the bottom end of the market, Richards began to go downhill. Merger with **Rodgers-Wostenholm,** then ownership by U.S. Imperial Knife, followed by Western Knives was a disaster, with insolvency, then closure in 1983 & demolition in 1985. A depressing big shed called Wickes is now on the site. The top quality names, **Rodgers & Wostenholm (qv)** survive, fortunately, back under Sheffield ownership.

The once regarded as "cheap tack" **Richards** knives,with pictures of Bournemouth, Bridlington, Blackpool etc. now command £5-£10 each in second hand shops.

Ringinglow an interesting little settlement at the extreme western heights of Sheffield just outside the **Peak Park,** yet, a milestone tells us, only 5 miles from the Town Hall. A 3 storey former tollhouse called the **Round House** (even though it's octagonal) stands at the crossroads, opposite a nice solid stone pub/hotel called the **Norfolk Arms.** A horse riding school, an alpaca farm and café, a ski and sledging slope into the **Mayfield Valley,** and a rockinghorse factory are near to hand. **Ringinglow** is a high point on the 14 mile **Round Walk** and you can either follow the little river **Porter** down towards **Hunters Bar**, or the **Limb Valley** down through **Whirlow Park** and **Ecclesall Woods** to **Abbeydale.**

Sheep farming is the main occupation in the idyllic **Mayfield Valley** and on the slopes up to and beyond **Ringinglow Road** which heads in a straight line from near the **Hammer & Pincers** right up to the **Norfolk Arms;** so straight that I once told my 5 year old daughter that Roman soldiers had probably marched up here 2000 years earlier. "Did they have a picnic?" she asked. I was reminded of this when we took an Italian along the road and he said, with the green fields bounded by stone walls containing hundreds of sheep, it was **"paraiso."** This was despite gangs of spring lambs racing round the flocks, and, on the road, motorists **trazzing** along at 90 m.p.h.

Away from the road and surveying the bucolic scene it is hard to imagine that the area once housed important industries. To the east of **Ringinglow** the ruins of

Copperas House stand near the head of **Limb Brook,** and **Smeltings Farm** is off the **Ringinglow Road;** to the west hidden in the moors are the **Brownhills Quarries,** now home, in Spring to a pair or two of ring ousels. At **Ringinglow** itself there were once coal mines and a wire mill. **Robert Cook(e)** of **Hathersage (qv)** owned the wire mill, off **Fulwood Lane,** in the early 19th century till 1855 when it was taken over by Mr. Broomhead, also of **Hathersage.** It was last worked by **George Winterbottom** of Batley, possibly related to **Hy. Winterbottom** of **Oxspring Works,** who were taken over by **Unsco** of **Kiveton** in 2004. **Robert Cooke** discovered **coyal** in his mill yard and sank a 60 yard shaft, but had too many problems with **watter,** so filled it in. A more successful mine was the **Deep Sick Mine,** which was somewhere between the little church on **Sheephill Road** (see **"lad"** for an anecdote by a Victorian preacher here), and **Moorcot,** the house with the ultra-neat hedges before the junction with the rough track called **Houndkirk Road,** which winds its way towards **Fox House. Muriel Hall** tells us that **Deep Sick Mine** was dug by **Robert Trotter** whose parents had come from Scotland to Durham in 1750. Astonishingly, **Robert** had been kidnapped by colliers and brought to **Barnsley** to work, before escaping to sink his own pit by **Ringinglow Road.** He must have achieved some wealth since he lived at **Moorcock Hall** (sounds better than **Grouse Hall),** last inhabited by **Hiram Trotter** in 1892 and demolished in 1911, the stone being used to build **Moorcot.**

Rivelin one of the tumbling streams, now, like the **Loxley**, **Porter,** & **Moss** valleys, breathtakingly beautiful, that fuelled Sheffield's industrial prowess right to mid-late 19th century, when steam and then, much later, gas & electricity took over - see **Sheffield Rivers.**

Robbo Robinson

Robbo's **Robinson's** factory in **Chesterfield,** well known for medical dressings, bandages, and packaging.

Robertus le Coteler has the honour of being the earliest Sheffield knife maker of whom we have written evidence (1297 AD). There were probably many more knifesmiths of his and earlier generations, and he is listed along with three or four named scissorsmiths. Certainly, enough knives were made here and of good enough quality to be sold around the kingdom, and to be both listed in the inventory of **Edward 111's (qv)** wardrobe, and get a mention in **Chaucer (qv).**

Rockingham Pottery at **Swinton, Rotherham 1745-1842** and from **1826-1842** fine porcelain including a 200 piece dessert service for William 1V. There is a fine collection at **Clifton Park Museum, Rotherham,** including the massive 'rhinocerous' vase.

Rockley Furnace solid stone built remains of a blast furnace, originally about 25 ft. high rescued from dereliction by **Sheffield Trades Historical Society** (now S.Y.Industrial History Soc.) Built in 1652 by Lionel Copley, it is believed to be the oldest surviving bast furnace in Britain, and possibly Europe. Copley & his successors made use of local iron ore and wood from the surrounding forest, converted to charcoal. Charcoal heated by powerful bellows (**belluses**) worked by a **watter wheel,** reached 1100 degrees C causing the iron to melt and collect at the bottom of the furnace. After running slag off this was periodically **tapped** =run along a channel into **pigs,** or **sowes,** and from these into a series of smaller moulds ressembling piglets. Production of **cast iron (=pig iron)** was ca. 400 tons p.a. much of it used at **Rockley Smithies** and **Wortley Forge (qv).**

Rocko short form for **Rockingham Street** said by the many hundreds of **light trade** workers in the vicinity, e.g. **Bill Thornton,** silverware **saw piercer,** quoted by **Valerie Answer**.

Joseph Rodgers for several hundred years was the most famous cutlery firm in the world, and the biggest. Most famous for pen & pocket knives, their **Star & Maltese Cross** trademark dates from 1682. By 1870 **Rodgers** employed 1200 who made weekly**:** 5000 dozen table knives & forks**;** 1500 pairs of carvers**;** 1500 dozen pocket knives**;** 1200 dozen razors**;** & 1200 dozen scissors. In the last week of 1870 10 tons of cutlery was despatched to the U.S.A.= one seventh of all Sheffield's trade. Imagine the upset when the American government periodically doubled import duty to protect their own manufacturers.

Their name became synonymous with the very best quality around the world**; Rodgers** 'best cutlery' is mentioned in ' Moby Dick' (1851)**;** In his book 'Hindoo Holiday- an Indian Journey' (revised 1952), J.R. Ackerley quotes an old man who begged medicine for his sick wife, the best medicine, **'Rogers medecine.'** The author explained this meant medicine as good as the steel articles (from **Rodgers, Sheffield).**

Pocket knives marked with **Rodgers No 6 Norfolk St.** address are highly prized by collectors. This, **Rodgers'** main factory, head office and magnificent showroom was opposite the G.P.O., which now awaits redevelopment. (It was a characteristic of many Sheffield cutlers to stamp or etch their name and address, as well as trade mark on blades, which, as well as showing absolute confidence in quality, was a nice form of advertising for further business.)

See fine examples of **Rodgers** work in the **Millennium Galleries,** and stand in amazement before **the Year Knife** with its 2000 blades, now in the trust of the **Hawley Collection (qv),** and **the Norfolk Knife,** 3ft. x 75 blades 'multum in parvo' **sportsman's knife** with exquisite etchings of the White House, Crystal Palace, Chatsworth, Arundel & Windsor castles + Queen Victoria etc. in **the Cutlers' Hall.**

roller the man in charge of a **teeam** rolling steel.

rolling mills **Hadfields; Brown Bayley; Neepsend Forge & Rolling Mills; Rotherham Forge & Rolling Mills; Sheffield Rolling Mills; Andrews Toledo** and many others towered above the Sheffield scene in the past. **Continuous mills** at **Corus; Alloy Steel Rod; Firth Rixson; Brinsworth; Sheffield Special Strip** and others keep on rolling and there are several **hand mills,** including **Bedford Steels** and **Pro-Roll** producing smaller lots of very special metals.

rolls set in pairs one on top of the other, solid, hardened cylindrical polished steel, cast or forged, through which steel billets, bars, strip etc. are rolled.

rooad road; roadway (in a mine). **In' rooad** in the way; **Gerraht o'rooad; Ah'll pay these bills, then th're aht o'rooad- done wee.** (out of the way- done with). An old **Fulwoodite** quoted in Muriel Hall's 'More of Mayfield Valley' says of three sons of a local farmer, **'Th're like horse muck- all o'er rooad.'** (The three were said to be 'the Three Merry Lads' of the **Lodge Moor** pub sign.

rooak, roke fault iside a knife or steel bar, billet etc. found by **grinding** (knife), or **chipping/deseaming** (billet).

rooarin' crying (babies); **He's allus rooarin'** not to be confused with:

rooartin', roartin', rortin' yelling out, bawling out in vulgar fashion. Said of immature young men when, for example, binge drinking along **West Street,** or on the way from **Hillsborough** or **Bramall Lane.** See also **blartin'.** (Note in Collins **rort** is given as an Australian word for a rowdy party). In **Chaucer's** 'The Reeve's Tale' ca **1386**, the rough Miller (he who carried a Sheffield knife), after supping too much ale, "snorteth" in his sleep "as an horse" while his wife accompanies him so loudly "Men might hir **routing** heeren a furlong." **Routing** here appears to mean snoring, but the word has a resonance with the Sheffielders' **rooartin'** don't you think?

The Rotherham Plough a lighter, horse pulled plough patented in 1730 by **Joseph Foljambe** of **Eastwood** & **Disney Staniforth** of **Firbeck.-** see sample in **Clifton Park Museum (qv).**

roughers men/women **buffers** who do the basic **buffing** or **roughing** of spoons, forks & holloware, getting rid of marks and indentations.

'Round Walk a 14 mile walk in Sheffield's often picturesque, always hilly south west. Called the **Sheffield Round Walk** but the full walk around the city is 54 miles. The original south west walk, **Hunters' Bar** to **Graves Park** via **Ringinglow, Ecclesall Woods** & **Beauchief Abbey** was 10 miles, and was thanks largely to the generosity of silverware manufacturer turned mail order pioneer, **J.G.Graves.** A few years ago the walk was extended from **Graves Park** through woodland (unfortunately very heavily littered by uncaring, undisiplined schoolchildren), to **Meersbrook Park, Brincliffe Edge Woods** & **Chelsea Park** back to **Hunter's Bar**.

rozzil, rozzel **resin** boiled in a small saucepan mixed with whitening & ash to make it bind, like sand & cement. It is used to fix tangs of blades on to a handle (**xylo,** stag, wood, pearl etc.), the handle being **rozziled on. Roughers** would also use molten **resin,** dribbling it on a leather **buff** to give the leather a hard glazed edge.

rubbin' rag . He gus all round 'houses an' ends up wi 'rubbin' rag. Irate Park Gate Iron & Steel Co. employee who has to field off an irate buyer ringing down the grades; sales director, sales manager, office manager until he found someone to deal with his call.

I want rubbin' aht & drawin' ageean long suffering patient to G.P.

rubbin' stooan for whitening stone doorsteps, sills etc.. Made from bits of old grindstone if not the propriety brand **Donkey stooan (qv).**

John Ruskin (1819-1900) Victorian artist & writer, a mini Leonardo da Vinci with a multitude of interests, a social reformer whose influence is still felt today- see **Freeman College.** He was both horrified by Sheffield's smoke and heavy industrialisation, and impressed by the independence & skills of men in the cutlery trade. When asked why he had set up his museum in Sheffield he replied: **In cutler's ironwork we have (in the town of Sheffield) at this epoch of our history, the best of its kind done by English hands, unsurpassable, I presume, when the workman chooses to do all he knows, by that of any living nation.** (See also **bloody minded!)**

His 1875 museum and home for some years was at **Walkley Bank,** between **Bole Hill Road** & **Bell Hagg Road,** & the stone building is still called **Ruskin House.** He moved his collection to the larger red brick building**Meersbrook Hall** in 1890 where it stayed until 1953. (This fine building in **Meersbrook Park** is now the Park Department's H.Q.) The Guild of St. George founded by **Ruskin** to oversee the collection then moved it to Reading before bringing it back to Sheffield, first to **Norfolk Street,** then to the **Millenium Galleries.**

S

Salmon Pastures area by the **Don** at Attercliffe, named when it was a salmon river, and apprentices are on record as complaining that they were given too much of the fish.

sam collect, get hold of; "**Sam up yon hammer. Sam 'od will tha.**" Take hold (of it) will you; German **sammeln**

same as I say as I say.

sand rat **moulder** in a **casting shop.**

Sanderson Kayser formed by the merger of two fine **crucible,** then **electric arc** steelmakers **Sanderson Brothers & Newbould** and **Kayser Ellison (qv)** in 1960. **Sanderson** were founded in 1776 and became known for fine saws as well as for crucible steel. The American steel & bearings manufacturer, Timken, bought the merged firm out about ten years ago and have their European office on **Newall Rd.,** but closed the Sheffield factories down. Fortunately the sites are mostly reoccupied by genuine Sheffield-owned firms, such as **Mayflower Engineering,** who have custody over a large 19th century **crucible shop,** which is grade 11 listed by English Heritage.

Sanderson's fine saws, with their **Pax** trademark are now made by **Garlick** in the city.

saw grinder a tough job especially considering it could involve **pit saws** with 6 ft. blades and **circular saws** up to 6 ft. diameter, used in woodyards or for cutting steel **billets** etc. (see **brat, armoured).**

Attempts in mid-Victorian times to mechanise grinding led to the **Sheffield Outrages (qv)** instigated by the **saw grinders union** secretary, **William Broadhead.** The saw grinders regarded themselves as the aristocrats of the Sheffield trades doing work that involves considerable skill as well as strength. Take a modern hand ground **Garlick** hand saw and see how it is finely taper ground from handle to tip, as well as from back to cutting edge.

G. Calvert Holland (qv), Sheffield Physician in his 1843 report wrote**: "** The saw making branch may be regarded as generally healthy. It is an occupation in which considerable muscular exertion is required, and yet the labour is not so severe as to make an undue call upon the energy of the system. The men are mostly well-formed and strong, and live to a fair average age. The saw grinders are among the most powerful of the artisans......a great part of the labour is heavy, but several circumstances concur to prevent this exhausting the vital powers. The wheels....are mostly propelled by water...,in the exquisitively beautiful situations within a few miles of the town**;** consequently the artisans are liable to numerous interruptions either from too much or too little water, (leading) many of them to add to this employment the cultivation of the soil.They have frequently either small farms, or plots of ground for garden purposes. The wheels are always well ventilated in consequence of dilapidated windows and roofs, for they are proverbially in a bad condition." Being in the country and with good wages they lived well. Wages could not be suppressed by boys doing the job because the articles were too heavy for lads "of tender age or delicate constitution" to hold. As with all grinding there was the danger of an exploding stone, but saw grinding was healthier than in other trades because it was done "on a wet stone & the position of the grinder is standing, so that the lungs have free play."

saw piercer craftsman who uses a fine fretsaw to cut decorative patterns in silver spoon & fork handles, fish eaters, fruit bowls etc. Long production runs would tend to be stamped out by machine and there is not enough demand for 'one-offs', or short runs to justify a firm specialising in the craft today. **Taylor & Taylor** was such a firm on **Button Lane** many decades ago, though the art can still be found, done surprisingly fast and accurately by, for example, silversmith **Graham Madin** at **Hugh Crawshaw Silversmiths.**

saw setter skilled man who **sets** a saw's teeth alternatively to one side then the other, using a special hammer.

saw smither hammering, or **smithing** a saw so that it lies flat, straight.& stress free is another very skilled job. Without the **smithers** intimate knowledge of steels and his ability to make the blade run true by flattening it & relieving stresses within it, a large 5ft. diameter saw, for example, could wobble uncontrollably & dangerously in use. **Ken Hawley** quotes words to the effect that for every pound the **smither** earns, a **bob** is for hitting the saw, and 19 **bob** is for knowing where to hit it.

scale oxide coating that forms on hot metal. **Scale** has to be constantly brushed away during **hot forging** to ensure it doesn't get embedded into the forging. At **Kelham Island museum** see the film of men dealing with scale forming during **rolling** at the **heavy plate mill**, **River Don Works** by throwing bundles of birch twigs onto the hot steel before it enters the rolls. The sap in the twigs explodes on contact with the steel blasting off the constantly & rapidly forming scale before it is embedded in the steel. A modern method of removing scale- e.g. at **Brinsworth Hot Strip Mill** is by directing multiple jets of water down on to the strip as it emerges rapidly from the **train** of **rolls** and heads for the **coiling machine.**

scale tang knife flat tanged knife with wooden, **xylo, bone,** etc. handle.

scales **covering (qv)** = handles of wood, **bone, xylo, antler** etc. on **pocket knives,** or butcher's, cook's knives etc.

scallops as well as meaning slices of potatoes fried in the chip pan this can also refer to the edging on a **Granton** knife (still made at their factory off the Parkway).

Scarlett & Whiting were Sheffield's last specialist **horn cutters** who closed in 1977. **Stag & buffalo horn** handled cutlery & pocket knives are still made on a small scale & cutlers cut & shape their own pieces, some shed from Scottish deer but most from two types of Indian deer. (Indian deer antlers are not so pithy, but the government there controls supply to keep prices high, and has a 'take it or leave it' attitude). **Buffalo, bull & cow horn, walrus & elephant's tusks** are not shed, unlike **deer** which shed their antlers annually. Despite this an Italian woman, confronted with piles of antlers at **Mitchell's** sword, dirk, hunting & bowie knife manufacturers, enquired anxiously whether any cruelty was involved in obtaining them. "Don't worry," Stuart kidded her, "I go to **Chatsworth** at dead of night & shoot them myself."

Pairing & matching pieces of **stag horn** for products as varied as **pocket knife coverings, steak knife** or **carving knife, fork & steel** handles is quite a task with various shapes, surfaces and colouring to contend with.

Cow, ox & buffalo horn is malleable when heated, and can be pressed to various shapes in moulds. There is little demand today but **horn pressing** was once a specialist trade & there was even a pub in **Burngreave** called **the Presser's Arms.**

scissors (sithers q.v.) putter-togetherer skilled man who assembles the traditional forged steel scissors.

scissors (sithers) setter another skilled job involving slightly bending & twisting scissor blades by hammering, to ensure the edges meet all way down at the cutting point. (Applies to the traditional forged steel scissors only).

scissors' stick (sithers' stick) a steel rod looped at the end holding by their **bows** up to, say, 60 pairs of scissors for carrying from **forger** to **hardener** to **grinder** to **putter-togetherer.** Formerly carried on his shoulder by a man on foot, or in a cart, and now occasionally seen being put in the boot of a car.

scoff to eat heartily. Used nationally but included here in memory of an old walking friend who, regretting his inability to get down a substantial three-course meal said; **'As a lad tha could scoff 'lot.'**

scopperel heard used in the phrase **'running about like a scopperel.'**

scoppodile overactive child

scorch overheat a blade when **grinding,** spoiling its **temper.**

scraps (in 'chip oyal) bits of fried batter free with an order, or sold separately to lads who would ask for **'Ayporth o' scraps please, Missis.'**

scratted bone scored bone **scales** of a knife to give a good grip, often dyed brown to imitate stag horn.

scroam, scrome, scrooam to climb over, clamber over (awkwardly), to wriggle about, usually of a small child or toddler. **He's forever scrooamin' o'er 'furniture: Stop scrooamin' about or I'll put you down: She loves scroamin' up 'rocks at Stanage. (Hunter's "Hallamshire Glossary" 1828** gives "to walk or climb with long strides & awkwardly).

Scunny, sunny Scunny Scunthorpe, Lincolnshire town to the north east of Sheffield. If Sheffield/ Rotherham is the **special steels** jewel in the crown of British steelmaking, **Scunny** is its **bulk steels** jewel. New plant to roll **railway lines** has recently been installed. (This product was a speciality of the big Sheffield firms in Victorian times until production was moved to Workington, which, in turn, has now lost the business to **Scunny - see Cammell).**

scutch glancing blow to the back of the top of the head, given to an errant boy by parents, teacher or policeman. This instant justice, nipping trouble in the bud, if used today would save police time & paperwork and free them from costly hovering lawyers.

The meaning has altered over the years, since **Hunter (1828)** gives **scutch** "to strike with a thin switch, which is often done to snakes by cruel boys." He goes on to quote Macbeth**:** "We have **scotched** the snake, not killed it."

scythes these & other agricultural tools such as **sickles, grass hooks, hay & straw knives** etc.were a **Hallamshire** speciality established in settlements in Derbyshire around Sheffield such as **Dore, Dronfield, Norton, Eckington, Ridgeway, Mosborough, Moss valley, Troway** as well as **Conisborough (Staniforth,s Severquik works), & Norton Lees (Linley's** at **Bole Hill,** top of Cobnar Rd. by **Graves Park).** The trade came to be dominated by large firms such as **Tyzack Sons & Turner** of **Abbeydale & Little London Works, Spear & Jackson, Robert Sorby & Skelton's.** Sheffield remains the centre of U.K. manufacturing though demand is reduced to a comparative trickle thanks to mechanisation in agriculture. Names such as **Tyzack; Spear & Jackson & Sorby Hutton** survive and if you are lucky you can see **Ron Staley** grinding scythes & hay knives at **Abbeydale Hamlet** for **Tyzack's. Ron** carries on the tradition of doing sub contract work, previously done at the **Hamlet** by **Ron Wilkinson** and, before him, **Wilf**

Coates. They have all worked with artificial grindstones, **carborundum** etc. **Wilf's** father & grandfather worked with sandstone wheels and both died of silicosis.

The big scythes with blades today, say 3 or 4 foot long and American ash, or aluminium **snaths** = handles, are **patented scythes.** These have thin sheet steel blades riveted to a forged steel or iron back for strength.

Crown scythes had blades up to 5 foot long **forged** from **crucible steel** up to the 1940's/1950's, then from **high frequency** or **electric arc steel.** Since **crucible steel** was expensive it was often used for the cutting edge only, being **forge-welded** in a sandwich between 2 **wrought iron** flat bars. We read that the scythes were **forge-welded** by water-power, first under the **steeling hammer** at 126 blows a minute, then, after reheating, under a **plating hammer** at 65 blows a minute. Blades would then be straightened, hardened in oil and ground.

Himsworth, in his 1953 book, **'The Story of Cutlery'** quotes a nice epitaph, which I've not been able to trace, in **Norton** churchyard commemorating the death of scythe-maker, **Mark Tyzack** in 1795:

My scythe and hammer lie reclin'd
My bellows too has lost his wind
My iron is spent my steel is gone
My scythes are set my work is done
My fire's extinct my forge decayed
My body in the dust is laid.

seconds knives, tools etc. rejected by quality control after manufacture. Applies around the country to manufactured goods, usually textiles, though it is interesting to read **Hunter's 1828** definition as "flour not of the finest quality." He quotes Shakespeare: (Flour) **'**that is not mixed with **seconds.'**

selt sold

sempt seemed**; he sempt orreight to me.**

sen self, an essential word in Sheffield grammar**: missen, thissen, yersen, hissen, hersen, ussen(s), yersens, thersen(s).**

sit thissen dahn; 'I used to car missen dahn' (on a rug in front o'fire)- Harry Brearley, inventor of **stainless steel.**

- here' s to me, mi father's son, not forgerrin missen.

- "Hear all, see all, say nowt; Eight (eat) **all, sup all, pay nowt; An' if tha ever does owt for nowt, allus do it for thissen."** (Yorkshireman's motto).

set team of men on a **forge** or in a **rolling mill.** See Karl Marx and reference to boys working on the night **sets.**

set pot also known as **'copper** = big copper or cast iron pot, perhaps 2ft. wide x 2ft. deep, set in brickwork above a firegrate in the corner of the kitchen to wash clothes in, or bathe babies and toddlers.

He's a 'eead as big as a set pot said of an opinionated, boastful chappie.

coil set **bars** or **strips** of steel, after being cut to length from **coil,** especially those cut from the end of the **coil,** can assume a bent shape, i.e take the **coil set.** I saw this problem on a sales visit to Caterpillar France, Grenoble 20 or so years ago. The top strip of a bundle 0.70/0.80% carbon , cut to length and all perfectly flat on leaving **Brinsworth hot strip mill** had experienced a pronounced bow.

wheel set assembled 4 or 6-wheeled bogie at each end of a railway carriage.

setter man who sets up machinery in a **steel** or **tool works.** See also **saw setter & scissor setter.**

setting in assembling an **open razor.**

S.H. One T quality poor quality steel, bulk steel - see **clog iron.**

shadow pen knife without **bowsters (bolsters).**

shank part of a pair of scissors between **bows** and blades.

sham pin a pin in a table knife handle that does not pass through the **tang**. It serves no purpose appart from making the knife seem higher quality than it is.

shant (pronounce as in **ant,** not shan't) used in the phrase, **all o'er shant**= all over the place. (H)**er clooers are all o'er shant.**

sharra, sharrabang charabanc, touring bus, coach.

Sheaf see **Sheffield rivers**

Sheaf Works like **Green Lane Works** & **Globe Works,** a classical building which resembles a country house, but was in fact part of an early, 1820's, integrated tool & steel works. It was built to take advantage of the proposed **Sheffield & Tinsley canal** by **Wm. Greaves** who had previously set up as a steelmaker, first on **Hollis Croft,** then on **Division Street** The **Greaves & Stephenson Blake (type foundry)** families intermarried and the successor firm, **Thomas Turton** was in the **Stephenson Blake** group of companies until quite recently. See the fine building, now occupied by **Ant Marketing** near the **canal basin,** and close to a firm busily making **steel narrow boats. (Turton Springs** in **Neepsend** make heavy **coiled springs** for railways & commercial vehicles, as well as **anti-roll bars** for such as Rolls Royce, Aston Martin & Lotus. I believe their pedigree to be, however, **The Neepsend Steel** group rather than the **Stephenson Blake.** The neat factory on **Burton Street** is a world away from **Turton Bros. & Matthews** on **Neepsend Lane,** which I never passed as a boy in the upstairs **back bay** of a tram without peering through their steel-barred, glass-free windows, seeing men **hot coiling springs**, and whistling; **"And was Jerusalem builded here, among those dark satanic mills.")**

shear steel **blister steel** flat bars produced in **cementation furnaces (qv)** were heated & hammered together (forge welded) to produce the raw material for the famous Sheffield **shear steel** knives. Often, **shear steel** bars were reheated, folded and hammered again to give the doubly sought after **double shear steel,** a steel of more uniform quality that could take a most wicked edge. A metallurgist today would find **shear/ double shear steels** 'dirty', with too many non-metallic inclusions, and though 'cleaner' **crucible cast steels** never fully superseded them, **electrically melted stainless steels** eventually did from the 1920's onward. **Shear/double shear steel knives** would rust if not cared for, and if not rusted would develop a greyish patina in your kitchen drawer, sometimes, unlike the hygenic **stainless steel,** harbouring the smell of food. And yet! And yet! A few strokes with a steel would give the old knives the edge that gave Sheffield its reputation for sharp knives. **Crucible cast steel** knives were, and **stainless** knives are often as sharp, but never sharper than the standard consistently achieved by **shear/double shear.** So many of us have samples, or memories of ordinary table or dessert knives stamped **shear** or **double shear steel, Sheffield** worn to a thin strip and so flexible that it can/could be almost bent double, still slicing & cutting after so many decades of use by mothers, grandmothers, great grandmothers back to the time it was made, usually in Victorian times. Pick up a knife for a couple of quid, stamped **Joseph Rodgers, Cutlers to Her Majesty** and it is **VR,** not **E11R.** Ninety-nine out of every hundred knives sold in Great Britain in the late Victorian era were reputed to be made in Sheffield and all the best makers; **Joseph Rodgers; Walker & Hall; Mappin & Webb; George Wostenholm; Taylor's Eye Witness; Michael Hunter; Brookes & Crookes; W & S Butcher; Christopher Johnson; Thomas Turner; Harrison Brothers & Howson** etc. etc. boasted that their knives were hand -forged, hand-ground **shear** or **double shear steel.** A grinder, complimenting another grinder in a **Walker & Hall** brochure of the time is captioned saying; **'Tha'rt as sharp as ahr double shear steel.'**
Look for knives of this era- though they may be stamped with the name & address of a shop in Leeds or Leamington, London or Lewes, they would have been made in Sheffield- and admire how the blades are forged & ground using hand, eye, & touch, finely tapering both from back of blade to cutting edge, and along the length from bolster to tip. Note the flexible blade and the vicious edge after a few strokes of the steel.

A sure way of checking that a knife is made from **shear** or **double shear steel** is by the faint **'thumb' (qv)** imprint on the base of the blade where it joins the bolster, on the **pile side (qv)**= reverse side (= side opposite the **mark side).** This was formed when the **iron bolster** was forge-welded on to the blade, the imprint lingering despite subsequent **grinding & buffing**.

sheepfoot pocket knife with a straight, tapering blade larger, naturally, than a **lambfoot.**

Sheffield Assay Office Silver knife handles had been made in Sheffield since at least the 1600's but it was thanks to **Thomas Boulsover's (qv)** invention of what became known as **Old Sheffield Plate,** that the silverware trade was brought to town. By the 1760's **Old Sheffield Plate** manufacturers were also making silverware and resentment grew that these goods had to be sent by stagecoach to London for assaying and hallmarking. A petition was eventually presented to Parliament by Sheffield & Birmingham silversmiths and, depite keen opposition from the London Goldsmiths' Company, an act was passed in 1773 allowing the two upstart towns to set up their own **Assay Offices.** It helped their case that Goldsmiths' Hall were proved to have stamped goods below the legal standards as silver. Legend has it that the Sheffield & Brummie silversmiths celebrated at the Crown & Anchor pub off the Strand, and while there Sheffield chose a **crown** as its **hallmark,** and Brum chose an anchor. Pieces in **Old Sheffield Plate** and **sterling silver** of exquisite quality from these early times can be seen in museums made by a raft of companies, most new to the town: **Mathew Fenton, Richard Creswick, Tudor & Leader, John Winter, Thos. Bradbury** and **Sissons,** etc. **Tudor & Leader** are remembered by a square and a house respectively, **Bradbury** by the definitive book on **Old Sheffield Plate** and the standard booklet on British hallmarks. **Sissons** Victorian premises still stand on **St. Mary's Road** amidst a furry of early 21st century redevelopment- see the stone pitchers, bowls etc. on the roof reminding us of the building's silversmithing past.The firm's metalworking skills are still alive, though, like many other traditional Sheffield firms they changed tack, moving to the big stone-built ex-cotton mill at **Calver,** then to **Chesterfield** making stainless steel wash basins and urinals. The firm are now owned by Swiss firm, Franke.

Sheffield's Office has been in various parts of town including; **Fargate, Leopold Street (1881-1958)** & **Portobello Street,** and will shortly move to new workshops, laboratories and offices at **Owlerton.** In the late Victorian/ early Edwardian era when silver cutlery & holloware was the height of fashion satisfied by major firms such as **James Dixon; Walker & Hall; Mappin & Webb,** some exceptional orders were handled by the **Assay Office,** then on **Leopold Street.** Biggest of all was a bedroom suite made totally in sterling silver by **Mappin & Webb** for an Indian Maharaja, including a four–poster bed that had to be manhandled through a window with frame removed.

The E.C. has cast a baleful, envious eye on the British hallmarking system. Their standards are often lower than ours- e.g. German standard for silver goods is either 400 or 800 parts per 1000 whereas British standards are 925 (sterling silver) or 985 (Britannia silver). In January 1999 in the name of "free competition" within the E.C. the standard per 1000 stamped on an item replaced the sterling silver **lion** mark & the **britannia** mark**;** the date letter became voluntary, & the **town mark (**in Sheffield's case, now a Yorkshire rose for silver) is the same for British & foreign products. When Italy held the presidency they wanted even this watered -down hallmarking system to be abolished, deeming that the manufacturers can be relied upon to keep the standards. This from a country whose prime minister had been accused of corruption!

Sheffield is currently the busiest of Britain's 4 Assay Offices accounting for 34% of the trade. Back in 2001 13 million items were assayed and stamped, or laser etched with the hallmark. Of course, now all have the one **town** mark we no longer know which are foreign and which Sheffield made, but there are grounds for optimism**:**

When demand for silverware declined after WW2, being largely replaced by stainless steel, and the largest firm, **British Silverware Ltd. (**comprising **Mappin & Webb, Walker & Hall** plus **Elkington's** from Brum) eventually closed their factory on **Queen's Road,** the future for the industry seemed bleak, especially taken together with **Dixon's** subsequent closure of their **Cornish Works.** However, many craftsmen from these & other big companies, set up on their own, surviving to this day on top quality work. **Hugh Crawshaw Silversmiths, Perry Glossop, Malcolm Marsden, Bob Lamb, Keith Tyssen, Camelot Silverware,** & **Jim Porteus** spring to mind. Some of their more intricate, one-off work such as model jet aircraft, the steam engine Flying Scotsman & Supertram etc.etc. match anything the Victorian craftsman could do.

Carr's of Sheffield have bucked the 'downsizing' trend to become one of the largest manufacturing silversmiths in Europe and, together with **Hallam University,** have developed a non-tarnishing silver. Meanwhile **British Silverware** have been revived in **Attercliffe** keeping some grand old names such as **James Dixon** & **Cooper-Cobb** alive.

Finally, a stream of new silversmithing talent, nutured largely at **Hallam University's Psalter Lane** site, are working in the city at, for example, **Persistence Works.** The new **Freeman College,** too, promises to train silversmiths, as well as pewterers & cutlers.

All the above trends and developments are relevant to this section because the **Sheffield Assay Office,** under **Assay Master, Ashley Carson** has constantly sponsored & publicised the trade, commissioning trophies, supplying silver for competitions, financing a workshop at **Persistence Works** for metalwork graduates starting out in business, etc. etc.

Sheffield Bus Museum formerly located, ironically, in **Tinsley Tram Sheds,** they moved to **Rotherham** in 2007 and are now **South Yorkshire Bus Museum.**

Sheffield car industry with its steel industry and engineering expertise Sheffield could have been the centre of the British car industry rather than Coventry & Brum- and a better job would have been made of it, I hear you cry. **Henry Austin** was a local lad who set out to rival Ford, but in Oxford, and steel firm **Hadfield's** took over Bean's, who made cars in the West Midlands- a very unsuccessful venture. More important as far as the Steel City is concerned, are the cars of extraordinary variety made in Sheffield in the first half of the 20th century, examples of which are on display at **Kelham Island Museum,** hopefully having escaped the ravages of the **2007** flood. These range from the **Ne'er a car,** which was midway between a car and a motor bike, to the **Sheffield Simplex,** which rivalled Rolls Royce. The **Simplex** was made at **Tinsley** at a factory adjacent to the 'Sheffield end' of **Steel Peech & Tozer,** and the owner, **Earl Fitzwilliam** vetted prospective customers to ensure they were suitable persons to drive his cars. (**Fitzwilliam** works still exist, now occupied by **Darwin's** who make steel castings). Only three of the hundreds of beautiful **Sheffield Simplex** machines made exist today, of which one is on show at **Kelham,** another has pride of place at the **Powerhouse Museum, Sydney,** and the third is privately owned. At the other end of the scale, though not as small as the **Ne'er a car** was **Richardson Cars** produced in some volume on **Aizelwood Road-** once again, an example can be seen at **Kelham. Laycock-Charron** (or was it **Charron-Laycock?)** an Anglo-French high quality car was made on **Archer Road (**see **Laycock's).**

Sheffield Castle by 1116 the Norman **William de Lovetot** was lord of **Hallamshire** and was probably the builder of the original mott and bailey castle, which was destroyed in 1266 during the Barons' War. Four years later **Thomas de Furnival** was given permission to build a substantial stone castle on the same site and this dominated Sheffield for almost 4 centuries, largely under the **Shrewsbury** dynasty (qv). The huge building, as big as Warwick Castle, was razed on orders from Parliament in 1649-50, and Sheffielders lugged away as much stone as they could, leaving only the most massive foundation stones lurking under the current **Castle Market.** Hopefully, when the market is relocated to the **Moor,** the castle remains will be preserved & displayed to give us and future generations some idea of the powerful building that dominated the small town at the junction of the **Don** and the **Sheaf.** See also **Sheffield Manor.**

Sheffield Cathedral of St. Peter & St. Paul was built in 1430, on the site of an earlier church dedicated by the Archbishop of York in 1280. The site was said to have been a place of worship since 800AD and a church built about 1100AD. An Anglo-Saxon elaborately carved cross, made about 900AD & now in the British Museum, probably came from the site. It was found in a cutler's workshop, one side hollowed out for use as a trough! Obviously the London museum thought it was too valuable an artefact to leave with people of such a practical frame of mind, though we have got a replica in Weson Park museum. The spires of Victorian **St. John's**, Ranmoor, and **St. Marie's Roman Catholic Cathedral** are equally impressive, and the whole of the venerable **Rotherham Minster** perhaps even more so, but walk into **Sheffield Cathedral** and you walk with our history, from the tombs of the mighty **Talbots** (see **Shrewsbury**) to tributes to the Royal Navy **H.M.S. Sheffield** ships, to the 1996 extensions & 1998 **Lantern,** to today's new building facing **Campo Lane** housing the **Archer Project** for the homeless.

Sheffield City Hall completed in 1932 and refurbished in 2006/7, this fine building of Darley Dale stone has a main Oval Hall seating 2000+, a ballroom underneath it, and a smaller **Memorial Hall** to the rear commemorating the dead of WW2. Two huge stone lions once dominated the stage but the conductor, Sir John Barbarolli, as well as others complained that they ruined the acoustics, so they now grace the entrance to Tarmac's head office in Wolverhampton.

Sheffield College of Art was on **Arundel Street,** alongside its **Junior Art Department,** which had evolved after the **1902** Education Act, and which was permeated with the Ruskinian concept of bringing art to Sheffield's future workers. The **College** itself was, of course older, founded **1843,** with, this being Sheffield, a strong craft bias. Our hero **David Mellor,** the U.K.'s foremost industrial designer, and master silversmith & metalworker, was at **J.A.D.** then at the **College;** taught by **William E. Bennett** who had been a pupil of the famous Arts & Crafts silversmith, **Omar Ramsden (1873-1939),** who had trained at **Sheffield School of Art** in the **1890's. Charles Green (1836-1916)** founded the **Sheffield Arts & Crafts Guild** in **1894** and work of the most exquisite craftsmanship was produced over the years- see the work of **Helena Ibbotson (1877-1962), Joyce Himsworth** and **Godfrey Sykes (1825-1866)** at the **Millennium Galleries. Sykes'** paintings too, in **Weston Park Museum** are worth seeing. **George Fullard,** the sculptor, whose 'Walking Man' can be seen, striding in front of the **Winter Garden,** and 'Woman with Child' seated in the nice yard in front of the **Unitarian Chapel** on **Norfolk Street,** was a pupil at **Sheffield College of Art,** as was artist **Kenneth Steel. Steel (1906-1970)** is best known for a series of 'See Britain by Train' posters for British Railways, nostalgic reminders of a vanished era, that adorned platforms & waiting rooms in the mid 20th century. A copy of his poster 'Over the Sea to Skye' realised £1,015 in 2004. The happy scenes hid a dreadful personal tragedy when both his wife and his mother were killed in the **Sheffield Blitz.** **The Sheffield College** was also bombed in the **Blitz** and, after a wartime temporary home, set up on **Psalter Lane** at the former **Bluecoat School (q.v.)** A move back to town is now imminent in **2008** under the aegis of **Sheffield Hallam University.** The **College** has always been best known for its silversmiths and, as well as **David Mellor; Brian Asquith, Keith Tyssen, Roy Risdale, Malcolm Marsden** & **Peter Devine** have made a name for themselves. In their footsteps are a great number of younger craftsmen & women, who have gained prizes & commissions throughout the U.K., helped by mentors such as **Bob Lamb** & **Keith Tyssen** & by **Assay Master, Ashley Carson.** Here are some of them: **Brett Payne, Chris Knight, Alex Brogden, Victoria Kershaw, Owen Waterhouse, Paul Butler, Suzie Horan, Katey Felton, Rebecca Joselyn, Jessica Briggs, Rebecca Lawley, Amba McNamara, Brian Saynor.** So , if you want a future family heirloom, seek them out.

Sheffield Flood when Sheffielders in the late Victorian & the Edwardian eras talked of life 'before the Flood' they weren't referring back to Biblical times, but to the disastrous breaching of the **Dale Dyke** dam embankment, battered by a storm on the night of 11 March 1864. Over a hundred million gallons of water roared down the **Loxley Valley** into the **Don Valley** drowning 240 people, probably three times that number of cattle & other animals, as well as destroying mill wheels, houses, factories and bridges that stood in its path. A body was later found as far downstream as Aldwarke, beyond Rotherham, where the Don now makes its way quietly through the huge steelworks there. We have now, of course, another great **Sheffield Flood** to talk about- the overflowing of the **Don, Sheaf, Rother** and smaller streams in June 2007 after days of continuous heavy rain. Scenes of helicopter rescues & floodwater in **Forgemasters** and **Meadowhall,** at the **Wednesday** ground, on the **Wicker,** at **Catcliffe** and at **Toll Bar** in **Donny** were shown around the world.

Sheffield Football Club **'The Club'** have the honour of being the world's first football club, being established 24th October 1857 and currently commemorating their 150th anniversary, along with **Sheffield Chamber of Commerce,** who were founded in the same year. Two men of the Sheffield metal trades, **William Prest & Nathaniel Creswick,** cricketers with **Sheffield United Cricket Club** at **Bramall Lane** since it opened in 1855, were instigators of **'The Club'** with the twin aims of keeping the men together with the winter game, and keeping them fit for the cricket season. Another man in the metal trades, **Asline Ward,** let the football club have use of his potting shed & greenhouse on **East Bank Road** as H.Q., and over the years matches have been played at various sites including **Owlerton, Bramall Lane, Abbeydale** (for 60 years), &, more recently, **Don Valley Stadium.** There have been some low points- at one game at **Don Valley** there was only one paying spectator- but now, with the help of sponsors, especially **Bright Finance,** they have their own stadium, **the Bright Finance Stadium** at **Dronfield,** and have achieved promotion as well as world-wide publicity in their anniversary year.

Initially **'The Club'** played matches among themselves; married men v single; workers v managers etc.but when **Hallam Football Club,** the world's second, were formed in 1860, came the world's first inter-club match, won by **Sheffield 2-0.** The rivalry of this **'Rules'** derby continues to this day.

'The Club' pioneered many rules & features of the modern game such as solid crossbars, free kicks, corner kicks, throw-ins and heading the ball. When they went to the Oval to play London, the Cockney players and fans were reduced to hysterics at the sight of the Sheffielders butting the ball with their head!

In **1878** **'The Club'** with the **Sheffield F.A.** held the world's first floodlit match at **Bramall Lane** and 20,000 turned up to watch. The London Daily Telegraph reported that "the players of Sheffield took to this science-provided sport as naturally as though they had been born in electrical phenomena." The article ended, " The good folk of Sheffield are so far in advance....that they are prepared to accept and make the best use of everything which science provides; and as the new electric light, with its wonderful powers, comes before them, they utilise it for the sturdy game which Englishmen love so well."

The city may not be the power it was in football, but it may be noted that the head of the F.A.; the chairman of the Premier League; and the chairman of the referees' association are all Sheffielders. Mention, finally, should be made of a previous President of the F.A. **Sir Charles Clegg,** who played along with his brother for **Sheffield F.C.;** played in the world's first international England v Scotland in **1872,** and later as a referee, was in charge of the **1882, 1892** and **1923** Cup Finals. Locally, **Clegg House,** home to the **Sheffield & Hallamshire Football Association** honours his name.

Sheffield Forgemasters with 7 factories & now, thankfully, back in sound Sheffield hands. Walk past their big shed opposite the **Hallam FM Arena** and you will hear the characteristic powerful hum of their **electric melting shop** that makes the steel for some of the world's biggest castings & forgings. Recent orders have been for huge castings up to 325 tons for parts for forging presses in South Korea & Austria, for mill housings for Chinese plate mills, and for up to 150 forged steel 61 ton vessels to carry nuclear waste between Germany & France. In the early 1990's they made huge forgings for the petro- chemical industry, the biggest of forged tubes machined so beautifully that **Forgemasters** had it on film to get further orders round the world. Unfortunately they had been duped & the parts were, in fact, for Saddam Hussein of Iraq's Super Gun, the orders being received in Sheffield via Brum & Belgium. It caused quite a stir at the time with parts held at U.K docks, MI 5 & 6 involved & the inventor of the Super Gun, a Canadian called Bull shot dead in Belgium by the Israeli secret service. It was claimed the Gun could have had civil use- to fire satellites into space, being much cheaper than using rockets. The only good from the sorry tale was that **Forgemasters'** craftsmanship was given worldwide publicity and they had been paid for the work by letter of credit.

Sheffield Forgemasters most famous site is the canyon formed on **Brightside Lane** by their **River Don Works.** Look into their yard and you are likely to see some huge pieces of steel- some are placed on transporters with 72 wheels to take them overnight to the docks on the Humber, or locally, to **Davy-Markham** for machining.The impressive three storey red brick listed offices, originally built for **Vickers (qv)** sometime after they moved here in 1864 from **Millsands,** are no longer used by **Forgemasters,** but the firm are a worthy successor to the Victorian giant. Anyone who is lucky enough to see a massive glowing hot octagonal ingot being forged in their **10,000 ton forging press,** which stands like an altar in the middle of a huge shed the size of a cathedral nave, can see why **Sheffield** retains its name for steel. A man stands before the ingot, silhouetted black against its yellow heat, making small movements with his hands & fingers- signals for another man in a glass-protected pulpit on high to operate machinery to move the beast. Move & press, move & press, the forging gradually takes shape under their watchful eyes. Occasionally the **forgemaster** will approach to measure the forging with a giant pair of callipers, then hastens back before he catches fire **.........** Are such men well paid for such a responsible, hazardous job? We trust so, but probably not as much as M.P.'s claim on expenses.

Sheffield Outrages violent disputes in the Victorian era involving non-union workshops &/or machine grinding taking over from hand grinding, principally in the saw trade. There was **rattening** of non-union shops, line shafting belts were cut, dynamite put in grinder's **trows** for it to ignite when the grinder set to work and the first sparks flew. When problems escalated, men injured & intimidated, & bosses were shot at a Royal Commission into the violence was set up in 1867. See **Abbeydale Hamlet** & **Wm. Broadhead.**

Sheffield Manor was situated at a high point in the middle of the 2000 acre deer park of the Lords of the Manor. It began as a medieval hunting lodge, then in 1516 the 4th **Earl Shrewsbury** decided to build a sustantial residence in brick and stone as an alternative to his mighty **Sheffield Castle** at the bottom end of the deer park, at the junction of the **Sheaf** & the **Don.** While the **Talbots, Earls of Shrewsbury, Lords of the Manor** lived in Sheffield from 1406 to 1617 their properties were well cared for, their industrial enterprises flourished, and the Sheffield cutlers were well regulated & protected. The **Turret House,** a hunting lodge, renovated in Victorian times, standing in the outer courtyard is the only roofed building remaining on the 4 acre site. See also **Shrewsbury** and **Mary Queen of Scots.**

Sheffield Newspapers **The Sheffield Daily Telegraph - (**now only weekly, unfortunately, as the **Sheffield Telegraph)** since 1855, and **The Star** since 1885 have kept Sheffielders up to date on the local news. Some prefer to buy the weekly paper only, with more subjects in depth and less coverage of depressing gory crime, but the **Star** has some excellent features, covers industry & women's interests well, and the Diary under **Martin Dawes** keeps a wry, amused eye on interesting people in the Sheffield region. Older people recall perhaps most of all brilliant cartoonists such as **Whitworth 1925-1998 (Telegraph)** and **Harry Heap 1901-1968 (Star** and **Green 'Un).** In his **History of Sheffield, David Hey** covers an earlier press over some tumultuous times, especially in the 1790's round about the time of the French Revolution, with **Joseph Gales,** radical editor of the **Sheffield Register,** founded 1787,; printer of a sixpenny pamphlet edition of **Paine's "Rights of Man";** fleeing to America in 1794 to avoid arrest; his paper becoming the **Iris** under his former assistant, **James Montgomery (qv),** who was also arrested in due course. There was mob violence against the enclosure of **Crookesmoor** and against town magistrate **Vicar Wilkinson** at **Broom Hall.** A man was hanged; a **Colonel Athorpe** rode into crowds waving his sword leading to the death of two men. There was much cause for anger; ancient rights were being ignored; the price of corn was sky high; and, of course, Sheffield wasn't represented in Parliament.

Sheffield Pewter if **Sheffield Plate** became known as the poor man's silver, is pewter the even poorer man's plate? Be that as it may, there is much skill involved in the various processes carried out today by a score of firms here which dominate the U.K. trade.The leading companies are **English Pewter Co.** based in the former **Brown-Firth Research** building on **Princess Street,** where **Harry Brearley** discovered stainless steel; **Wentworth's (qv)** at **Darnall; Edwin Blyde** on **Little London Road;** & **Pinder's** on **Arundel Street.** Traditional pewter had high lead content and was cast into plates and tankards etc., mainly in the city of London. As with silver, the pewter trade came to Sheffield in the 18th century, though the metal used wasn't called pewter but **britannia metal,** or **white metal.** This, not to be confused with **britannia silver,** was an alloy with **92% tin** and the rest copper and antimony, invented by **James Vickers** of **Garden Street.** This metal was capable of being spun into goblets, tankards, coffee pots etc. and is, in fact, today's **pewter.** Some of the larger silversmiths and cutlers such as **James Dixon** and **Cooper Brothers** had large pewter departments well into the 20th century, but the different metals needed different techniques, e.g. care had to be taken when soldering pewter in view of its low melting point, and now the trades are separate. See **Wentworth's.**

Sheffield Plate; Old Sheffield Plate see **Fusion Plate; Fused Plate** and **Thos Boulsover.**

Sheffield Rivers the **river Don,** along with its tributaries **Sheaf, Porter, Rivelin/Loxley** with smaller streams **Limb Brook, Blackburn Brook** and the **Moss** were instrumental in Sheffield's growth and fame. Their 'tumbling water' sustained over a hundred mill sites over the centuries providing power to roll, forge, & grind steel, giving the small town an unassailable lead, in knife-making especially, despite its geographical isolation.

Sheffield Silver see **Sheffield Assay Office** above.

Sheffield & South Yorkshire Navigation during the 16th century the **Talbots, Earls of Shrewsbury (qv)** based at **Sheffield Castle** had looked after the interests of Sheffield cutlers and, since English iron ore had low iron content, say 22% Fe, had arranged for Spanish iron, made from iron ore with ca. 70% Fe to be imported by water to Bawtry. This entailed a final 20 mile journey overland to Sheffield and in 1696 the cutlers petitioned parliament for the river Don to be made navigable, both for the import of iron and the export of their finished goods.**Gilbert Talbot,** the 7th, and last, **Earl of Shrewsbury** had died in 1617 and his successors the **Howards,** Earls of Arundel & Surrey, later becoming the **Dukes of Norfolk,** lived on their estate in Sussex and had no interest in the cutlers' trade. David Hey quotes Francis Foljambe in 1723:

"I do not know any persons of fortune or substance concerned in the prosecution of this scheme but the **fiery blades of Hallamshire (**who, as my **Lord Howard** calls them) a pack of beggarly rascalls that cannot finish their church and yet must be for making the river navigable, purely to gratifie a conceited humour that they may appear great in their opposing the gentlemen of the country."

The **Duke of Norfolk** had thwarted a Bill championed by the **Cutlers' Company** in Parliament in 1721, fearful that water supply to his dams & **Attercliffe Forge** would be affected, but reached a compromise with the **Company** that the Navigation should end at **Tinsley.** Acts of Parliament in 1726 & 1727 gave the **Company** responsibility for making the **Don** navigable from **Doncaster** to **Tinsley Wharf,** which scheme was completed in 1751. Eventually the **Sheffield Canal** was constructed, avoiding the **Don,** involving a flight of locks up from **Tinsley,** then a level 3 mile run to the **Canal Basin,** which opened to huge celebrations in 1819. The impressive **Sheaf Works** (see above) took advantage of the **Navigation,** as did subsequent huge steel concerns such as **Thomas Firth** who had their own wharf to handle iron from Sweden for them to convert to Sheffield steel. In general though, the celebrations were overly optimistic since the finish of the canal coincided with the start of the railway boom, and finished goods, and of course people, from Sheffield were overwhelmingly carried by rail.

The canal remained best for bulk traffic; iron of course, but also flour, limestone, aggregates and, above all, coal and **Sheffield & South Yorkshire Navigation**

Co. was formed in 1889 with the grand aim of deepening the waterway to enable 500 ton vessels reach the centre of Sheffield. The **Navigation** went from Sheffield to Tinsley to Rotherham to **Swinton** (with **Dearne & Dove** branch from Barnsley & minor, but important, waterways to **Elsecar** & **Wosborough collieries);** to Doncaster, then after Barnby Dunn via the **New Junction canal** straight north-east to join the Aire & Calder Navigation to Goole & Hull on the Humber, or east via the **Stainforth & Keadby canal** to the Trent. **Swinton** is highlighted above because it is home to the **Waddingtons,** boat builders and carriers as well as being tireless campaigners for the waterways over the years.

Waddingtons were instrumental in getting government approval for improvements along the canal as far as Rotherham in the early 1970's (though not the Tinsley-Sheffield section which is hindered by the Flight of locks at Tinsley). Estimations of potential trade were optimistic however, and plans to take thousands of tons a year of steel bars & coils, mainly from the 11inch continuous bar mill at **Roundwood** for export to Germany by a BACAT scheme = barge aboard catamaran, in 1974 were scuppered by Hull dockers. This wonderful scheme would have allowed barges to sail directly onto the catamaran and sail off up the Rhine from Holland to Germany, without any handling at the Humber or Dutch ports, but in those days unions were bolshie and all powerful.

The huge steelworks at **Aldwarke (qv)** now exports a hundred thousand tons per year to Germany and the same amount to the U.S.A. via the Humber. **Waddingtons** operate a new wharf at the plant, built 2006, to shift 500 ton bargeloads to the docks. Hopefully this will be profitable for the works and the carrier, though water transport has to be subsidised to compete with road & rail. In the other direction the press reports that a 600 ton bargeload of machine oil is shipped from Hull to Rotherham weekly.

Boatbuilding has featured prominently along the Navigation right to the Humber ports & in his 'Industrial History of South Yorkshire' Derek Bayliss tells us of a disaster memorial in **Rotherham Minster** to 50 people, many of them children, drowned in 1841 when a boat overturned on being launched into the Don at **Masborough.** Though Sheffield to Tinsley is a backwater for freight with its 90 ton load limit it is a haven for narrow boats & pleasure boats, two of which can be used as floating hotel alternatives to the nearby Hilton. The **Canal Basin,** now renovated & called **Victoria Quays,** houses shops, offices and appartments and just beyond the **Wicker Viaduct** is narrow boat builder **John Wilson,** manufacturing steel bodied boats. On passing by in 2007 there were about half a dozen in various stages of manufacture from steel bodies to finished, painted and polished craft. The firm supply completed vessels as well as the shells for other firms to complete.

Sheffield stand a comparatively new expression for a steel bicycle rack, named after the silver toast rack. Boris Johnson, prospective new mayor of London, has written that more **Sheffield stands** are needed in the capital to reduce the epidemic of bike theft. (He'd just had another stolen).

Sheffield steel, tools and cutlery we must pay tribute to the many hundreds of thousands of people over the years, whose products, made with such skill, have ensured, and still ensure the development of the region, and have played no small part in the advance of civilisation. If steel could talk - what a story! Our industrial history should include the **Tankersley seam** of **iron ore** worked from prehistory to Anglo-Saxon times; Romans working at **Templeborough;** then, ignoring the Dark Ages to mention the **Cisterian monks**, from Kirkstead Abbey who brought iron working to **Abbey Grange, Rotherham** in **1116,** and then to **Wadsley, Chapletown, Attercliffe** & **Wardsend.** The monks of **Beauchief Abbey (q.v.)** worked iron at **Greenhill** and **Norton** in the 14th century, but after the Dissolution of the Monasteries, control of ironmaking passed from the religious orders to landowners & aristocrats. **Sir Francis Wortley;** the **Sitwells** at **Renishaw;** the **Spencers** at **Cannon Hall, Cawthorne-**all were involved in the iron trade. Towering over them all locally were the **Shrewsburys,** with **iron forges** on the **Don** at **Oxspring, Wadsley** and **Attercliffe,** controlled from their imposing **Sheffield Castle.** Contemporary with the development of these industrial enterprises there was the rise of the small manufacturer; the **Little Mester,** the knife and scissor makers, who would need little more than a **stiddy(q.v.),** hammers and **belluses(q.v.)** and fuel to work in a **smithy,** probably attached to their house. The first printed evidence of this sturdy breed of independent craftsmen is in tax returns of **1297.** There was reference to **Sheffield cutlery** in an inventory of King Edward 111's possessions at the Tower of London in **1340,** and, of course, the well-known reference to a **Sheffield whittle** in Chaucer. The best known **Talbot,** the 6th **Earl of Shrewsbury,** apart from the strain of being married to **Bess of Hardwick,** and having to hold **Mary Queen of Scots** prisoner for 14 years, & on top of his iron enterprises, kept a close, sympathetic eye on the development of the cutlery trade; on quality, apprenticeships, conditions, holidays etc. **Wheels** were built on the fast flowing streams, and **trows (q.v.)** were hired out to self-employed **grinders.** In **1575,** when the industry was already being described as ancient, the **Earl** is recorded as giving a case of **Sheffield knives** to Lord Burghley, being "such things as my poor country affordeth **with**

fame throughout the realm." The local cutlers eventually overtook all English competitors to become, by the end of the Victorian era, the largest cutlery manufacturing centre in the world.

The first written evidence of **cementation steel (q.v.)** manufacture in Sheffield are the furnaces of **Samuel Shore** (ancestor of **Florence Nightingale)** in **1705.** The manufacture of the celebrated product of the **cementation furnaces; shear steel (q.v.)** advanced because cutlery flourished, and **Huntsman (q.v.)** came to Sheffield & invented **crucible steel** here ca. **1740** because it was becoming the nation's steelmaking centre. **Crucible steel** was the world's first 'proper,' reliable steel, melted to consistent qualities, and such was Sheffield's dominance that by **1843** the town produced 90% of British steel, & 50% of Europe's. **Cementation & crucible** steel making became known as the **'Sheffield methods.' Harry Brearley (q.v.),** though working in a laboratory, had a brother and a father who were **crucible steel melters,** and he never ceased to admire the skills, passed down the generations, in the industry. He set down his opinion that Sheffield's prosperity **"depends more on the acute observations of workmen, or of managers who have been workmen than on anything else.The pivot of the business lies in the workmen, and it lies in his brainy distinction between good and ill & not merely in his brawn & muscle." Crucible steel** was essential for hard wearing parts of machinery feeding the industrial revolution, for dies and tools, and was even used for huge castings when, say, a thousand **crucibles** would be wheeled to the casting pit. The giants of Sheffield steel: **Vickers, John Brown, Cammell, Firth, Hadfield, Jessop, Steel, Peech & Tozer** etc.etc. spread down the **Don Valley,** the first three having their own shipyards at Barrow, on the Tyne, on the Clyde, and on the Mersey. However, **crucible steel** was much too expensive for bulk items, such as railway lines & ships plates, and iron was used for these, until **Henry Bessemer** came along in the **1850's,** with his revolutionary method of making mild steel in bulk. When the Sheffield men proved reluctant to try his method, he decided to 'beard the lion in its den' and built his own works right between **John Brown's** and **Cammell's.**

On to the great **alloy steel** discoveries: **Osborn** produced & developed **Mushet's** tungsten high-speed steels; **1882/3 Hadfield** invented manganese & silicon steels; **1913 Brearley** invented & developed carbon-chromium steels; **1920 Hatfield, Brearley's** successor at **Brown-Firth Research** developed the celebrated **18/8 Firth Staybrite stainless.** From the **1930's** right up to today there has been & still is research in steels and alloys for the most exacting purposes, from Frank Whittle's jet engine, to **2007** collaboration with **Boeing** and **Messier-Dowty** for titanium landing gear.

"If a steel product in service must withstand continuous high stress; if it must operate without distortion or softening at high temperatures; if it must not corrode with heat or acid or both; if it must not expand appreciably under the combined influences of high stress & high temperature, then it is likely to be made in Sheffield, of Sheffield steel." When **W.D. Hargreaves** of the **British Iron & Steel Federation** wrote this for the British Association for the Advancement of Science, in **1956,** he gave the number of men in **1954** producing & shaping steel as **41,617,** & those converting it to a machined product as **51,349=** two fifths of the employed population of the city. The quality & the huge amount of steel & products made today still hold true, but total employed is, perhaps, a quarter of the number in **1954.**

With the dominance & romance of **steel** the **Light Trades** have lost out in this little survey**:** suffice to say that various firms have their own small sections, and names of manufacturers, and their products are recalled with affection & pride. Across the little river **Porter** from **Waard's Brewery** the multi-storey factories of **James Neill & Dormer Tools** seemed to be the size of a small town, smell of machine oil in the air, and sounds of steel being worked in the production of their beautifully engineered tools. Best auger bits, **Gilbow?;** best saws, **Sanderson,** or **Spear & Jackson?;** best spanners, **Bedford,** or **Gordon Tools?;** best files **Ralston** or **Bedford?, Firth Brown** or **E.S.C.?;** best wood chisels, **Marples** or **Stormont Archer?;** best cold chisels, **Jenkinson?;** best wood-carving tools, **Hy. Taylor** or **Marples?;** best planes, **Record** or **Stanley?;** best screwdrivers, **Stead?;** best vices & clamps, **Record?;** best hacksaws **Neill's 'Eclipse'?** There is no question, none were made better in the world, and the firms that remain still make the best, though the world hankers after the cheapest. And we can't even begin to list the myriad of firms making a multitude of cutting, drilling & milling tools, and machine knives. We should mention that whereas **steel & engineering** is very much a man's world, outside the offices, in the **Light Trades** women come into their own & are more than a match to the men. As for the **cutlery firms,** such a vast number of firms have kept the tradition of fine craftsmanship alive from generation to generation that we can only mention a selection; **Butler's** inc. **Leppingtons; Rodgers; Ibberson; Wostenholm; Walker & Hall; Mappin & Webb; Taylor's Eye Witness; Harrison Brothers & Howson; Christopher Johnson; Wm.Hutton; Thos. Turner; James Dixon .....** Look in your cutlery drawer and if you can't find any Sheffield items go to one of the specialist shops and buy some, before it's all gone! No apologies are made for stressing the **steel & allied trades:** if you're a Sheffielder, even if don't work with metal, you will have had plenty of friends & relatives who did, and we honour them all.

Sheffield stout a black beer, the best known of which was **Jubilee stout,** made at **Hope & Anchor** brewery. See **breweries.**

Sheffield Town Hall imposing and confident Victorian architecture designed by **Mountford** and built of **Grindleford stone**, Sheffielders joked that they thought it was made of **coyal** before it was cleaned up following the Clean Air Act. When Queen Victoria pressed a button to open the building in 1893 while sitting in her carriage at the town hall steps, she little realised that the automatic electrically-operated door mechanism didn't work, and two blokes hidden behind the doors pulled them open at a given signal. A smart stone sculpture celebrating **Sheffield trades** such as **saw grinding & crucible steel melting** forms a frieze and the statues of Queen Victoria, and way up high atop the 210 ft.tower, Vulcan himself might be pleasantly surprised to see nowadays a crisp new union jack flying proudly.

The **Sheffield Trades** the **metal trades; heavy** is heavy and **light** is light and never the twain should meet- but they did of course, quite often, and still do to a certain extent: The **'Heavy Trades'** are **steel & engineering**, the **'Light Trades'** are traditionally **tools & cutlery, pewter & silverware-** though today we should add products as diverse as **ice skates, scalpel blades, jewellery, & gripples (qv). Heavy & Light** met when almost every steelworks had a tool department making **cutting tools, files,** etc: **Samuel Osborn, Neepsend Steel & Tool, Jonas & Colver, Firth Brown** spring to mind. (Oh yes, many made **springs** also) A general rule of crushed thumb is; **"If tha can pick it up it's 'Light Trades, if tha can't it's 'Heavy Trades."**

Sheffield Trades Technical Society was formed in 1918 under the aegis of the **Faculty of Engineering** at the **University of Sheffield.** They were pioneers in giving the man & woman in the street an insight into what went on behind the sometimes forbidding walls of Sheffield industry. Works' visits in the early 1960's are recalled as magical, with, for e.g., heated tank tracks being dropped into an oil-quenching bath at **Annealers Ltd., Penistone Road:** gruesome medical instruments being ground at **Eschmann Brothers & Walsh** on **Corporation Street: Stanley planes** being assembled on **Rutland Road.** The Sheffield society had led to the formation of the **National Trades Technical Society** with branches in other great industrial areas, but they gradually folded or were superseded. **Sheffield Trades "Tech."** ended in **1966** when their exhibition tent off **Devonshire Street** (now **Devonshire Green)** blew over in a gale, leaving them with debts of £3000. They left a vigorous offshoot however, formed in **1933** by some of their members, and members of the **Cutlers' Company**, concerned that, with the speed of progress, many Sheffield tools of the trades and machines were becoming obsolete. This **Society for the Preservation of Old Sheffield Tools** has the honour of being the world's oldest local industrial history & preservation society. How many of us have seen, even today, some of the thousands of metalworking firms, when relocating, shutting down, changing product emphasis, or replacing machinery, chucking the old into a skip or on a low loader to get it weighed in at an East End scrap firm for grading & subsequent melting in **arc furnaces,** (where it becomes nice new **Sheffield steel.)** They **'get rid'** as **Ken Hawley** says- unless **Ken** or other members of the Society get there first. (see also; the **Hawley Collection).** The Society changed its name to **The Sheffield Trades Historical Society** in **1949** and is now **The South Yorkshire Industrial History Society.** Over the years, as well as tools & machinery, it has been instrumental in saving buildings which are unique, and of world industrial sigificance. See **Abbeydale Industrial Hamlet; Wortley Forge; Shepherd Wheel & Rockley Furnace.**

Sheffield United & Wednesday Football Clubs see **Blades & Owls.**

shek shake. **'Shek thissen'**= look lively.

Sheldon a quiet, unspoilt village on a hillside that drops down to the river **Wye,** the A6 and **Ashford in the Water,** it is best known for the stone ruins of the **Magpie lead mine** that stand on top of the hill, on a plateau rather, looking strange in the middle of fields populated by sheep & cows. It is at its eeriest when seen in a mist or against a darkening sky, especially if you're aware of tales of ghosts of murdered miners from a neighbouring mine, victims of fire & smoke in disputed seams. The imposing stone remains have been described as the best example in Britain of a 19th century lead mine, surpassing **Lathkill Mine** or any in Cornwall. A connection with the **Steel City** is that the last owner,in 1923/4 was **Garlick,** the Sheffield sawmaker.

Sheldon knife a pocket knife, without a spring, usually with **lambfoot (qv)** or **pruning blade,** that can be opened, used, and shut again using one hand only.

Shepherd Wheel a venerable water-powered **grinding hull (qv)** in **Whiteley Woods** in the **Porter Valley.** The earliest reference to it is in the will of **Wm. Beighton, cutler** of **Stumperlowe,** who, in **1584** bequeathed his sons "all my interest......in...one **watter whele** called **Potar wheel...**which I have of the grant of the said Lord." (= **George Talbot,** the **6th Earl of Shrewsbury).** A Mr. Shepherd owned the wheel in **1794** and had a **teeam** of self-employed **grinders** working there. Grinding continued at the wheel right up to the 1930's when it was under the protection of the forerunners of the **Sheffield Trades Historical Society (qv).** It is now, along with **Abbeydale Hamlet** and **Kelham Island Museum** part of **Sheffield Industrial Museums.**

Shevvild, Old Shevvil' old pronunciation of the **Steel City.** Not so common now, but still heard **'if tha keeps thi lug oyals oppen.'**

Shiny Sheff nickname of the first **H.M.S. Sheffield,** a cruiser in WW2, so called because so many of its artefacts were made of stainless steel, many given by the city. See the ship's bell, memorials and flags in the **cathedral,** honouring the men of this cruiser and the destroyer **H.M.S. Sheffield** which was lost in the

Falklands war.

Shiregreen once a small settlement of farmers and people in the cutlery trade, mainly making **forks,** it is now the site of a large, generally well-tended, housing estate. It was the dream of many a house-proud woman in the little terraced houses with outside toilets & no bath, built cheek-by-jowl alongside huge black corrugated sheds of the steelworks, to get a nice council house, **up Shiregreen.** The estate was built on rolling hills with the 200 acre **Concord Park** on high, dropping down to **Woolley Wood** on its northeastern slopes. This ancient woodland with its sessile oak, yew and wild cherry is best remembered by **Old Firpanians** for its beds of bluebells, and the insistent boom of **Shardlow's drop hammer** making **crankshafts** in the valley bottom. Now, unfortunately, you are more likely to hear the insistent swish of traffic on the M1. (Read: **Woolley Wood** ancient bluebell wood **FUELLING A REVOLUTION** The woods that founded the steel country, by **Mel & Joan Jones).**

shop workshop of varying size for e.g. an **engraver,** a **cutler, grinder, buffer, silversmith etc** or groups of craftsmen; a **(machine) shop,** say at **Davy-Markham** or **Fooargemasters** can be huge, and biggest of all, larger than a cathedral's nave is the **melting shop** at, for e.g. **Aldwarke.**

shop flooer shop floor, usually of steel & engineering works- see **flooer.** **shop flooer talk** rumour or gossip, sometimes rude, rarely malicious. A friend tells of when he worked at **Metros (qv)** and two men habitually indulged in **shop flooer talk,** the rest would sing loudly above the hum and clash of machinery a rousing chorus of the hymn **"Tell me the old, old story- tell me the old, old story-tell me the old, old story, of Jesus and his love."**

shooers shoes: **Get thi shooers on if tha'rt gooin' in 'yaard.**

shot blades **shear steel blades** hot forge-welded to an iron bolster & tang. **shot sithers** scissors with **bows** of iron forge-welded to steel blades.

shot blasting ; shot peening similar processes, angular **shot** used for the former, spherical **shot** (steel balls of various sizes) for the latter. The cold working effect of **shot peening,** as well as cleaning the steel being treated, improves its fatigue limit or endurance.

shove 'a'penny a national game which **Bramall Woodware, Mary Street,** made until spring 2007. Instead of a halfpenny, Shakespeare tells of **shove-groat,** and now it should be shove-pound to keep up with inflation.

Captain Percy **Sillitoe** big & bold chief constable who quelled vicious gangs in Glasgow and Sheffield in the 1920's. No pussy-footing then; no greedy, hovering lawyers, bent on securing taxpayers money to defend criminals. Big coppers were sent in, if necessary roughing-up the evil-doers. **Sillitoe** later became first head of MI 5.

The **Talbots; Earls of Shrewsbury** when **Waltheof,** anglo-saxon Earl of Northumberland and **Lord of Hallamshire** was beheaded in 1076, despite being married to a niece of William the Conqueror; a Norman, **Wm. De Lovetot** became Lord and began a blood line with property & influence in our area that extends right to the **Duke of Norfolk** today. The **Lovetots** became the **Furnivals (see Sheffield Castle),** then, briefly, the **Nevilles** before the **Talbots,** the mightiest and most influential of them all, burst on the scene.

John Talbot, who had married Maud, daughter of Sir Thomas **Neville** & Joan **de Furnival,** became **Lord of Hallamshire** in 1410, though, since he had properties around England, especially in Shropshire, and since he spent much of his life in the Army, he probably saw little of his formidable keep at the junction of the Sheaf & the Don. He served as Lord Lieutenant in Ireland 1414-1419; led the Army in France 1428; was knighted, then in 1442 made **Earl of Shrewsbury** and finally was killed in battle in France in 1453. His son, **John Talbot** was also a soldier and was killed at the battle of Northampton in 1460 (and is buried at **Worksop**), but Shakespeare in Henry V1 part 1 has him cradled, dead, in his dying father's arms in the battle in France. Indeed the Bard's play centres so much on the heroism of the first **Earl of Shrewsbury** it could as well be titled **Talbot!** It tells of his valour with 6000 men surrounded by 23,000 French as he "Enacted wonders with his sword and lance: Hundreds he sent to hell, and none durst stand him;....." "His soldiers spying his undaunted spirit, **A Talbot! A Talbot!** Cried out amain, and rush'd into the bowels of the battle." Sir John Fastolfe should have defended the rear but had run away (was this Falstaff, Shakespeare's buffoon?), and **Talbot** was speared in the back by a "base Walloon" and taken prisoner. He lives to fight again, skirmishing with Joan of Arc - not very chivalrous here, calling her a witch & a strumpet; his soldiers put terror in the French by crying out his name; as one puts it: **"The cry of Talbot** serves me for a sword **." ....**When the Countess of Auvergne asks to see **Talbot** so "That she may boast she hath beheld the man Whose glory fills the world with loud report" he senses a plot and has soldiers on call when he visits her. She scorns him when she sees him:

" Is this the scourge of France? Is this the **Talbot,** so much fear'd abroad That with his name the mothers still their babes? I see report is fabulous and false: I thought I should have seen seen some Hercules, A second Hector, for his grim aspect, And large proportion of his strong-knit limbs. Alas, this is a child, a silly dwarf! It cannot be this weak and writhled shrimp Should strike such terror to his enemies."

(Was **Talbot** like so many military heroes from Caesar

to Napoleon, Nelson to Montgomery, small in stature and not particularly good-looking, but capable of inspiring intense loyalty in his men?)

The Countess prepares to chain his arms & legs "That hast by tyranny these many years Wasted our country, slain our citizens, And sent our sons and husbands captive." At this **Talbot** calls in his soldiers explaining that these are "his substance, sinews and strength, With which he yoketh your rebellious necks, Razeth your cities and subverts your towns And in a moment makes them desolate."

She immediately weakens, & apologises; he insists he is not offended by the 'fair lady' and wants nothing more from her than good food and wine for his men. "With all my heart, and think me honoured To feast so great a warrior in my house" –are her closing words.

King Henry V1 receives him in Paris & in gratitude for **Talbot** reclaiming 50 fortresses, 12 cities, & 7 walled towns plus 500 'prisoners of esteem', gives him the title of **Earl of Shrewsbury.**

When he is finally killed in battle his honours & titles are listed, including, as well as **Earl of Shrewsbury** and **Knight of the noble order of Saint George;** Lord Cromwell of **Wingfield** and **Lord Furnival of Sheffield,** but Joan of Arc brings the defeated English back down to earth with: **"**Him that thou magnifiest with all these titles Stinking and fly-blown lies here at our feet."

The first three **Earls of Shrewsbury,** though **Lords of Hallamshire,** didn't live in their castle at Sheffield, but the 4th, 5th, 6th, & 7th **Earls** lived in the castle or in the magnificent **Manor** house, built by **George Talbot,** the 4th **Earl.** All four were buried in the **Shrewsbury Chapel** in **Sheffield Cathedral** –see the fine alabaster tombs and effigies of the 4th and 6th **Earls** there.

George Talbot (1468-1538) put up Cardinal Wolsey, Henry V111's Lord Chancellor, in his new **Sheffield Manor** for 18 days in 1530, breaking the Cardinal's journey from York to London, where he faced charges of treason. He died in Leicester 4 days afterwards, but we can't blame the 4th **Earl** for that.

Francis Talbot (b.Sheffield Castle 1500-d.Manor 1560) The 5th **Earl** was President of the Council of the North and a member of Queen Elizabeth's Privy Council, but, more important to the town, his Manor Court recorded the first **Sheffield cutlers' marks.** The first logged was that of **Wm. Elles** consisting of 2 triangles point-to-point in 1554.

George Talbot (1528-1599) the 6th **Earl of Shrewsbury** at the height of his powers was the richest, most powerful nobleman of the whole of the Midlands and the North; Earl Marshal of England (after the Duke Of Norfolk's execution in 1572) was just one title; **Sheffield Castle & Manor, Worksop, Wingfield,** Tutbury & Pontefract castles, **Chatsworth,** were just some of his properties. David Hey (History of Sheffield) comments that his portrait shows his 'hard and gloomy nature', but he seemed to buckle towards the end of his life, buffeted as he had been over the years by powerful women. He married first, Gertrude Manners of **Haddon Hall,** but it was his second, **Elizabeth,** now better known as **Bess of Hardwick** who showed a formidable character right from the start by insisting that their children by previous marriages should marry at the same time in **Sheffield Parish Church** (today's **Cathedral): her** eldest son **Hy. Cavendish** marrying his eldest daughter **Grace Talbot;** her youngest daughter **Mary Cavendish** marrying his second son **Gilbert Talbot.** (see **Bess of Hardwick).** Then the most powerful woman of all, **Queen Elizabeth the First** asked **Shrewsbury** to hold **Mary Queen of Scots** in custody, and for 14 long years, from 1570 to 1584 **Mary** and her retinue were unwilling Sheffielders held at the Earl's **Castle** & **Manor** here. (see **Mary Queen of Scots).** This duty must have put a great strain upon **Shrewsbury** & **Bess.** There have been suggestions that he took a fancy to the headstrong red-haired Scottish queen, but on the other hand, if he had been a strict gaoler, what would his position have been if any of the plots to free her and set her on the English throne had been successful? Conjecture apart, when they were finally able to pass **Mary** on to others to guard, their marriagc brokc up; hc married & set up home at **Handsworth** with a former servant girl (who 'took him to the cleaners'); **Bess** moved back to her ancestral home at Hardwick, later supervising the building of a new **Hardwick Hall.** (This is the hall that is 'more glass than wall' which has **ES =Elizabeth Shrewsbury** prominent in stone on high).

More important to the development of Sheffield and so to national progress than all the above, however, were **the 6th Earl's** industrial interests, and especially his nurture & protection of the cutlery trade. After all, a thriving cutlery trade led to Benjamin Huntsman researching and perfecting his **crucible steel** here, which led to **Bessemer** and the giants of Victorian steelmaking underpinning the industrial revolution, the railways, shipbuilding and the projection of British power around the world. **Sheffield steel** was essential for Britain in two world wars, and today remains essential in generating power, in operating theatres, or jetting us abroad-and landing us safely, etc.etc.etc. All this can be traced in a line from **Shrewsbury's** support of the early knife makers, just as surely as his blood line can be traced to today's royalty.

Like other local and national aristocrats **George Talbot** built and operated **furnaces** & **forges** and mined **coal-** the former at **Attercliffe, Kimberworth** & **Wadsley,** the latter under his own **Sheffield Park.** His interest in and development of a specific trade**:** knife-making was, however, unique. Marks were assigned by the Lord's **Manor Court** to **cutlers-** e.g. 25 in 1565- and though the men worked in a trade under the ultimate control as well as protection by the **Lord of Hallamshire** they had a remarkable degree of independence. A jury of 12 **cutlers** were appointed who decreed: - No work should be done from August 8th for 28 days, nor from Christmas to January 23rd. Before a man could work on his own he had to undertake a 7-year apprenticeship. - There was a £5 fee to enter the trade, half to the **Earl of Shrewsbury,** half to help relieve poor cutlers and their families. – Wages, prices, production and quality was regulated. Cutlers had to live in **Hallamshire,** and had to have their own mark registered.

These ordinances were restrictive but ensured quality was maintained, & the **Earl's** benign paternalism was such that the turnout for his funeral emptied homes, smithies & **wheels** throughout the town and its environs. Some lads standing in a tree for a better view over the crowds thronged in the forecourt of the parish church, died when a branch collapsed under their weight.

When **Gilbert Talbot (1553-1616), the 7th Earl of Shrewsbury** died the **Talbot** dynasty in Sheffield & overlordship of the **cutlery industry** died with him. His estates were shared by his three daughters, with the Sheffield & Derbyshire properties going to **Alethea,** wife of **Thomas Howard, Earl of Arundel & Surrey.** Her grandson was named the **5th Duke of Norfolk** and like her, through the centuries to the current incumbent,was based in Sussex. The manorial system of control of the cutlery trades had gone, though the absent **Howards** still profited as landlords. A surveyor, **John Harrison,** employed by them listed not only the timber, deer, coal & ironstone on their **Hallamshire** estates, but also the mills and 'Cutler wheeles' turned by 'streames, which weeles are imployed for the grinding of knives by four or five hundred Master Workmen.'

There were powerful and malignant obstacles to Sheffield cutlers' progress to dominance of the trade in England over the years, an ever present one, of course, being the taxman, another being the London cutlers who used all means, fair or foul, to keep their monopoly of trade in the capital. Fortunately, our cutlers didn't lose out when the **Talbots** faded from the scene. They acted to replace the **manorial court** by their own **Company of Cutlers in Hallamshire (qv),** incorporated by act of parliament in **1624**.

shufflin'; a'tha shufflin'? are you playing at dominoes? (or cards).

shunkle to shine (of jewellery or dress)
shunkley bright, shining, gaudy (of jewellery, dress etc.).

side or **sidy** to clear up pots, tidy a table. " **Side** (or **sidy) 'table will tha?**

side area of workbench for **cutler** , **buffer girl** etc. in a large establishment. If they are independent self-employed craftsmen they pay a rent for their **side.** An errand girl promoted to a **buffer girl** expressed pride that she was now **workin' on 'side** = on her own section of bench.

sile; siling rain; raining

It,s black o'er Bill's mother's (= o'er yonder) **It's goointer sile it dahn. It's silin' it dahn; chuckin' it dahn; raining stairods=** raining heavily. A Norwegian told me they used a similar word to mean rain heavily,'like a **foss'** (= **watter fall). Hunter's "Hallamshire Glossary** of **1828,** however, gives the meaning of **sile** as a fine sieve through which milk was passed to free it from hairs & other impurities. **siling up** in **Barnsley** means going deolali.

silent morn said of someone who doesn't say much.

silver chaser whereas a **hand engraver** cuts patterns in silver or gold, the **chaser** uses small tools to push the metal into shape. To see work such as **Bill Richardson's** picture of St. Peter's, Rome, is magical.

Simkins boiled **spice** (sweets) made in **Hillsborough,** sold in round tins as travel sweets.

Sissons were **Sheffield Plate** & silversmiths on **St. Mary's Road.** If you look up to the top of their building you can see stone representations of silver trophies, wine coolers etc. - this despite part of the building being bombed in the **Blitz.** They had to do war work and eventually moved to the huge **Calver Mill** to make stainless steel sinks, urinals etc. They are now Swiss owned and based at **Sheepbridge,** and still hopefully thriving, despite having suffered a major fire. **Julie Bunting,** in her book **Bygone Industries of the Peak** tell of how a lead miner's style of hat, the **Bradda Beaver,** was used for the design of the **Tommies helmets** in WW1. This was thanks to **Walter Sissons jnr.,** who lived in **Bradwell.** The Trench Warfare Department placed an initial order for one million helmets at 4s 6d each- unfortunately not with the **Sissons St. Mary's Road** factory, but with **Viners** at a new plant on **John St.**

sithee, (pronounced **sithi)** or, as the **dee-dah** Sheffielder says **sidee, (**pronounced **sidi)** a Sheffield region classic, meaning **look**, or exactly like the Welsh, **look you = see thee.**

He's at it ageean sithee/ ah'll sithee terneet/ he's neshed it sithee/ sithee at this sithee the last example has two **sithees** for emphasis**:** = just look at this, will tha. Say **sidee (sidi)** with a soft "d" if you're trying to imitate a **Dee-dah. (qv)**

sithers scissors

skelp to hit, slap, **bray**

C.T. Skelton a fine agricultural & garden tool manufacturer who were taken over by **Spear &**

Jackson (see **Neill's).** What Sheffielder in the 1940's to the 60's could restrain feelings of pride and amusement, as the train gathered speed through **Heeley,** hardly giving time to read the big advertisement, painted in black and white on **Sketon's** red brick wall: **SPADES & SHOVELS, HAY & MANURE FORKS....** Probably **SLASHERS & BILLHOOKS** also, but the train went too fast and the memory goes too slow. (On a 2005 **Sheaf Valley** walk the advert could still be discerned above a rash of ugly graffitti). The building, **Sheaf Bank Works** is now home to an assortment of (hopefully) vigorous firms.

skinny mean

skoyal; skosh school, or even university. **A tha(r) still skoyalin' ? (art thou...) A yor still skoyalin'? (are you)...**still at school, or university? : **Skoyal ageean!...** the daily lament of the schoolboy getting the tram, as he goes unwillingly to **skoyal.**

slagger off lad who held back the **slag** with a steel rod, when **crucible steel** was **teemed.** See the fine bronze statue of a **crucible teeam** at **Meadowhall.**

slair to drag your feet on the ground."**Stop slairin', pick thi feet up.";** to slide, preferably on ice, but lads in the 1940's & thereabouts used to take a fearless run and **slair** as far as they could in their hob-nailed boots in the ashphalted school playground.

sleeve board penknife with blades at each end, and when closed the **covering (scales)** is broader at one end, than the other,like an ironing board.

slinger man who loads steel bars, billets etc. onto road trailers or railway wagons, using cranes & chains, ropes, wire rope etc.

slop dosh mud, played with by children**; e.g.** for making dams in the gutter when it rained.

sluthery slippy, muddy, **clarty**

smarrerwee 'im? What's the matter with him?

Smoky Sheffield like Edinburgh (Auld Reekie) and London (The Smoke), Sheffield had a well deserved reputation for smoke, thanks to its houses, but thanks even more to its world famous industry. This reputation clung to the town from, at least, the **1540's** and to the city right up to the **1980's-** even though the Clean Air Act had given us smoke-free housing & steelworks from the late **1950's.** (Though Sheffield & Rotherham between them make as much steel as ever= ca. 2,300,000 tons p.a., there are still old Sheffielders who shuffle about saying **"it's all gone, there's nowt left"** just because they can't see smoke **putherin'** out over the **East End.** If you lived to the west of the city or on the hills- say **up Crookes,** or at **'Lane Top-** with the prevailing winds blowing industrial and household smoke eastwards down the **Don Valley** you would be less likely to suffer from bronchitis & other lung ailments, though there were Sheffielders who were almost proud of the city's smoke. It was, along with the reassuring sounds of steel production, a sign that men were at work, earning decent wages, making first class products of which they, and indeed the whole city were extremely proud. Though everyone knew someone who was riddled with lung disease, there was a belief held by many that our smoke was a barrier against infectious diseases & fevers. Sundry **Smoky Sheffield** snippets: **ca. 1540-** John Leland**: " Hallamshire** hath plenti of woode, and yet ther is burnid much se cole." **1606-** a knight at the Royal court wrote to **Gilbert, 7th Earl of Shrewsbury** arranging to meet him in Sheffield **"where I look to be half choked with town smoke." 1722-** Daniel Defoe set out on his journeys through Great Britain and, after leaving **Donny,** "had a fair view of that ancient **whittle making, cutlering** town, called Sheffield. This town is very populous and large, the streets narrow, and the houses dark and black, occasioned by the **continuous smoke** of the **forges,** which are always at work. **1794-** the **Iris** newspaper commented; **"...**infectious distempers are not apt to spread in this place. The **smoke, produced by the manufactories**, is thought by many persons to be sericeable in this view. **1884-** John Singer Sargent, an American artist living in Paris, came to **Bolsover Hill,** the grand home at **Page Hall** of **Thomas Edward Vickers,** to paint his three daughters, **Florence, Mabel & Clara.** In a letter from Paris to Maine, U.S.A., he wrote, **"..** I am to paint**....** 3 ugly young women at Sheffield, **dingy hole."** It might have been a dingy hole in those days, but the young women weren't ugly- far from it. See the picture at **Graves Art Gallery,** along with another of **Ronald & Francis Vickers. (**He also painted **Mr. & Mrs. Albert Vickers** at dinner at night, but you'd have to go to San Francisco Fine Art Museum to see this). **1930's -** T.S.Elliott spoke about his muse falling silent in the Sheffield air and George Orwell was even more scathing in his essay "North & South," **(1937): "**even Wigan is beautiful compared with Sheffield**.....** Sheffield, I suppose, could justly claim to be called the ugliest town in the Old World**:** its inhabitants, who want it to be pre-eminent in everything, very likely do make that claim for it**.......** Once I halted in the street & counted the factory chimneys I could see**:** there were 33 of them, but there would have been far more if the air had not been obscured by smoke." Perhaps we should take what he wrote with a pinch of salt, because when he describes our industry he gets it completely wrong, showing he had learned **nowt** from his few days spent in **Neepsend. 1974- Basil Boothroyd,** the humourist wrote a much more sympathetic, and technically accurate article in Punch magazine, capturing the overwhelming noise & power & heat of an **arc melting shop,** and the pride of Sheffielders in their industry and their urge to be the best. Even that**: "**It was probably a blow for Sheffielders when they stopped being the dirtiest city in the world**" (**after homes & works became smokeless).

snap food packed up for work, in a **snap tin,** similar to an army mess tin, but now usually plastic.

snath, snaith the big, shaped handle of a scythe, made to curve round the hip in use.Traditionally made of ash, it is now also madelighter of aluminium tubing. Not a word unique to Sheffield but since **Hallamshire** was the leading centre for scythe-making,and now is the **only** centre in the U.K. (**Tyzack's & Sorby-Hutton)** it is worthy of inclusion. Visit **Abbeydale Hamlet.**

sneck door latch...**put sneck on will tha.**
snecklifter pint of beer (originally bought for a poor man, allowing him to stay in the pub).

snicket alleyway; path between buildings or hedges, perhaps more common in Rotherham & Barnsley. The more usual word in Sheffield is **jennel (qv).**

snided wi' , snided wee full of; infested with:
- **apple tree snided wi' woolly aphids**
- **pond snided wi' taddies**
- **rooad snided wi' traffic**
- **Parliament's snided wi' lawyers**

snot a vulgar word nationally, but two phrases, dredged from a **Neepsend** childhood are only used in Sheffield, to my knowledge - **he wain't part wi' snot from his nooase** he's very mean - **he's a long streeak o' donkey snot** he's a very tall (& thin) bloke

snotty Oliver an unfriendly, snooty cove; a clever dick

snotty wheel a **grinding wheel** clogged up with **swarf** needed **feying (feighing)=** cleaning up. **Billy Hukin,** Sheffield's last **open razor grinder,** who used this word, said locally made **Abrafact** or **Jowitt wheels** worked better than Norton, American-made wheels.

snurp (up) ; snurped (up) turned up; wrinkled up of cloth, sometimes caused by faulty stitching

soaking uniform heating of **blades** in a cutlery or tool works, or of **billets, slabs ingots etc.** in **soaking pits** in a steelworks, prior to further **rolling** or **forging.**

Henry Clifton Sorby (1826-1908) scientist, geologist, botanist (the **Sorby Natural History Society** flourishes to this day), but most importantly to human progress, a pioneering **metallurgist.** He was scornfully referred to as "the man who looked at mountains through a microscope," but by looking at polished steel samples through his microscope he helped to make steelmaking more of a science, less of an art. A certain stage in the heat treatment of steel is called **sorbite** in his name. **Sorby** is not an uncommon name in Sheffield- there was a maker of a wide range of excellent tools, & today a **Sorby** makes **high speed steel tools** at **Handsworth,** and **Sorby 'Kangaroo Brand'** agricultural & hand tools ex-**Wellington Street;** ex-**Woodseats** soldier on, now merged as **Sorby-Hutton** at **Dronfield.** (If you're quick, before the area is re-developed, you can see the original stone carved kangaroo above an archway on **Wellington Street).**

sough drain, for water from coal or lead mines, e.g. **Calver Sough**

sours; souring in cutlery trade = goods paid for in advance; drawing pay for work not yet done. See **sweets.**

South Yorkshire Fire Service Museum in a sturdy Victorian, listed building on **West Bar;** sturdy machines + fire and police service artefacts maintained by sturdy volunteers. Look on top of the building and you can see a wood & glass look-out post, where a Victorian fireman would keep his eyes open for fires.

South Yorkshire Railway **Meadowall sidings, Barrow Road, Wincobank** maintained by enthusiasts who hope, eventually to run services to **Chapeltown.**

sowder solder**; soft sowder** = lead plus tin**: hard sowder** = copper + zinc (+ silver).

spanish liquorice. **Gi us a stick o'spanish**

spark tester skilled man who can touch steel with a grinder and tell by the pattern of the sparks what type of steel it is. Different steels give off different patterns, and he was usually brought in if their was a quality mix.

spell splinter of wood lodged in a finger. (Could be related to a spill). Also **spelk.**

spice sweets, sometimes even chocolate. Local **spice** factories include **Bassett's (qv); Thornton's** ,now with nationwide **spice** (chocolate) shops, they moved to deepest Derbyshire when they weren't allowed to expand on their **Archer Road** site; **Maxon's-Dixon's,** famous for **mint rock (qv)** -that Sheffield delicacy; & **Simpkin's** travel **spice** in a tin. See **Granelli's** shop on **Broad Street** with its sign, **"Old fashioned spice at an old fashioned price."**
spogs **Mexborough** variant on **spice.**

spinner a skilled man forming flat sheet **blanks** of **pewter, nickel silver,** or **silver,** into goblets, tankards, vases, trophies etc. using **nylon** or **wooden chucks** & a **spinning lathe.** Often self-employed and working for several firms, one at least, **Stephen Gifford** who trained at **James Dixon's,** formed a successful company along with silversmith **Ernest Lacey: Camelot Silverware** who have become one of Sheffield's leading firms specialising in small batch, or one-off trophies.

splash booard wooden board set in a grinder's **trow** to catch the **wheel swarf (qv).**

splodgin' fishing; see **plodgin'.**
"Weer's tha beean?"
"Splodgin' "
"Caughtowt?"
"Couple o' breeam....otherwise watter-licked."

sprottle, sprottled (out), sprottlin' like the caelocanth, presumed extinct, but trawl around the depths of Sheffield & district and you find this marvellous word is widely known, if not widely used. It can mean being hamfisted; doing something awkwardly; being spread out on a settee or on the floor, blocking the way; leaving someone speechless; or even backfiring, of a motorbike. Examples heard, or reported: " Did you see Schmeichel, **sprottlin' about** in 'goalmouth?" (Man Utd. Goalkeeper). " What tha **sprottlin'** at? Here, let me show thi what to do.Gawky teenager, in the way **" sprottled out** on **'flooer."** If there are two of them they could be said to be **"sprottled out,** like **lamb & lettuce."** " William Hague hasn't got 'image, but if you actually listen to what he says, he leaves Blair **sprottlin'."** "He went off, lad, like a **chuffin'** rocket, t'owd B.S.A. **sprottlin'** away."

Hunter (1828) gives **sprottle** as "to struggle with inefficacious vehemence."

stainless steel **12% Cr stainless** was invented by **Harry Brearley (qv)** at **Brown-Firth Research, Princess Street** in **1913** (see tribute etched on stainless steel at the corner of the building, now occupied by **English Pewter Company). 18/8 % Cr Nickel stainless** was perfected by his successor at the **Brown-Firth** laboratorie **Dr. Hatfield (qv)** in the **1920's,** which became known world-wide as **Firth Staybrite steel**

Stainless Stephen (1892-1971) pioneering radio comic with Sheffield station 2FL before heading south to the B.B.C. He would begin: "Good evening, comma, this is Stainless, semi-colon, semi-concious Stephen, comma, speaking to you....", a routine inspired by a 1914-1918 wartime signalling course, and much later used by Danish comedian, Victor Borge. For music hall acts he wore a bowler hat, a revolving bow tie and a stainless steel waistcoat made by **Firth Vickers** for him.

After the Great War he had taught at the **Crookes Endowed School** for 17 years, which, no doubt, provided him with plenty of material. A highlight in his subsequent career was performing at the 1945 Royal Command Performance. When he retired in 1952 to be a farmer in Kent, he described himself as "stainless, painless, brainless, shameless, aimless, semi-concious and approaching semi-dotage." (This information thanks to **Martin Dawes,** the **Star,** August 2006).

stake silversmith's anvil

stalled (of) tired of; fed up with: surfeited. Very seldom heard now, though an aunt at **Holme Lane** told my wife of her granddaughter being **'stalled of salmon.'** **Hunter** in his **'Hallamshire Glossary',** **1828** lists the word, and a quotation from 'Julius Caesar.' Further down the centuries a character in Emily Bronte's 'Wuthering Heights' complains, **"I'm stalled of doing naught."**= I'm fed up wi' doin' nowt.

Stanage Edge a three mile sandstone (**millstone grit)** escarpment, a climbing edge famous throughout the world among people who enjoy the sport. Many students come to study in Sheffield attracted most of all by the proximity of **Stanage,** and other nearby edges in the **Peak District.** Sheffield, and more precisely **Hunter's Bar** is the location of choice for the U.K.'s climbing fraternity. **High Neb,** halfway along the **Edge** was thought, by yours truly, to be the highest point, at 1502 feet (458m), in the city of Sheffield, but the honour goes to **Margery Hill,** between **Derwent** and **Langsett** reservoirs, at 1793 feet (546m). See the abandoned millstones, mostly about 5 feet diameter x ca. 10 inch width, chiselled out by some mute, inglorious, Victorian craftsmen, their work still seeming to be in prime condition for scythe grinding & other trades. The stones litter the base of the Edge, and the craftsmen got **nowt** for these impressive works of art, victims, perhaps of the new, artificial, **patent** wheel technology. See also the strange, numbered, chiselled channels & hollows on flat, or slightly sloping stones along the top of the Edge. It is said they were to collect water for the grouse, to tide them over the odd drought, & keep them fit enough to be shot later in the year on the glorious 12th, or whenever. There are some interesting stones set at intervals through the heather at the north end of **Stanage,** and further on, across the **Snake Road** through more heather up to **Derwent Edge.** Most are hidden, but if I remember **reight** many have a **W** initial on one side and **M F** on the other, marking the limits of the **Wilson (snuff mill)** family grouse moors, and **Mark Firth's (qv).** Just across the **Snake** stands an impressive stone built house, **Moscar Lodge,** marked **M F 1872,** which seems big enough to entertain the largest of hunting parties. At some time over the years it has passed from the **Firths'** to the **Wilsons' ownership. Robin Hood's Cave** affords a good view from a face of the **Edge** and a vantage point from March to September for sightings of ring ouzels, lapwings and curlews.

Standing around like **tripe on a shutter,** or, as my sister described her husband when he stood in goal on a frozen Sheffield pitch: like **a frozzen turd!**

Stanley Tools Ltd. with H.Q. in Connecticut, U.S.A., in **1936** they bought out Sheffield firm **Chapman Tool, (est.1888),** best known as a high quality brace and plane manufacturer on **Rutland Road, Woodside.** When walking up this steep road in the **1950's** ears were assailed by loud music, and the clash of steel being worked above the constant hum of machinery, emanating from **Stanley's** four-storey glass & brick building. Extensions seemed to be built into the hillside every year,and further plants were built at **Ecclesfield** (hammers) & **Hackenthorpe** (screwdrivers). As well as the above products they were noted for tape measures & rules, taking over **Rabone-Chesterman,** before transferring production of these to France. They took over, too, production of **Surforms** from its inventors, **Firth Brown Tools,** but this development of the wood plane became, as did so many hand tools, victim of the craze for power tools. **Stanley's** best known tool is the **Stanley knife,** now the generic name for trimming knives. It was invented in the U.S.A. but developed in Sheffield using, at first, **Swann-Morton** blades, before making their own from **Stocksbridge** precision strip. They bought & shut down a French blade-making firm and their large factory at **Hellaby,** which has replaced the other three Sheffield factories, is said to produce 3,500,000 blades a week. An unfortunate consequence of its success are the frequent references to **Stanley knives** in criminal case: **"**he was heard to cry ' **Stanley him,**' M'lud.**"** Like most British manufacturing firms, hit by cheap labour overseas, and by red-tape, heavy tax load, high pound and hovering H.& S. lawyers in the U.K. **Stanley U.K.** have downsized with just one factory **(Hellaby)** and European head office **(Sheffield Airport Park).**

starved, starving can mean **frozen** as well as hungry. I'm **starved to deeath=** I'm chilled to the bone. Collins gives it as archaic, but it's not round here **owd luv.** Used around Leicester too & no doubt elsewhere. Occurs quite often with the **frozen** meaning in Emily Bronte's 'Wuthering Heights'.

steeam hammer **forging hammer** powered by a steam engine

steeam wheel when steam engines superseded **water wheels** in powering the cutlery trade, there was a movement of factories from the rivers to the town centre. Works could be made bigger and more efficient, freed from the vagaries of water power and the cost of maintaining **dams & goyts,** as well as the wheels & associated machinery. The new works were often still called **wheels- e.g.** the huge **Butchers' Wheel** on **Arundel Street.** The works was refurbished in **2007,** though, unfortunately, the historical word **Wheel** has been dropped. See **W. & S. Butcher.**

Steel City although Sheffield is no longer overwhelmingly dominated by the **Steel and Allied Trades,** production of its special steels remains as high as ever, and, together with **Rotherham** makes a far higher percentage of U.K. total steel production than it did when bulk steel plants were found in almost every industrial conurbation in England, Scotland and Wales. (If we add **Scunthorpe,** the area now dominates U.K. production., though, of course, the U.K. total at,say 10 million tons, is peanuts compared with the world's burgeoning total = over **one thousand million** tons p.a.).

Nearby cities, Manchester & Leeds have long lost their fame as 'Cottonopolis' and suitmaker to the world respectively, and draw pride from being second to London in service industries; in having buildings up to 50 storeys high, and in having a football brand, and a branch of a posh London frock shop respectively.

Sheffield pushes its two million trees and that a third of the city lies in the Peak District; its prowess in music & sport, but it doesn't need to reinvent itself. If a local person, or team does well- e.g. Sheffield United beating Arsenal in 2006- the national press invariably refer to a performance showing **Sheffield steel.** United v Wednesday is always the **Steel City** derby, & the book of their rivalry is **The Steel City Divide.** Among acknowledgements to Sheffield industry received from Aussies, Yanks, Japanese, Russians etc. when selling products of the **Light Trades** on **Ecclesall Road,** the nicest was from an Indian doctor who said he'd **heard so much about Sheffield steel, when growing up** (in India) **it was almost a religious experience to come here!** (Tata of India has now bought our two largest plants- at **Aldwarke** & **Stocksbridge -** but that's another story). Locally, anyone reading the press, or wandering around the city in the last few years, can't fail to have noticed how many businesses & organisations show their pride in the **Steel City,** by using it in their title**:** There's **Steel City** ABC Boxing Clubs, and Angling Club**; Steel City** Beer Festival, and Concert Band**; Steel City** Crown Green Bowling Club, and Championship Cup (Napoleon's- poker)**; Steel City** Cruisers- Classic Customised Cars, and Guitars, and Gymnasium**; Steel City** Ghost Tours**; Steel City** Mortgages, and **Steel City** Salsa**; Steel City** Sax (girl band) and **Steel City** Scholars (University of Sheffield centenary book)**; Steel City** Striders (running club), and Scaffolding**; Steel City** Tatoos, and Tilings, and Telecom….. I'm sure you can find more.

Steelers **Sheffield Steelers** ice hockey team

Stephenson Blake Ltd. at **Upper Allen Street** were Britain's last traditional printers' type founders, established **1818** by **Joseph Blake,** file maker, **Wm. Garnett,** silversmith, and **John Stephenson,** tool & mark maker, breaking a London monopoly. **John Blake** was **Master Cutler** in **1832** when he died in a cholera epidemic- see **Cholera Monument** & his gravestone on the hill behind the **(Midland) Railway Station.** The **Blake's** family homes were **Upperthorpe Villa** (later let to **Ebeneezer Elliott,** the Corn Law Rhymer); then **Sharrow House;** then **Mylnhurst,** an early **1880's** stone, neo-gothic mansion with castellated tower, now a Catholic school. See "A South Yorkshire family of type-founders", by **Wm. Greaves Blake, 1999.**

Steelo's **Steel Peech & Tozer,** the massive **Rotherham** firm, whose towering black corrugated sheds that were the **Templeborough Melting Shop,** now house **Magna Science Adventure Centre. S.P.T.** merged with **Park Gate Iron & Steel** on nationalisation to become **British Steel Rotherham Works,** and now, with production consolidated at the thousand acre **Aldwarke (q.v.)** site (with aerospace &

other exotic steels made at **Stocksbridge),** they are known as **Corus Engineering Steels.** Ultimate ownership is now with the Tata Steel Co. of India.

Steels **Stocksbridge F.C.**

stint a shift. A poem in "**Sheffieldish**"; **Dreeamin'**, by **'Totley' Tom Hague, coyal** miner, begins: **"Ah wor wukkin' in mi stint wun day, Twor in t'owd Silkstun seeam...."**

stithy; stiddy anvil; in general **stithy** is the larger one, **stiddy** the smaller, e.g. the **cutler's stiddy.** Collins gives **stithy** as archaic, and there is reference to **Vulcan's stithy** in Hamlet. My theory is that just as Sheffielders developed **thee** into **dee, stithy** became **stiddy,** a word unknown outside the town. A bit of practice for you: **Sithi at this stithy, sithi; Siddi at dis stiddy, siddi.** Just look at this anvil!

stock sandstone or oak tree stump used as a base for the **stithy/ stiddy** (anvil), which was recessed in.Tinder-dry horse muck was put in the recess under the anvil, which acted as a shock absorber to help prevent **hand forger's 'dropped wrist'** (= a rheumatic condition, or repetitive strain injury, common in the trade).

stooan stone; grindstone.The **Stooan man** was the man who came to collect a weekly payment for the **grinder's** < **6ft.** diameter **stone,** bought on the never-never. (**Housley** tells us they cost **£80-£90** each in the **1930's** and, by then, all stones were artificial = **patent stooans,** with, happily, less danger from breaking, and no danger of **silica dust).**

Stooanses **Stones bitter,** from the **Cannon Brewery, Rutland Road, Neepsend.** Sometimes known as **Jungle-Juice,** it was nevertheless the workers' favouite- now R.I.P. See **Breweries.**

Stooers the Co-op store; **the Corporative** (with stress on the **a**).

stool the **three-legged stool,** whilst not exclusive to the cutlery trade, was widely used in older workshops, where it was ideal for uneven wooden or stone-flagged floors. Some are still around. Shakespeare in "A Midsummer Night's Dream", written 1594-5, mentions one as Puck, mischievous & "merry wanderer of the night" says: **"**The wisest aunt, telling the saddest tale, sometime for three-foot stool mistaketh me**;** Then slip I from her bum, down topples she."

stoup stone guidepost, often 5 or 6 foot high x about 1 foot square, erected ca. **1730** when a law decreed that directions should be shown at remote crossroads, pack-horse ways etc. See examples at **Strines & Longshaw** where the destinations chiselled out include **Sheffeild Rode.**

stravegin' wandering around aimlessly. (Collins gives **stravaig** as Scots & N.English for the verb to wander aimlessly).

striker the **hammerman,** using a heavy **striking hammer** to assist the **forger (makker)** in two-handed hot forging, working on larger butchers' & cooks' knives for example. By using two men hitting the blade alternatively & at speed, while the steel is hot, they can quickly get the shape right before it needs re-heating. To see **Harry Drabble** and his **makker** working at speed, and in unison, filmed by **Ken Hawley,** is magical.

summat something; **summat fer nowt; summat's up 'eer; Is summat up or summat?; It's neether nowt nor summat=** It's something trifling.

Supwithee? Supwidee? What's the matter with you? (A glib answer could be; "Ah'll sup wi anybody.") **Ah tha suppin' terneet?...**are you going out for a drink tonight? **We've supped some stuff terneet.......sup up an' shurrup.** A **"sup"** of molten steel into your clog was a hazard, especially in a **crucible steel melting shop.**

surrey; serri form of address, c.f. sirrah. (Hamlet to grave-digger**:** "Whose grave's this, sirrah?**")** Heard in **Mexborough** but more common south of Sheffield, in north Notts. & Derbys. My mother's father, a grinder on Hollis Croft, addressed everyone as **surrey,** but he was from Matlock. **Creswell colliery** young miner shouting after the London waiter, who'd brought him black coffee: **"Ey up surrey, tha's put no milk in this."** Read D.H. Lawrence.

sustificate certificate

swaarf; swarf waste metal from engineering works,or, if from a **grinder's trow,** a mixture of metal & stone particles in mud form**;** see **wheel swarf.**

swage chamfered edge down the back of the blade of a best quality table, dessert, or tea knife, aiding both its looks, and its balance.

Swann Morton an honourable firm owned by its workers, promoting from within - the current managing director started work there as a shop floor electrician. Big modern buildings at **Owlerton** house spotless factories and offices. They are the world's leading **scalpel blade manufacturer** producing **one and a half MILLION** per day.

sweepings accumulated particles, shavings, off-cuts etc., usually of silver after engraving, saw piercing & other processes. This is swept up and bagged & sold to such as **Sheffield Smelting Co. (THESSCO)** for weighing, re-melting, casting or rolling for resale.

sweets are easy jobs in the cutlery trade, or jobs done & delivered, but not yet paid for. Jobs not done, but paid for in advance are **sours (q.v.).**

Swinden House in Rotherham, formerly the H.Q. of the metallurgical laboratories of **United Steel Companies;** the restored Jacobean style mansion, built **1860,** is now home to the **National Metals Technology Centre (NAMTEC).**

T

tabs ears. **Tha shunt be flappin' thi tabs=** you shouldn't be eaves dropping.

taddies tadpoles

takkin' ageean file trade's equivalent of the cutlers' **cuckoo (qv)** = faulty work needing correcting.

tang the pointed end of a chisel, file, knife etc. that fits into the handle. A **through tang** goes to the end of a knife handle, and is often pinned in – but see **sham pin.**

tap to pour iron or steel. This was achieved at, e.g., **Park Gate Iron & Steel Co.'s blast furnaces** by drilling a hole through the **gannister** at the base of the furnaces, to allow the molten iron to run out into **pigs,** or into a ladle to be transferred to a **mixer,** a holding furnace, prior to its use for steel making. **Electric Arc steel making furnaces** in contrast, are **tapped** by tilting the furnace one way to pour off the **slag,** and tilting the other way to pour the steel. One of the most exciting events in the drama that is steelmaking is **to see 'em tappin' furnaces. Tap to tap** time, the time taken from one **melt** of steel to the next, which was 8 to 10 hours in the **Siemens Martin Open Hearth** furnaces, came down to ca. 6 hours when big **arc** furnaces replaced them in the 1960's/ 1970's. I understand that the huge 180 ton **arc furnaces** at **Aldwarke** now only take 60 to 90 minutes from one **tapping** to the next- incredible when you take into account that this involves **fettling** (=repairing) the furnace lining where necessary; **charging** (= putting in) the base metal, selected scrap; adding limestone as a flux + any alloying elements applicable; swinging the furnace roof on and lowering three carbon electrodes through holes in the roof; switching on the electricity which leaps in an **arc** from the electrodes to the **charge,** which generates a heat of 3000 degrees centigrade at the point of contact; melting & refining, alloying and testing and **tapping** once more. To save time refining is sometimes done in the ladle. Get a party of 8 plus and you may be allowed to look round **Aldwarke.** It's every bit as impressive as seeing Mount Aetna, and cheaper too.

Taylor's Eye Witness were absorbed into **Harrison Fisher** in **1975;** two famous names in the Sheffield cutlery trade, now trading under the **Eye Witness** brand, with **Eye** trademark granted **1838.** The firm are notable for fine cutlery in beautiful modern style, as well as traditional patterns, in stainless & silver plate; for a wide range of kitchen knives & scissors; for trade knives (e.g. oyster knives) and pocket knives. All these are made in their fine old works on **Milton Street,** though with nearby works'conversions and 'new build' appartments sprouting up, they may be persuaded to relocate, say to the East End.

tea cake a plain bread cake (not the national teacake with raisins in). **he's no tea cake** = he's no fool.

teagle hoist for lifting grindstones up to upper floors in multi-storey cutlery factory.

teem, teeam to pour steel; **teemer** = melter. **C.f. to ladle and teem**= to balance things out.

teeam team. The **Blades,** with star player **Jimmy Hagan** in the **1940's/1950's** were dismissed by **Wednesdayites** as **'a one-man teeam.' teeam** also applies to a **set** of men at a **forge, foundry, rolling mill, melting shop** etc.

teeamin' it dahn raining **stair rods; siling it dahn**

tek thi 'ook go away; clear off

telewag pole telegraph pole

temper **hardening** in oil or, more severely, in water or even iced brine makes steel & steel products very hard, but brittle. **Tempering** to a set heat (perhaps between 250/330 degrees centigrade in the case of table knife blades), then allowing to cool slowly in air, retains most hardness & strength while avoiding brittleness, & recovering some of the steel's ductility& toughness. Processes are now automated in the steel industry, but when the tempering colours of the steel had to be judged by eye, it took a good un' to differentiate the 10 degrees between 'straw' & 'yellow', or 'cornflower blue' & 'light blue'.

terneet tonight

that can be used instead of 'so'**: 'Puddin' were that good, I had another 'elpin'.**

That ball, Mester! (when ball is hit or kicked over a fence, railings etc.: "Would you please throw- or kick-the ball back to us, kind Sir.")

tha what? pardon?

the, in Sheffield & district speech, is replaced by a **glottal stop (q.v.),** represented in print by an apostrophe **'. Gerron 'bus.** NOT **Gerron t' bus.** Sheffielders have advanced linguistically, though the **t** is retained in some phrases because it sounds **reight:** It's **neether** one thing, nor **t'other. T'Wikker weer t'watter runs o'er t'weer** = The **Wicker** where the water runs over the weir.

theein' & thouin' despite the constant onslaught over the years of standard, or 'estuary' English on radio, film & television, as well as in schools and colleges; despite local disapproval by those who think using the familiar form of address is, at best, the next stop towards effin' & blindin', or at worst, a barrier to 'getting on in the world'; despite all this the true **Sheffielder** obstinately continues to **thee & thou.** Collins gives it as 'archaic' & only used by 'The Society of Friends.' Not 'ere it in't, **old luv,** nor in **Rotherham,** and who are the Society of Friends **when they're at 'ooam?** The Dutch, the French, the Russians, the Germans, the Italians, the Spanish have all retained the familiar form, & so have we. The French **tutoyer,** and the German **duzen** mean to **thee & thou,** and the usage is the same**:** among friends & fellow workers, among family siblings, father to child etc. but **not** child to parents, pupil to teacher, worker to boss **unless** wishing to insult. An angry Sheffield father scolded his rebellious son**: "Don't thee thee-thar me, thee thee-thar thissen."** (The rebellious son, after being given a list of his faults, including being late for **skoyal,** countered**: "Way** (well)**, it's thee-thar-thissen that's made mi late for skoyal!**

In the WW1 German classic on the futility of the Great War, " All Quiet on the Western Front" the troops in grey dream of a deep trench & English corned beef, and one insults a corporal by addressing him as **du.** The corporal snaps back "**Seit wann duzen wir uns denn?"** Since when are we **theeing & thouing?=** Less of the familiarity**!** Sheffield usage & susceptibilities would be exactly the same. 400 years after the death of Shakespeare Sheffielders' usage is exactly the same as in those tumultuous days: in Othello, written **1604,** higher class Brabantio addresses lower class Iago; **"Thou** art a villain." Iago replies; **"You** are - a senator."

So, if you want to learn the language keep your ears alert in pubs & clubs and at football matches, on trams & buses, at fairs & markets, in factories & offices, schools & colleges, shopping **on' Moor** or at **Meadowhell.** You will hear **Thee; thou=tha,** or **thar (thou art= tha'rt=**you are); **thy= thi; thine; thissen=** yourself. Examples: It's up to **thee** that. Use **thi** common (sense). Look after **thissen.** If **tha** wants owt doin', do it **thissen.** "What's **thine's** mine, and what's mine's mi own." **Tha'rt** daft, **thee.** You're silly, you are. Childish banter, **Neepsend 1940's: " Does tha know what? ....**(What?)**... Tha'rt daft an' I'm not." Tha what?** pardon? (Or today's annoying), sorry? Note that a true Sheffielder, especially one born within earshot of **drop hammers** by the **Don,** is **always** grammatically correct when **theeing & thouing,** even if he claims to know nothing of grammar. He would consider the journalists quoting Sheffielders wrongly, as in the following, to be guilty of gross ignorance: "Are **thee** Yorkshire? Are **thee** Lancashire?" (Sunday Times, at a Roses match, at **'Lane,** long ago.) =Do you support Yorks., or Lancs. The Sheffielder would say**; A' tha(r)** (supporting) Yorkshire= **art thou.** " Get **thee** booits on." (Sheffield History Reporter, who ought to know better) should be **thi= thy. "**Get **tha** coat on.**" (Star,** August **2007)** Terrible grammar; it should be, of course**: "**Get **thi cooat** on." **"Tha's** a **reet un"** instead of the correct, **tha'rt a reight un'=** you are a right one. **Tha's** is short for **thou hast=** familiar form of **you have,** as in; **"Tha's gorrit cumin' to thi."** Or **"Tha's gone an' dunnit nah, sithee!"** (Don't be confused, incidentally, if you find **thi** meaning **they** or **there: Thi** not cumin' **a'thi?** They're not coming, are they? **Thi int owt** left. There isn't anything left).

There are Sheffielders who are more advanced linguistically, or who are lazier, who have developed the **th** sound to a soft **d. Thee and tha (thou)** becomes **dee an'da(h).** This is such a localised development, capturing the imagination of surrounding towns so much, that they are inspired to call all Sheffielders **Dee-Dahs.** See **dee.** The peculiarity extends beyond **dee, dah, dine, dissen (NB dine=thine** is exactly the same meaning and pronunciation as the German **dein);** it extends to all words beginning with **th: "**Where are the deer at Chatsworth?**" "Di dahn deer,'deer."** (They're down there, the deer). .... Wunderbar!

theer there**:** Purrit o'er **theer,** will tha.

a time or two often

think on think about it**; think on, owd lad,** or, as **Freddie Trueman** said to an Australian batsman coming out to the crease**; "Think on, tha'rt next."**

thoil to suffer, endure, bear**; he can't thoil spendin' owt** but, on the other hand **he'd thoil owt for his lasses.** C.f. Robbie Burns' harvest mouse left homeless by the plough "To **thole** the winter's sleety dribble."

thraipin' a good hiding

throng busy. **Harry Brearley,** inventor of stainless steel, wrote of his mother as 'always **throng' (** he was the sickly one, with nine brothers & sisters). **Throng** as **Throp's** wife.

throoat (Sheffield & Rotherham), **throit (**Chapeltown & Barnsley) throat Mi belly thinks mi **throoat's** cut = I'm hungry.

thrustened up well wrapped up

thumb mark, thumbprint mark on the back of a **shear steel** knife blade where it joins the bolster, caused when the **iron bolster** with tang was welded by **hot forging** to the **shear steel** blade. Look for the **shear steel/double shear steel** marks on Sheffield table or dessert knives made around the Victorian era- many, many millions were made & you can find them for a couple of quid on market stalls. (They may have a shop name stamped on, such as Harrod's, Garrard's or Gamages but would have been made in Sheffield). Turn them over to the **pile side**= that without the mark, and you will see the faint, or strong thumb-shaped imprint, which had remained even after **glazing. Shear steel (qv)** was preferred for sharp knives right up to the advent of **Brearley's Firth Stainless** blades in the **1920's,** so look for the mark, look for the thumbprint, give the edge a few strokes with your steel- and watch your fingers!

thwitel knife, **whittle (q.v.).** Chaucer, in the Reeve's Tale ca. **1385** tells of the rough Miller carrying a **Sheffeld thwitel,** the first mention of a Sheffield knife in English literature, showing that the town's industry was already widely known.

Tidders; Tidza Tideswell

tiggy children's game of chase. The one who was 'on' ran to **tig** (tap) another, who was then 'on' in his/her place, unless he/she shouted **'Kings'** and froze. Out of danger from being **tigged,** the frozen one would shout **'Queens'** and run off again. Teachers & the gauleiters of the Health & Safety Executive, mindful of hovering lawyers, have now, no doubt, banned this dangerous sport.

tilt, tilting large hammer; forging by the **tilting** action of the **helve** (oak beam); the **tup** (hammer) at the end of the **helve** falling onto the hot steel or iron. C.f. **'to go full tilt.'** Also known as a **falling hammer** or **drop hammer.** Go to **Wortley Forge** or **Abbeydale Hamlet** to see wonderful examples. The late **Professor Francis Evans,** himself a fine engineer, enjoyed quoting from Abraham Rees' 'Cyclopaedia' **1819,** which paints a nice picture of Sheffielders' skills in forging steel.: "The perfection of **tilting steel,** depends upon drawing out a rod perfectly straight to the same size in every part of its length. Many workmen, particularly at Sheffield, have acquired such skill & dexterity in the management of the rod while under the **tilt,** that their work is as straight & even as though it had been drawn through a steel-plate, in the same manner as wire, and all its angles perfectly square: its surface is of a black polish, and as smooth as though it had been filed. All artists use the square steel rods for making their tools; and the straightness & regularity of the rods are such, that a person who has not been an eyewitness of the operation, would scarcely believe it possible to produce such accurate work from the blows of a hammer." **Francis** in **2001,** added: "Historians of fine art & design limit their admiration to the fine work of the cutlers; yet surely the man who could forge such true bars was also an artist."

'Tin Chapel **1902** corrugated iron Wycliffe Mission chapel on Hickmott Road, alongside the bubbling River Porter. (Now newly brick-built.) In the **1920's Rev. 'Daddy' Vince,** a bearded, firebrand, Old Testament prophet-like man, used to take groceries from local shops for the poor, with the reassurance; "If I don't pay you God will." A local shopkeeper, fed up with these raids came back at him with; "Well God can get his money out, because **tha'rt** havin' **nowt** until it's paid for."

tin'tin'tin (the second ' indicates a **glottal stop)** it isn't in the tin.

togger football. **Atha playin' togger terneet?**

tommied-on bowsters bolsters hammered or pressed on to the tang of a knife, or pinned onto the scales of a pocket knife. Not an **integral bolsters**

tooers toes. **His big tooer's peepin' aht o' ris sock, sithi.**

top cooat; top rod (Sheffield/Rotherham). **Top coit** (Chapeltown/Barnsley) overcoat **It's a top cooat cowder on 'Tops;** e.g. **up Kinder** etc. Above a certain height on the moors, depending on the weather & season, you need an extra layer of clothing. Sheffield rises from about 200 feet above sea level in the lower **Don Valley** to 1500 feet in the far west at **High Neb, Stanage Edge,** and to 1700 feet at **Margery Hill,** so the saying is quite common.

Top mill nice stone buildings, once **Wilson's snuff mill,** at the top of **Sharrow Vale Road,** now offices. See **Bottom Mill.**

Totley suburb at the foot of **Blacka Hill** & **Totley Moor** in the beautiful **West End** of Sheffield, often coupled with another former Derbyshire village, **Dore**. The railway station for the **Hope Valley** is called **Dore & Totley** and trains go under **Totley Moor** to **Grindleford, Hope & Edale,** before entering another long tunnel under **Kinder** towards Manchester. **Totley Tunnel,** built **1893,** is the second longest tunnel on the railway network, after the Severn Tunnel.

tow to be a **reight tow** is said of toddler, for e.g. who has to be urged on or carried. Also heard used along with a **toil** for an old person, failing in mind & body: "Mi mother's gerrin to be a **reight tow;** a **reight toil."**

tozzin' very good; **'We had a tozzin' game o' togger.'**

Traditional Heritage Museum a little gem at 605 **Ecclesall Road** connected to the **University of Sheffield's** National Centre for English Cultural Tradition. Old shops are represented, including **Leclere's** silversmiths; **Pollard's** coffee retailers; **Austin & Dobson** file workshop; **George Wostenholm's** work's office; & **Hawley's** ('we sell nowt but') **Tools** shop. Run by volunteers, it is open one day a month, usually on the last Saturday in the month.

tranklements knick-knacks; bits and pieces; odds & ends, usually cheap jewellery or ornaments.

trazzin' going very fast

tripe 'ound idiot

trough to eat; a word known nationally, used locally in expressions **" Atha troughing?"**= are you going to lunch? **"Get thi nooase aht o'trough**= Don't be greedy. **"They've all got their nooases in 'trough"** can be used disparagingly of Euro, U.K & local politicians, lawyers, stockbrokers etc. to mean money-grubbing.

trow trough, water-filled for grindstone to run in; for **quenching** hot steel items, or, in a **crucible shop,** for dousing the **melter** against searing heat.

truing up **'racing'** a worn grindstone with an **Abrafact** or **John Watts** tool to level out any uneveness on the stone.

trump to fart (loudly); see **fluff** for the 'silent-but-deadly' (S.B.D.) variety.

in **tucks** laughing

Tudor Square & the nearby **Leader House Tudor & Leader** were a firm of fine silversmiths attracted from London in the **1770's** to our burgeoning new industry, following **Boulsover's** invention of **fused plate (q.v.)** ca. **1740.** See examples of their work in the **Millennium Galleries.**

Tuesday miners who were **laikin'** Mondays (= couldn't face going down the pit after a free week-end), said they got that **'Tuesday morning feeling'** going back to work.

tup hammer head in a **drop fooarge;** a ram, **Derbyshire tup.** (The Rams= Derby F.C.).

Turner Museum of Glass entrance free in the **University of Sheffield Robert Hadfield building; comprises** the collection of a former professor of **Glass Technology.** Like Pittsburgh, Sheffield is a centre for glass research, as well as steel, and **the British Glass Industry Research Assn.** was nearby alongside the **Goodwin Sports Centre. B.G.I.R.A.** has now moved to **Chapeltown** taking advantage of the cost of land in **S 10** to sell the site. Sheffield was also the centre of the British spectacle lens industry. Numerous glassworks were, and are, nearby. Once at **Bolsterstone (q.v.), Catcliffe (q.v.), Whittington, Silkstone, Wentworth,** & until recently at the big **Dema** glass tableware site at **Chesterfield** (soon to be the new home of **Chesterfield F.C.),** big works remain at **Rotherham, Barnsley** & **Doncaster. Beatson Clarke** at **Rotherham,** specialising in glass containers for the pharmaceutical trade among others, are still going strong after more than **200** years.

Turret House the hunting lodge in the outer courtyard of the **Sheffield Manor House (q.v.)** It is the only roofed building surviving on the four acre site.

Twerlies name given by bus drivers for pensioners with bus passes, who would say "Am I **too early"** when getting on a bus before cheap-fare time.

Twikker The **Wicker,** now a bit shabby with fast food litter carried onto the **Five Weirs Walk** by the **Don,** new roadworks dissecting it, & then flooded & churned up to boot in June **2007,** it has nonetheless a bright future. New buildings at the **Blonk Street** corner, coupled with the impressive **1853** former steel firm **Shortridge Howell & Co.'s** H.Q. (See **Samuel Osborn)-** now an Afro-Caribbean Centre, plus a couple of pubs and a couple of fishing tackle emporiums, lead to the formidable **Wicker Arches.** These with the long viaduct across the **Don Valley,** designed by Sheffield engineer, **Sir John Fowler** & built **1840,** served the L.N.E.R. and the **Victoria Railway Station.**

twilly-toed having toes pointing inwards

Tyke a Yorkshireman; a character**; a reight tyke.**
little tyke a little terror (small boy)
Toby Tyke **Barnsley F.C.** mascot

Tyzack the name resounds over three centuries of Sheffield tool making, and if you go to **Abbeydale Hamlet** today you may be lucky enough to see **Ron Staley** bent over a revolving stone, grinding **scythes** & other agricultural blades in the time-honoured way for **Tyzack.**

Where did **Tyzack** originate with a name like that? **Don Tyzack,** in his **1995** book, **"Glass, Tools & Tyzacks"** tells us it was Lorraine where branches of the family were glassmakers from the **1400's** under a variety of spellings of the name**; Thysac, Tixot, Thisac, Tyson, Tissau, Tissat** & **Tizak.** Towards the end of the **1500's** there was evidence of emigration to England where glassworks were set up in Gloucester, Newcastle, Sussex, and most importantly in Stourbridge, Staffordshire. It has been assumed that, with their Huguenot background, religious persecution was the reason for the exodus of several **Tyzacks** to England. However, as **Don Tyzack** points out, economic factors played just as large a part. Trade was sometimes poor in Lorraine, more money could be earned in England &, in those far off days, taxes were less here. Also, in at least one case, a **Tyzack** took refuge in England to escape a murder charge in Lorraine.

It has also been assumed by some, that Huguenots such as the **Tyzacks,** brought the **scythe** trade to England, and they point out as proof that in the Sheffield scythe trade the grindstone revolves **towards** the grinder, continental fashion, whereas in all the other metal trades here, the stone turns **away** from the man. **J.G. Timmins** (The Forge & the Wheel, **1968)** and others, including **Don Tyzack** scotch this claim, pointing out that scythe makers , all with English names & of English origin were already well established in areas such as **Norton.** At **Norton** the earliest mention is of **John Parker,** who leased a building for **scythemaking** in **1459** on the **Beauchief Abbey estate.** By **1718** a **Benjamin Tyzack** was living in **Norton** and was a **scythesmith.** This branch of the family had moved from glass to steel, and **Tyzacks** made **scythes** at various sites in the parish of **Norton,** including **Abbeydale Works.** The **Tyzacks** expanded in the Sheffield area in almost bewildering fashion, making a huge variety of steel products; **scythes, sickles, hay knives, reaper blades, files, saws, hammers, mower blades, builders tools, harrow discs, bacon slicers** were just a few. Many are still made by descendants of their firms. Their works, over the years, were scattered around west & central Sheffield; **South Street** (later called the **Moor), Sharrow Lane, Old Hay, Totley, Rockingham Street, Smithy Wood, Abbeydale, Little London, Hereford Street, Valley Road** and more!

The **Tyzack** firms that have made an impact on the Sheffield scene in recent times are: **1. William Tyzack Sons & Turner** established **1812,** they moved down the **Sheaf Valley** over time from adjacent wheels **Old Hay** & **Totley Forge** down to **Abbeydale (q.v.),** eventually, concentrating all manufacture in the extensive **Little London Works.** Their **Nonpareil** and **Elephant** trademarks were known and respected around the world and there are nice tributes to their wide range of products on their former site. One, in brass and stainless steel highlights many of their tools **hammers, grass hooks, screwdrivers, cold chisels** and their famous **Elephant** brand **saws**. The other is a stainless steel **Sheaf Valley Walk** marker, opposite **Heeley Baths,** which points out local wildlife etc. as well as honouring the firm.

W.A. Tyzack there are some beautiful table knives with their top-hatted **horseman** trade mark, marked **double shear** steel, to be found in antique shops, if you're lucky. These are Victorian or Edwardian, but afterwards right up to the present time they decided to concentrate on tool manufacture, and today they are making machine knives under the **Miba-Tyzack** name. Miba, the owners, an Austrian firm with no allegiance to Sheffield, or sense of its history, are moving production to a cheap-labour country. Let's hope their business is taken by other Sheffield firms including another **Tyzack:**

Tyzack Machine Knives Ltd. at **Shepcote Lane.**

Mark Tyzack was a stainless steel fabrications business in the **East End.**

Needham, Veall & Tyzack made high quality cutlery and the mark is owned by **Taylor's Eye Witness** on **Milton Street.**

Joseph Tyzack their substantial red brick building on **Valley Road** now houses a variety of small firms but they have left their famous three-legged trade mark high on the wall. (They had some connection at one time with the Isle of Man Steam Packet Co.-hence the mark.) They were most famous for their range of builders' trowels, now made by **Spear & Jackson/ James Neill** in the **East End,** who took the firm over.

U

udge up; utch up move up, budge up

un' one. **Tha'rt a reight un' thee.** See **Green Un'**

under to be on the books of; She's **under** Dr. Thompson

United Steels Ltd the most powerful group of British steel companies with headquarters at **The Mount, Broomhill,** before being absorbed into that amorphous mass, with goverment control from London, that was **British Steel Corporation.** Made up of **Samuel Fox's** special steelworks at **Stocksbridge, Steel Peech & Tozer's** engineering steels at **Rotherham,** and **Appleby Frodingham's** bulk steels at **Scunthorpe, United Steels** were well run & efficient, inspiring intense loyalty among employees, (as did most other steel firms in the Sheffield region).

up used describing where someone lives ,etc.in the hillier parts of Sheffield, or upstream of one of the rivers. Sheffield rises from about **200** ft. to ca. **1000** ft at the western limit of the suburbs; to **1500** ft. at **Stanage Edge,** and to over **1700** ft. at **Margery Hill.** So, they live **up Bradfield; up Crosspool; up Crookes; up Gleadless; up Fulwood; up Lodge Moor; up Norton; up Walkley; up Worrall. Kids** at **Neepsend** would ask, **"Atha gooin' up Rivelin fishin'? "**

Note, rather than **up,** it is more common to say they live **on' estates; on' Manor; on' Cross** (on **Parson Cross),** and **on Heeley Bottom,** (possibly **at the top of Heeley Bottom).** Though the people of **Attercliffe Common** might say that they live **on' Common,** everyone else says they live **dahn Attercliffe.** They live **dahn Rotherham way.**

us (pronounced **uz)** can mean me, to me, our. **Gie it us**= give it to me. **We're gooin' on us own**= we're going on our own. **Us sens**= ourselves. See **sen. Save us 'core** = save me the apple core (hungry, or greedy lads in **1940's Neepsend).**

V

Vickers Brothers **Thomas Edward 1833-1915 & Albert 1838-1919** were giants of Victorian Sheffield steelmaking. From making **cast steel bells** at **Millsands** under the name of **Naylor Vickers** (see examples in the **Millennium Galleries)** they moved to the **River Don Works** in **1863** to become the leading **steel and armaments** company in Britain, along with such as **Cammell** and **John Brown,** underpinning British naval & industrial power. (**Vickers** capital in **1912** was **£20 million,** compared with **£4 million** each **Cammell & John Brown). Tweedale** quotes a man who used to visit the firm about the time of the Great War: **"I have never entered without a curious feeling of awe, for I have heard in my inner ear the throbbings of thousands of great steel hammers, seen the lakes of molten metal, caught echoes of the great guns that fired from battery on land or from Dreadnought on sea; and now and then the echoes of the tread of the mighty army of workers who throng to and from their works in almost all quarters of the globe".**

Imagine the skill and military precision involved in making, say, a 25 ton casting for one of their ships built at Barrow or on the Tyne. This might involve about 600 crucible pots, each containing ca. 100 lbs of molten steel & pushed from the melting shop on a small barrow, to be emptied into the casting pit at a rate of one pot every half second. Were the **Vickers Brothers** alive today they would be impressed how their firm's descendants, **Sheffield Forgemasters** can melt 100 ton casts of steel in an **arc furnace** and can produce some of the world's largest forgings & castings. With Britain's decline as a world power **Forgemasters** have to rely on overseas orders for 80% of their business, but the former **Vickers** shipyard still makes submarines at **Vickerstown** (the only place named after a Sheffielder?) opposite Barrow-in-Furness. **Vickers** were associated with American machine gun inventor **Maxim,** (see the cast steel **V's & VSM's** set in the lintels of their huge **Brightside Lane** offices) and with the north-east armaments firm **Armstrong.** When they became the biggest conglomerate in Britain **Vickers** were making warships on the Tyne & on the Clyde, submarines at Barrow, torpedoes at Weymouth, aircraft, cars (Woseley) & office machines at various sites, & latterly medical scanners. Their core business, steel, after WW2 when they were known as **English Steel Corporation (q.v.),** was nationalised, along with other Sheffield firms, by the Labour Government who wanted control of the 'commanding heights of the economy.' Thus the direction of Sheffield's main industry, built up over centuries by Sheffield men, bringing wealth and fame to the city, was, at a stroke of Attlee's pen transferred to civil servants in London. A comparatively small reflection of **Vickers'** influence is seen in **Tapton Hall,** currently home to Sheffield's masons, which was rebuilt in **1855** by **Edward Vickers,** father of **Thomas & Albert,** and founder of the steel dynasty,

James Vickers no relation of the steelmen as far as is known, he invented **white metal** ca. **1770,** an alloy much more hygenic than pewter, and easier to work. This became known as **Britannia Metal** (not to be confused with Britannia Silver) –see selection in the **Millennium Galleries-** and with its **92% tin** plus copper & antimony, is, in fact, today's **pewter.** The original pewter with its high **lead** content (it had even been blamed for the decline of the Roman Empire!) has long since fallen out of favour.

Victoria Hall **Methodist Church** on **Norfolk Street.** Personal memories of youngsters running from **Neepsend** to **'Vic** along **Neepsend Lane,** by the **Don** on **Waterloo Walk,** along the sombre & forbidding **Cornish Street,** and up towards the town centre & **Norfolk Street.** Meetings were in the gym in the **basement;** drill, first aid, gymnastics, prayers, smell of polish, wood & sweat. We were in the Life Boys, the junior reserve of the Boys Brigade, thanks to pressure from my mother, who wanted to put lads on the right track. Tough little lads, especially the **Neepsend** contingent, football up at **Worrall** was a big attraction, winning results telephoned in to the **Green 'Un.**

village Sheffield is often described as the **world's largest village**. It's a very friendly city, people generally know a wide range of other Sheffielders, & are inquisitive about other people, usually in a kindly way. They were 'networking' here long before the word came into vogue. It can be a negative attitude, in that other cities sometimes seem to forge ahead leaving Sheffield to trundle on- for instance, whereas Leeds has a dozen buildings 30 to 54 storeys high, planned or being built, Sheffield has just one at 32 storeys under construction. Anyone who has been to such cities as Sydney can appreciate the beauty of a group of tall steel & glass buildings, but Sheffield planners, view up to recently, seemed to be reduce a proposed building down from, say, eleven storeys to seven, have a 'gull-winged' roof stuck on top, and call it 'iconic'. The following was written in **1887,** when, with a population grown to ca. 400,000, Sheffield was the most powerful steel city the world had ever seen, with world-wide trade & fame: **"**The population of Sheffield is, for so large a town, unique in its character, in fact it more closely resembles that of a village.....for over wide areas each person appears to be acquainted with every other, and to be interested with that other's concerns, a state of things leading to an amount of intercommunication such as is not, I believe, met with in other towns of similar size." These are the words of Dr. Frederick Barry in his report on an epidemic of smallpox in Sheffield during **1887-1888.** The 'intercommunication' spread smallpox in his view since "Heedlessness of danger was almost universal," children were allowed to play with friends who had smallpox victims in their families, and people almost dared each other to visit patiets.

Viners were a German-Jewish family who settled in England in the late 19th century –see their original **1908** electroplate factory, **Tiger Works** on **West Street. (**In recent cleaning & renovation the nicely-carved tiger has had the top of its head shaved off.) In **1914** the brothers were briefly interned, but were then entrusted to make British Army helmets- see **Sissons.** They expanded to employ over a thousand people in WW2 and in the **1950's** took over **Thos. Turner (**see a display of their products in the **Metalwork Gallery),** and **Harrison Brothers & Howson (**see their block with nicely carved **alpha** trademark plus date **1900** on Carver Street.) By **1965** they still employed 800 people and were Sheffield's largest cutlery factory. They specialised in **E.P.N.S.** trays, in tankards, & in **E.P.** & stainless cutlery. Some of their own designs, such as **Studio** pattern stainless cutlery by **Gerald Benney** were exquisite, meriting their advert, "so beautiful you want to lock it up." Their factory was good schooling for budding silversmiths etc., including **Malcolm Marsden, hand engraver.**

In the **1970's** especially, their fortune unravelled as British governments refused any help to beleagered industries such as cutlery, imports of Asian cutlery took most of the trade, and **Viners** made the disastrous decision to themselves import, thus losing their good name with those individuals & companies who were still prepared to pay more for British quality products. In **1982** the firm was shut down and the name bought by a London merchant, used to sell Far Eastern cutlery with ridiculous offers in the 'quality press." (£600 cutlery set offered for £99- and probably bought in Korea for £15, kind of thing).

W

Waard's Ward is a common name in Sheffield and this could be one of three well known firms. **1. Ward's Brewery** on **Ecclesall Road,** now converted to appartments- see **Breweries.** **2. Thomas Ward** on **Clough Road/ Countess Road** near the United ground , a razor blade manufacturer with trade mark **Wardonia.** They always advertised at the back of the **Blades** football programme, with the slogan**: We shave your team, why not you?** The firm have gone but their nice old building remains, built around a courtyard, Sheffield style, now without their long enamel sign and housing various small firms. **3. Thomas W. Ward,** the most famous of the three, with H.Q. on **Savile Street,** just beyond **'Wicker Arches,** their handsome **1902** 3-storey red brick building now home to the **Sheffield Chamber of Commerce.** The hanging clock which served the hordes of workers who funnelled through **'Wicker Arches** into **'East End** is now housed at the **Kelham Island Museum. Tommy Waard** who dismantled ships (their boardroom was lined with panelling from a great liner), sold scrap, made & sold machinery, quarried Shap granite, made **Ketton** cement, and had numerous other interests, were eventually swallowed up by Rio Tinto Zinc. **Tommy Waard's elephant, Liz** carted steel around during WW1 and in the **1920's,** when so many horses had been taken from Britain & lost on the battlefields. It was once as much a mark of the Sheffielder to remember **Tommy Waard's elephant,** as it was to recite, **"Twikker weer twatter runs o'er tweer."** A less ribald comparison was to have a **nooase** as long as **Tommy Waard's elephant's.**

Wadsley up the hill from **Hillsborough,** with interesting names such as **Rural Lane** & **Normandale;** along with **Loxley** has a collection of old stone buildings and it's worth a ramble around **Wadsley Common** & the adjacent **Loxley Common** & **Edge.** The mental hospital at **Middlewood (q.v.)** was often referred to as **Wadsley;** and **Wadsley flatbacks** were cheaply-made Victorian pocket knives, with the 'flat back' of knife, scales & spring all ground together after assembly.

wain't won't**: God knows- an' he wain't snitch (1940's** schoolboys' assertion). **They wain't have it,** e.g youngsters not wanting hard work. When a garage owner asked his apprentice what he had found wrong with a car, the lad replied, **" It wain't gu."**

walk and talk of a pen or pocket knife means to open & close sweetly.

Walker & Hall one of the great Sheffield **electro-plate & silverware** manufacturers, their mark now belongs to **Solpro/ Thessco.** Their multi-storey redbrick works with metal flag trade mark aloft, dominated the view as you walked up **Howard Street** from the station. **George Walker** was a pioneer of **electro plating,** though **Elkington** of Brum (now **Elkington of Sheffield,** also in the **Solpro/Thessco** group) has the credit. **Walker's** business partner, **Hall's** home is now the imposing stone-built **Fulwood Inn.**

Walkers' ironworks originally at **Grenoside,** tracing manufacture back to **1672,** they moved to **Masboro, Rotherham,** having seen "ye disadvantage of being so far from ye navigable river." Three brothers, **Jonathan 1711-78, Samuel 1715-82,** and **Aaron 1718-77,** built the firm up to be England's leading **cannon foundry.** They were the power behind Nelson's victory at Trafalgar, most of the Fleet's cannons being made in **Rotherham (79** out **83** cannon on H.M.S. Victory were **Walkers')** and it is said they could be fired faster & more safely than the French & Spanish cannon. On land, Wellington's victory at Waterloo owed as much to the **Rotherham foundry** as it did to the "playing fields of Eton." Production of cannon increased from **40 tons** in **1775;** to **1220 tons** in **1781,** at the time of the American War of Independence; to **26,000 tons** during the war against Napoleon. There was a slump after the Battle of Waterloo, which led to the demise of the Rotherham factory in **1820.** Their last cannon were produced in this year of George 111's death. **Walkers** also made bridges, a noble local speciality when subsequent famous engineers, **Sir William Fowler (**Forth Bridge) and **Sir Donald Bailey (q.v.)** are considered, leading to today's engineers at **Davy Markham. Walkers** made theirs from cast iron sections and between **1788** and **1791** employed **Thomas Paine (1737-1809),** author of "The Rights of Man," who invented a new type of iron bridge, in between being involved in the American & French revolutions. One of the largest bridges **Walkers** were involved with was one across the Thames at Southwark, but they were never paid for their castings, which also contributed to the firm's demise. Examples of **Walkers' cannons,** marked **Wco** on the trunnion can be seen at the Tower of London; Edinburgh Castle; St. Mary's, Isles of Scilly; H.M.S. Victory & at Rotherham Town Hall. A son of **Samuel Walker, Joshua 1750-1815,** had **Clifton House and gardens** built **1783-4,** which are now a **Rotherham** park and museum **(q.v.)**

Isaac & Israel Walker also of **Rotherham,** not related to the **'cannon kings'**, as far as I'm aware, but worth including if only for their splendid Old Testament names. A **1965 Rotherham Chamber of Commerce** booklet lists them as suppliers of **coal dust, charcoal, plumbage, black lead, ganister, etc.** and the company name was prominently painted in large letters, black on white- or was it white on black? -on their rather decrepit red brick factory, seen as you passed through Rotherham by rail.

Doris Walsh last of the independent **acid etchers,** she recalled on radio her memories of times past, including walking around the city centre in the early morning, with trays of goods in process from one firm to another, and with the constant sound of hammering, comparing Sheffield to a vast beating heart. The process lives on at **Wostenholm's** and you can see beautiful **bowie knives,** old as well as new, etched with Americana; -Bald Eagle, 'Remember the Alamo' etc. at the **Millennium Galleries.** In general, marking on metal is now done by **laser etching.**

wasters **1.** Rejects in manufacture of files, knives etc. **Andrews,** in his book, **"The Story of Wortley Ironworks"** describes iron cannon balls of the Civil War era found at **Wortley Low Forge** as 'possibly **wasters.'** **2.** Ne'er do wells.

waterloo bowster see **egg waterloo bolster**

watter **"Tha'rt as soft as Sheffield watter." tap watter** – see **'Corporation hair oil.'**

watter-licked fishing all day and caught nowt.

watterworks crying, weeping, **rooarin'**

watter wheels the Sheffield area made intensive use of water power, more than in any other part of Britain, and by **1770** there were more than 130 water wheels, mainly along the five fast-flowing streams; **Rivelin, Loxley, Sheaf, Porter & Don,** but also on the **Rother, Moss, Blackburn Brook & Limb Brook.** The monks of **Ecclesfield priory** built an early one to grind corn on **Blackburn Brook,** and the **Town Corn Mill** at **Millsands** stems from medieval times. Eventually there was a cotton & silk mill (**Cotton Mill Walk** off **Alma Street),** a fulling mill (**Walk Mill**), and a silver rolling mill **(Old Park Silver Mill),** but the vast majority of the mills were used to **forge, grind** and **roll steel. (By 1794 Vickers** had the **Town Mill** at **Millsands** with 38 men & 34 grinding **trows).** Water power led to Sheffield becoming the world's greatest cutlery producer, which continued & expanded in the age of steam, when the industry gradually moved from the rivers to the town centre. Interestingly, the sometimes very large steam-powered factories put up in town were still called **wheels: Butcher's Wheel, Petty's Wheel, Union Wheel, Kelham Island Wheel.**

There were three types of water wheels: **1.** an **overshot wheel,** which was worked by a high fall of water, regulated by a **sluice gate** into a **pen trough (qv),** onto the top of the wheel and into its buckets, thus setting it in motion. As can be seen at **Shepherd Wheel,** this system required a full level of water in the **dam (qv). 2.** a **breast wheel,** where the **pen trough** was behind the wheel, not above it, could be worked with a fairly low level of water in the **dam,** and its buckets were said to be filled more efficiently. Perhaps it couldn't turn as fast- otherwise why ever bother with any **overshot wheels.**

3. an **undershot wheel** didn't have buckets & didn't necessarily need a **dam,** since it relied on water in the mill race hitting its paddles and setting it in motion. However, it wasn't as efficient as the other two systems; only part of the water in the mill race hit its paddles, and the flow of water, and with it the speed of machinery, couldn't be controlled from within the works- see **pen trough.**

You could be excused from thinking that if water was free, why bother turning to steam power (and later gas & electricity)? Water may have been free but **feying** the **dam**= cleaning out accumulated sludge, stopping leaks, repairing walls etc. cost money, as did the upkeep of the **wheel,** which required a skilled millwright with knowledge of joinery & metalwork, as well as engineering. In addition the growing town needed more & more drinking water and reservoirs were being built, giving scope for disputes. Moreover, steam, then gas & electricity were more reliable than waterpower, giving more consistent & reliable machinery speeds. In **Valerie Answer's** book, **Sheffield's Traditional Craftsmen,** she interviewed **Mr. Alfred Timms,** foreman at **Kenyon's Rolling Mill** in the **Loxley Valley** who confirmed that water wasn't as reliable as steam or electricity. Water could dry up in summer, or freeze up the wheel in winter. More seriously, it could run the rolling mill somewhat erratically- sometimes so fast that a billet was drawn through much faster than expected & the **roller** or **back tonger** got burnt. **Kenyon's** mill, which eventually became owned by **Barworth Flockton** (now **Firth Rixson),** is now run by **Pro-Roll Ltd.** rolling very special metals. They are the only traditional manufacturing company in the now rural **Loxley Valley,** and have worked wonders preserving this fine old hand mill & buildings, now modernised & powered by electricity. Of course, in these lawless days they have had to surround the site with razor wire to keep out thieves and brainless, drugged up youths.

George Watts just one of many thousands of **Little Mesters** over the years, he was a skilled **hand forger** of blades as small as those in **pocket knives**, and as large as those in **bowies,** latterly working in **Kelham Island Museum** before he died, in **1985.** Speaking to me when I opened the **Sheffield Shop** in **1983** he said: "My advice to thee, or anybody in trade, is never cheat the public."

way well. **"Way, it's not reight, is it."**

wazz pee (verb & noun); more vulgar than tiddle, less vulgar than piss or slash.

wee, wi with; **gerraway withi!** get away with you! **oowashiwee?** who was she with? **washiwee 'ersen?** was she on her own? **supwithee?** what's the matter with you? (a flippant play on words in answer could be; **ah'll sup wi anybody!**

weer where, or weir; **Twikker, weer twatter runs o'er t'weer.** See **Wicker.** Little boy throws paper on the floor. Teacher; Where's the bin? Boy (puzzled); **I ampt been anyweer, miss.** (He had heard it as **'Weer's tha bin.'.......... does tha gerrit?)**

wellos wellington boots (never 'wellies')

Wentworth House "Wyteworth Wodehous" appears in a deed of **1303.** This house was replaced by a stone building for the Earl Of Stafford ca. **1630,** who was beheaded in **1641.** The present house, described as "the finest Georgian House in England", was built by **Watson Wentworth, Marquis of Rockingham** between **1730-1760.** It is the biggest stately home in the country, and said to be the biggest in Europe. The superb Palladian house, with its long façade and a thousand windows, is twice the size of Buckingham Palace, its stable block alone being bigger than many stately homes. The **Fitzwilliam** family inherited **Wentworth Woodhouse** in the late **18th** century, built canals & railways & exploited the **Barnsley** coal seam which extends under the estate. They rescued the pottery at **Swinton** which took the **Rockingham** name, and became famous for the finest china – see **Clifton Park Museum.** A 100 years ago when there were up to a million miners in Britain, with more than 2000 deaths in accidents a year, conditions down the mines were abysmal, danger was ever present, even though advances had been made – women and children no longer hauled tubs of coal. When GeorgeV stayed at **Wentworth** in **1912** as guest of the **7th Earl Fitzwilliam,** he woke to news of 61 dead in an explosion at nearby **Denaby colliery.** By contrast **Fitzwilliam's** own mines gave safety priority and he looked after his men. (When the **6th Earl** had died in **1902** a thousand miners led the mourners). The **7th Earl** urged his men to join the national **1926** General Strike; fed their **2500** children; turned **Wentworth** grounds into an amusement park for their families, offering in cricket matches on the lawn, **£25,** then a very big sum, to any miner who could slog the ball through one of the thousand windows. He also allowed striking colliers to dig through old workings on his land for coal for their families. When the mines were nationalised after WW2, and the very gardens of **Wentworth** itself were threatened by opencast mining, there was uproar against the plans, led by area N.U.M. president **Joe Hall: "**The mines in this area will go to almost any length rather than see **Wentworth House** destroyed. To many mining communities it is sacred ground." He called it sheer vandalism, more so when **Sheffield University** geologists and mining engineers confirmed that the coal to be opencast was poor quality, "not worth the getting." Unfortunately, a man called Manny Shinwell, a mini-Stalin, Clydeside socialist, was head of the Ministry of Fuel & Power (known locally as the **Ministry of Fools in Power)** and he was in vindictive mood, determined to destroy the estate. The bulldozers were sent in, and **98** acres of woodland, a similar area of grassland and manicured lawns, the formal gardens, and a 300 year old avenue of beech trees, were all destroyed, the mounds of earth reaching up to the **Earl's** bedroom window.**Peter, the 8th Earl Fitzwilliam,** a dashing cove, in S.O.E. during WW2, was killed in an air crash in **1948** along with his lover, **Kathleen 'Kick' Kennedy,** sister of Jack, the future U.S. president. The romance was hushed up- **Fitzwilliams** were staunch Protestants, and the **Kennedys** strong Catholics, of Irish descent. (Her father, American ambassador to Britain, was anti-British and had expected Britain to lose the war. He had told his daughter she would be disinherited if she married **Peter).** The Ministry of Health proposed taking over the House for "housing homeless industrial families", but **Peter's aunt, Lady Mabel,** an upper-crust socialist, persuaded West Riding County Council to lease it as a college. **Lady Mabel College of Physical Education** was born and lads from the **Park Gate Iron & Steel Works** in the **1960's,** freed from the dust & clamour of steel at lunchtime, occasionally went by the rolling wheat fields to the pub in the village of **Wentworth,** with a glance or two at healthy female limbs. In **1972,** the **10th** and last **Earl** had a bonfire of 16 tons of family papers, a fire that lasted three weeks destroying hundreds of years of history, including details of the **Kennedy** affair. The College was leased by **Sheffield Polytechnic** until **1988,** and when they left, the last **Earl's** daughter sold the House & what remained of the grounds. The businessman who bought it had ambitious plans, but after 10 years had debts of £13 million and the House was repossessed. The present owner, since **1999,** is reclusive Mr. Clifford Newbould, an architect from Highgate, who got England's biggest, but dilapidated, stately home, with its room for every day of the year, its thousand windows and 5 miles of underground passageways, for the knockdown price of **£1.5 million.** See "Black Diamonds: The Rise & Fall of an English Dynasty" by **Catherine Bailey**, and "Historic Houses in Rotherham District" by **Vernon Thornes.**

Wentworth Pewter one of about 20 pewter manufacturing firms they deserve a mention because of their exceptional quality, and for putting into production the drawings & one-off pieces of designer-craftsmen & women from around the country. The unusual vases designed by **Catherine Tutt,** and on show at the **Famous Sheffield Shop** are one example. Of course, it is one thing to design a piece, quite another to have the skills needed to produce them economically in volume. Sheffield pewterers have these skills.

Wentworth have also helped **Freeman College (qv)** by leaving some machinery in their former **Leadmill Road** works, now used by the college.

wesh wash (as in Chaucer)**; wesh-day** was **allus** on a Monday.

John & Charles Wesley founder & chief hymn-writer of **Methodism** were born at The Old Rectory, **Epworth,** north Lincolnshire, to the north-east of Sheffield. **John** was born in **1703,** a year before the father of Sheffield, and world **steel-making, Benjamin Huntsman (qv)** saw the light of day in the very same Lincolnshire village. As they grew up the young lads must have known each other. In **1709** a fire destroyed the **Wesley's** home and **John** escaped through a first floor window, his mother afterwards referring to him as "a brand plucked from the burning." The **Wesleyans** suffered some stoning & harassment from roughnecks in Sheffield, but nonetheless expanded rapidly in the town, and **John Wesley** had his biggest week-day audience when preaching in **Paradise Square.**

Weston Park & Museum nice small park opposite **'Children's,** with bandstand, pond, tennis courts, war memorial and statue of **Elliott (qv),** and bounded on the west by the **Museum** and on the east by the university's original redbrick **Firth** buildings on **Western Bank,** and the **Arts Tower & library** overlooking the pond. The **Museum** has been modernised and is clean and welcomingand politically correct. Even worldly-wise old Sheffielders are won over, while regretting the loss of all the wooden drawers you could slide open, revealing rows of insects, or **pocket knives.** (They may feel too that **Mappin (qv)** has been insufficiently honoured, and wonder what happened to the worlds's largest collection of **Old Sheffield Plate.)** A woman complained about **Abbeydale Hamlet (qv)** that there was **nowt theer,** and of course there isn't much, if you have no sense of history, nor wonderment of how our ancestors lived and worked, and you are as thick as a plank. This woman should like **Weston Park Museum** much better, with senses battered by impressions, sounds, voices, films, allowing of no silence or retreat into one's own thoughts.

Westbrook Mill 'Top Mill (qv), Sharrow Vale Road, was **J.& H. Wilson's snuff mill,** set up after a family quarrel as a steam powered mill in competition with the water powered **Bottom Mill (qv).** It was bought by Imperial Tobacco in **1953** and closed in **1989,** leaving the solid stone buildings to be converted into offices & apartments, and the **Bottom Mill** as the U.K.'s only surviving **snuff mill.**

whale oil once used to harden **saws** and **knives. Stan Shaw** used it right up to the **1980's** to harden his pocket knife blades. **Eddie Hudson** wrote of how, on the first day of his apprenticeship at **Tyzack Sons & Turner, Little London Road** works, he was draped from neck to foot with sacking, and had the job of retrieving the saws which had been put, red hot, into the oil quenching tank. He found the heat overpowering, the stench abominable.

wheel from its original meaning of a **water wheel** it came to mean the revolving **grindstones** that it powered, and the building they were housed in. By extension, when the industry moved from the rivers to steam powered buildings in town these were often still called **wheels.** See under **W.&S. Butcher; grinders & watter wheel.** **"Workin' in 'wheel"** could therefore mean doing a variety of jobs in a factory- say the steam powered **Butcher's Wheel,** where, to complicate things a little more, women could be working on **buffing wheels-** 10 inch diameter or so, wooden wheels, originally surfaced with buffalo hide. See **buff** & **buffer girls.**

wheel swaarf swarf or sludge in the **grinder's trow** (trough) formed by particles of steel & stone collecting as sediment in the water at the bottom of the trough during grinding. Not all settled peaceably in the trough, of course. Some were thrown against the **splash board,** and some onto the **grinder.** See **Yaller Belly.** Nothing was wasted in the Sheffield trades and **wheel swarf** was collected and caked on top of the charcoal-covered iron bars in **cementation (qv) furnaces** to seal them against oxidisation. The swarf produced a glassy slag called **crozzle (qv),** which was later cut up & sold on to put on top of walls.

whet to put the final cutting edge on a blade, which was often the job of the warehouse woman. If she was inexperienced, or poor at the job, she might have an insult, such as; **"tha can't whet lettuce"** thrown at her. **Whet,** of course, is a national word: **"thou whet'st a knife to kill thyself"** (Shakespeare Richard 111). **"I must go down to the seas again to the vagrant gypsy life, to the gull's way & the whale's way where the wind's like a whetted knife."** (John Masefield)

whetstone was a slab of fine grained **Brincliffe Blue** or **Wickersley** stone for the proficient warehouse woman to swish the knife edge along, to give a keen cutting blade.

while until; **working nine while five.** The story that a Sheffielder was killed on a level crossing after misunderstanding the sign, **"Do not cross while light is red",** is apocryphal and defamatory.

whin gorse. Generations of children know of the legend of a battle won & lost on **Win hill** & **Lose hill,** but is **Win hill** simply **gorse hill?** C.f. also **Whinfell gardens, Whirlow.**

"whip behind!" was the cry by a member of the public if he or she saw young lads leaping on the back of horse-drawn wagons labouring up steep slopes such as **Spital Hill.** The driver would flick his long whip behind &, **Bernard Whiting** tells us (in **Valerie Answer's** book) the "lads would get many a **scotch** on the legs." **The Star** occasionally reports young lads performing an up-to-date misdemeanour of clinging to the back of buses or trams - sadly without fear of punishment.

Whirlow a fine suburb where Sheffield meets the **Peak Park** with its own park & café, run by **Fretwell Downing,** having the busy little **Limb Brook,** and part of the **Round Walk** running through, and even a mill pond showing that Sheffield's early industry touched the uppermost reaches of **Hallamshire. Whinfell gardens,** mentioned under **whin** above, were established in an old quarry near the park entrance, and were given to the city by **James Neill** (famed for his high quality tools manufacture). One of Whirlow's grand houses, **Whirlow Court,** was built in the early **1880's** for **James & Mrs. Fawcett,** joint owners of silversmiths **James Dixon & Co.** Other owners included, from **1920, Arthur Davy,** grocer, baker & restaurant owner whose multi storey food factory was near **Howard Street,** and, from **1946 Lt.Colonel Maurice Batchelor,** of **Batchelor's Peas** fame. The house is now used by circuit judges, a far less productive breed. Among the houses on the other side of the road is a fine new, neo-Georgian home built for today's leading silverware manufacturer, **Ron Carr. Ron** has bucked the trend both in building up a large manufacturing firm when so many others have downsized, and in refusing to have his land smothered in new housing, unlike so many others in Sheffield's unsurpassable **West End** suburbs. **Whirlow Farm** on the edge of open countryside is a charity, like **Heeley City Farm,** which introduces children to fresh air, farmyard smells & life on a farm. There are residential courses for schoolchildren, with crops to plant & animals to look after. In summer there is a pick-your-own service with strawberries, raspberries etc. available for the general public. The man who did most for the farm trust was, perhaps, **Alan Aiken,** a Mancunian who first came to Sheffield to sell the Corporation's redundant gas lamps, and ended up building a thriving business, the **Pewter Manufacturing Company,** whose modern factory at **Darnall** now houses **Wentworth Pewter (qv).**

whitearse old name for the wheatear, a smart bird often seen on a rock among the heather moors in May-August. Notice the flash of white derriere as it flies away from you. The new name is probably a corruption of the old – note that the French keep with **cul-blanc.**

whittle **1.** A general workaday, all purpose knife, Sheffield's staple product along with scissors & pocket knives right from the thirteenth century. Every Sheffielder knows that **Chaucer's** tough miller, who could break any door down "at a running with his heed", carried one round with him in his sock, or waistband. **Whittle tang** knives were made until a few years ago when the cheap end of the market was finally overwhelmed by Far-Eastern knives. **Whittle tang** were Sheffield's cheapest knives, stamped out, both blade & tang from a sheet or strip of stainless steel, without a **bolster,** or with a **spelter bolster** which was mainly zinc, but could have contained at one time a small percentage of lead. The spelter was poured into **egg waterloo bowster (qv) dies** into which the **whittle tang** had been inserted, and the metal solidified around the tang forming a cheap, but secure **bolster.**

whittle **2.** To moan; go on & on complaining about something. If someone never stops **whittlin'** they are vulgarly known as a **whittle arse.**

wiaart **1.** without. Shafts of childish post-war wit?; First child (hesitant) "Well, well…well." Second child "What's use a well **wiaart** a bucket." First child (recovering his, or her aplomb) "It's enough to drown thee in!" **2.** unless; **not wiart** unless, or not unless. This usage used to be widespread: John Constable wrote; **"**I do not consider myself at work **without** I am before a six foot canvas."

wick **1.** lively, quick, alert. When Sheffielders say; **"Derbyshire born, Derbyshire bred – strong in 'arm, weak in 'head"** , should it be weak, or **wick,** as the **Rams** claim? **2. wick wi'** covered in; **snided with.** "Place were **wick wi'** flies."

Wicker Arches impressive Victorian stone railway arches, a wide & welcoming gateway to the **East End.** People used to talk about someone having "a grin as wide as **'Wicker Arches."** The line from **Victoria Station** to Manchester via new tunnels at **Woodhead** was electrified with journey time less than an hour for passengers, and not much more for freight. With the typical British short-sightedness of our days, the station and tunnels were closed, & the service transferred to the **Hope Valley** line. A few trains nightly use what's left of the track, between **Corus Aldwarke & Stocksbridge** works. See **Twikker** and **Sir John Fowler.**

Wickersley now an exclusive part of Rotherham, its quarries produced fine bluish-tinted sandstone **grindstones** which, along with **Brincliffe Blue (qv)** were regarded as the best for knife & razor grinding.

"One for Wigan!" cry at **Hillsborough,** the **Lane, Parkwood Rec.** or **Concord Park** etc. when the centre forward booted the ball, rugby-style, well over the crossbar.

Wiggies **Wigfalls** originally made bicycles, then became well kown throughout the region with shops selling household goods and furnishings, as well as cycles, supplied from their head office & warehouse on **Rutland Road.** They had a credit sceme and the **Wiggies man** would come round weekly for payment.

winder i pronounced as in win, not wine: **"**We got a **laddow** and **purrit up ageean 'winder"** –woman trying to enunciate 'correctly' when interviewed on B.B.C. T.V. at a time of flash flooding of the Meers brook in 1970's (?).

John Wilson the world's best & leading brand of ice skates, the choice of royalty & champions of speed and grace on the ice, world & olympic champions over the years. The Sunday Times, in an article on the last Winter Olmpics, pointed out that, although Britain didn't win a single medal, at least every one of the winners skated on **Sheffield Steel......** See the skates used by young Queen Victoria at **Kelham Island Museum.** A lesser brand of ice skates, for the mass market, **M.K. Skates** of Slough, with a local connection in that they bought steel strip from **Brinsworth,** are now merged with **Wilson's** under **H.D. Sports,** manufacturing at **Rutland Way, Sheffield. (H.D.** was previously **Hattersley & Davidson,** owning **Wilson's** and **Sorby Garden Tools** at **Woodseats,** then at **Greystoke Road** in the **East End.** I believe they also made agricultural discs, reaper blades, and grinding balls on **Clubmill Road, Neepsend,** but the agricultural implements are now made by **Chapman Tools** there. **Sorby Garden Tools** moved to **Dronfield.)**

James Wilkinson Vicar of Sheffield from **1753** to **1805,** was also Justice of the Peace, a hunting, shooting horseman, and a gentleman boxer. Sheffield was generally law-abiding then, which was fortunate since there were neither police nor army barracks, and only a handful of "decrepit watchmen who were far more afraid of evil-doers than evil-doers were of them." Most cases for **Mr. Justice Wilkinson** arose from civil disputes. Once called upon to arbitrate between a husband & wife, he ordered they should be locked up together until they could come to an agreement. **Hunter,** the historian, described **Wilkinson** as amiable and gentlemanlike **"**but shaken by a violent nervous complaint,**"** which led to his nickname **"Old Niddlety Nod."** Over his 50 years as Vicar there were, of course, some tumultuous events, local & national, that stirred the mostly peaceful town. First, was the agitation for revolution in Britain, to emulate the French. **James Montgomery,** editor of the **'Sheffield Iris,'** voiced support for the French Revolution as did many many inhabitants of the town, support which rapidly dwindled with news of atrocities committed by the revolutionaries. Locally, two events; the enclosure act for **Crookes Common,** and the widening of **Church Street** led to riots in **1791** and a mob set the Vicar's haystacks ablaze, and caused much damage at his home, **Broom Hall.** One man was subsequently hanged at York for this. The 'silent majority' of the day, however, were in favour of the old Vicar, who in **1792** was instrumental in the founding of the **Royal Infirmary.** There was a day of mourning when he died in **1805,** and tributes from all and sundry, including ertstwhile opponent, **James Montgomery.**

Wincobank hilly area overlooking the **Don Valley** with the **Tinsley Viaduct,** gas and steel works, sports facilities, **Meadowhall** shopping centre and the meandering **River Don** set out below. The high point and sentinel of the **East End** is **Wincobank Hill,** about 500 feet above sea level, with its iron age fortifications and views to the high moors in the west, and cooling towers grouped along the Trent in the east. (The local twin cooling towers were felled recently amid a burst of sentiment, to make way for a new, 'environmentally-friendly' power station). **Fred Dibnah,** guided by historian, **Peter Machen,** trundled his steam roller up **Wincobank Hill** for views of industrial Sheffield for a T.V. programme. Unfortunately it was damp and misty and with nothing much to be seen, he rolled the machine down again and then upstream to a modern forge, where the viewers could see old Sheffield skills- **Independent Forgings and Alloys Ltd.** The area was known for its iron ore, celebrated by ancient doggerel:

"Wincobank and Templeborough Can buy all England through and through."

Wincobank today is best known for **Brendan Ingle's gym,** which has nurtured boxing champions and responsible citizens, in equal measure.

winter(h)edge **clooers horse.** Clothes, sheets etc. were hung out on hedges in winter to dry - certainly up to the **1920's** (an amateur film of the era showed sheets hung over hawthorn bushes in Lancashire; possibly they still are in out of the way country areas). "White linen hung out on the sweet briar hedge"- Gaskell's ' North and South' describing Manchester of the **1850's.** When I lived in Manchester in the late **1950's** the indoor clothes horse was called a **maiden,** though **winteredge** still lingers on in Sheffield.

Winter Garden opened by the Queen in **2002** the plants give a tonic to tired eyes & lungs.

witch wooden wedge inserted temporarily between the scales of a pocket knife, to keep them from bending during rivetting, and prevent them being rivetted too tight.

Wolf Safety Lamp our interest starts with a **crucible steel & wire** company in the **1880's,** one of hundreds in Sheffield's history. An improved miner's safety lamp was made by a firm called **Wolf** in Germany and production was brought to Leeds in the **1880's.** The owner of the Sheffield steel & wire firm, **Wm.Maurice** took over the Leeds firm & transferred production to a new factory on Saxon Road, Heeley, in **1913.** Miners' lamps were still made there until the early **1990's,** and now the firm concentrates on special safety lamps for, e.g. oil tankers.

workboards wooden trays on which work in progress, pocket knife parts etc. is taken from person to person in various parts of a factory, or even to another workshop, in much the same way as **scissors** on a **scissor- stick (qv)** might be taken from forger to hardener.

works' weeks traditional steelworks' **shut down** in the last week of July and the first in August, when essential repair work to machinery is carried out, & furnaces and ladles are relined, where necessary, with new refractory bricks.

Worrall with other high Pennine villages to the north-west of Sheffield, such as **Bradfield, Stannington** & **Bolsterstone,** it is well-known for fresh air, high winds, and local Christmas carols, sung vigorously in pubs. It is also home to an isolated Carmelite convent. **Worrall** was also home in the **1940's & 1950's** to **Victoria Hall (qv) Methodist** Boys' Brigade and Life Boys football teams' ground. This, like so many pitches around Sheffield was on a slope on top of a windy hill, and it was not unknown for the heavy leather **casey,** upon being booted uphill into the wind by the **goalie,** to come sailing back and over his own crossbar. Once, with the wind in a particularly bad mood, we arrived to find that the wooden changing hut had been hurtled down the hill.

Worsborough Mill near **Barnsley** was listed in the Domesday survey of **1086** as **Wirceburg Mill;** the current 'Old Mill' was built **1625** and the 'New Mill' late **1880's,** the latter powered by steam. It is now a working museum.

Wortley Forge was operated by the **Spencer** partnership, which by **1695** had 8 blast furnaces and 11 iron forges in South Yorkshire. In the Victorian railway boom **Wortley** became renowned as a **wrought iron axle** manufacturer, using water power provided by three or four water wheels, from ca. **1835** to ca. **1908** when it closed & bigger, steel making businesses dominated the trade.There is evidence of two forges as early as **1638; Top Forge (**in **Hunshelf)** and **Low Forge (**in **Wortley)** and both sites were operated over the centuries by a succession of owners: the **Spencers** until the **1750's; Cockshutts** until the first half of the **19th century;** the **Andrews** from **1850** to **1906; Wortley Iron Company** from **1907** to the closure of **Top Forge** in **1912,** and the **Low Forge** in **1929.** The two forges had worked in tandem with **Low Forge** making **wrought iron** in **puddling furnaces** and **rolling** it into bars, and **Top Forge** doing the **forging.** Ca. **1879 Thomas Andrews, forgemaster,** claimed that **30,000** of the firm's axles were in use with various railway companies, operating under severe conditions and stress and not one had been returned broken. (**Firth Rixson,** may have a tenuous relationship with **Wortley,** in that they took over, among many other firms, **Walter Spencer** of **Warren Street, Norfolk Bridge,** founded **1778. Rixson** continue the local tradition of railway axle manufacture at their **Ickles** works.) **Low Forge** is now a ruin, but the **Top Forge** was saved by the efforts of, and is run by, the successors of the **Sheffield Trades Historical Society (qv).**

wortle plate steel plate, taper-pierced with different sized holes for drawing wire.

George Wostenholm world famous cutlery company, second only to **Joseph Rodgers,** were known in the trade as **Ooslams** or **Oosnams**. The first **George Wostenholme (** the final **e** was later dropped to fit easier across a pocket knife tang) established his business in **1745** in Stannington.The second **George Wostenholme** expanded the firm moving from **Garden Street,** to **Broad Lane,** then, sometime before **1815,** to **Rockingham Works,** known as **Rockingham Wheel,** even though it ran on steam power. The third **George Wostenholm (1800-1876),** with prodigious energy, made 30 sales visits across the Atlantic in his lifetime to build up a vast American trade, & built **Washington Works** on **Wellington Street** to become the world's second biggest cutlery factory. On top of this he bought an extensive area of **Nether Edge** and had large stone & brick houses built with gardens & tree-lined roads reminiscent of East Coast America. (Note **Washington Road** & **Kenwood Road).** His own home, designed by **Flockton (qv)** & built **1849** with **Stanton stone** was called **Kenwood** (as was a well known American electrical company he founded), and with parkland and pond planned by **Marnock** of **Botanical Gardens** fame now forms part of the **Marriott Hotel.** The firm was best known for **pen & pocket knives,** with a trade mark **I*XL** from **1787** being granted to them by the **Cutlers' Company;** for **bowie knives (qv)** using the same mark; & for razors with an even earlier mark, a **pipe** with the legend **True Pipe** from **1694** being granted. Sales of their **bowie knives** burgeoned in the United States after he sold some to American hero **Colonel Jim Bowie,** including twelve pearl handled, and Sheffield **bowies** from the **19**th century made by other firms as well as **Wostenholm** now command thousands of pounds in auctions. See a modern **I* XL bowie,** nicely etched with Americana, in the **Millennium Galleries,** and a roll-top desk used by **George Wostenholm,** which was made in Washington, U.S.A. and is now at the **Heritage Museum** on **Ecclesall Road. Wostenholm pen, pocket** and **hunting knives,** along with other famous brands **Rodgers & Ibberson,** are still made, now in a factory on **Garden Street,** with retained name **Washington Works.** They are in good Sheffield hands, owned by **Eggington** on **Allen Street,** after years of decline under American ownership.

Wrought iron **Cast iron** with about 4% **carbon** is too brittle to be **forged** or **rolled** so, before the almost universal use of steel, **wrought iron** held sway for a huge variety of engineering products- **railway axles**, to mention just one. (See **Wortley Forge,** above). It was a very low **carbon iron** obtained as a pasty sponge, by refining pig iron in a **puddling furnace.** This would be reheated & hot worked-usually hammered- to squeeze out much of the **slag** content , ensure even distribution of the rest, and develop the mechanical properties of formability, and resistance to rusting. Being easily forged & rolled while hot it was often used as the body of many tools, being **forge-welded** to a **crucible steel** cutting edge –as with **saws** and **scythes.** The strike-surface of **wrought iron hammers** would be **hard-faced** by **crucible steel.** The **wrought iron tang & bolster** of table knives would be **forge-welded** to **shear steel blades. Wrought iron** is no longer made, superseded by **mild steel,** so if you see **wrought iron gates** etc. advertised they are, strictly speaking, **mild steel.**

X

xylo; xylonite pronounced **zylo,** a trade name for a cellulose-based plastic celluloid, used for cheaper knife handles, replacing cow bone etc. (Better quality handles are still today made from **antler** or **horn,** and best quality from **silver** or **pearl,** and formerly from **ivory & tortoiseshell).** The **xylo** workshops were on the top floor of factories, so, in event of a fire, **xylo** being so flammable that a spark could ignite its dust, only the top floor would be destroyed. In a three storey building then, top floor = **xylo** shop; middle= **buffing** shop; bottom, and basement= heavy machinery shops for **grinding** and **stamping.** In our effete days of course, when even conkers are a health & safety risk, **xylo** is no longer used and handles, if not all metal, are made of acrylic, nylon, polypropylene, or polystyrene. Kitchen knife handles look good made of polished, brass-rivetted rosewood, but current thinking views wood as less hygenic than coloured plastic. Coloured polystyrene in powder form is injection-moulded, enabling different shapes & details to be incorporated into handles.

YZ

yaard o' pump watter thin.

Yarmouth beef when boats followed the shoals round our shores "red herrings" **(2-eyed beef steaks)** was the only 'beef' some cutlers could afford.

James Yates (1789-1881). **Yates** is a respected name in the Sheffield cutlery trade –see **Wm.Yates** building on Arundel Street- but Rotherham man **James** who took over the **Walker Iron Foundry (q.v.)** perhaps deserves more attention as a representative of the extensive cast iron trade in kitchen ranges, fireplaces and fenders etc. in the two towns. Gas cookers became popular in the **1880's,** and to produce these and other products **Yates & Harwood** had the new extensive **Effingham Works** built, with the foundry alone measuring 500 ft. x 70 ft., its roof supported on uninterrupted oak beams.

Year Knife made by **Joseph Rodgers** for an **1821** exhibition with a blade for every year of the Christian era. Blades have continued to be added each year with the last leading up to **2000** added by a **master cutler, Stan Shaw.** The **Knife** is now in the **Hawley**

Collection and can be seen currently, along with **Rodgers' Norfolk Knife** at the **Cutlers' Hall.**

Yeller Belly (sometimes **Yaller)** **1.** a **grinder,** so called because of the yellow swarf sprayed back at him when crouched at the wheel. **2.** a **Lincolnshire man** a rude **Lincolnshire** fellow at **Park Gate Iron & Steel** told me this was because "They wiped their arse the wrong way."

yitten **tha'rt yitten; tha'rt yeller; freetened; frit;** frightened.

yor; yo; yor lot; yo lot you; you lot.

"If yor lot had listened to us (British) **there'd have been no French Revolution." (Brinsworth** steelworker to a French woman working there.)

York **"Tha'll stand ('last) drop o' York."** You'll stand (for) anything. **Drop o' York=** execution by hanging.

Yorkshire Cricket Club founded **1838** at the **Adelphi** pub, where the **Crucible Theatre** now stands. They played at **Darnall,** then at **Hyde Park** before moving to **Bramall Lane** in **1863. Sheffield United Football Club** were founded in **1889** and though **'Lane** was the senior county cricket ground, there was pressure over the years & especially in the **1930's, 40's** & **50's** for conversion to a four sided football stadium, which it now is. The cricket pavilion clock remains-replaced in **2007**above the museum of football.

Yorkshireman Ken Dodd's way of telling one: listen for, **"Aaow much?"**,an expression of incredulity at the price of something. Another one of Doddy's, addressing an audience; **"Are there any Yorkshiremen in the audience? - Ah, there they are, grouped round the exit, in case there's a collection."**

Yorkshireman's motto:
" 'ear all, see all, say nowt,
eight all, sup all, pay nowt,
An if tha ever does owt for nowt
Allus do it for thissen."

Of course, since we have one foot in the Midlands, and both feet in **Hallamshire,** we're not like that**....** Are we?

young un' young child, youngster**; ahr young un', ahr kid (qv),** my little brother; our youngest child; or even, my,our eldest brother.

youth term of address as, **boss, surrey (qv), kiddo, laddo** (this when you don't know, or have forgotten a name), **squire.**

THAT'S IT OLD LUV.

Bibliography

Books consulted mainly for technical or for historical references:

The Cutting Edge. Hawley Collection.	Janet Barnes.
Sheffield Steel.	Ken Barraclough.
Industrial History of South Yorkshire.	Derek Bayliss
A South Yorkshire Family of Type Founders.	Wm. Greaves Blake.
Diamonds in Brown Paper.	Gill Booth.
Stainless Pioneer.	Harry Brearley.
Knotted String.	
Steel Makers.	
Mary Queen of Scots. The Captive Years.	Keith Cheetham.
Water Power on the Sheffield Rivers.	David Crossley, Jean Cass, Neville Flavell, Colin Turner.
Sheffield,Armourer to the British Empire.	Stewart Dalton.
Life at Stanage & the North Lees Estate.	Jeannie Edgar.
The Oldest Sheffield Plater. Thos. Boulsover	John & Julia Hatfield.
A History of Sheffield.	David Hey.
The Story of Cutlery.	J B Himsworth.
Back to the Grindstone.	Herbert Housley
"..A Most Enterprising Thing..." (history of **Newton Chambers**)	Joan & Mel Jones.
Forgeman at Jonas Colver.	David Jeffery.
The Sheffield Blitz. Operation Crucible.	Alistair Lofthouse
James Wilkinson.	Bishop David Lunn.
Where in Sheffield, 1989.	Konrad S. Manning.
Master Metalworker	biography of David Mellor
Iron & Steel Town.An Industrial History of Rotherham.	Anthony P. Munford.
Old Sharrow & Nether Edge	Nether Edge local history group
The Cutler's Tale	John Price
Damned Bad Place, Sheffield.	Sylvia Pybus.
Sheffield's Remarkable Houses.	Roger Redfearn.
Last of the Sheffield (independent) Horn Cutters.	W.H. Scarlett.
Chapter in 'The Cutting Edge',	Sheffield Trades Hist. Soc.journal.
The Cutlery Industry.	Peter Smithurst.
The Forge & The Wheel 1968	T.G. Timmins.
A Sheffield Anthology of photographs & words by the Cutlery Craftsmen 1978	C.A. Turner.
Giants of Sheffield Steel.	Geoffrey Tweedale.
The Sheffield Knife Book.	
Raiders over Sheffield	Mary Walton & J.P.Lamb.
One Great Workshop. English Heritage.	Wray, Hawkins, & Giles.